MEN
OF
DISHONOR

Other Books by Pino Arlacchi

Mafia Business:
The Mafia Ethic and the Spirit of Capitalism

MEN

OF

DISHONOR

Inside the Sicilian Mafia: An Account of Antonino Calderone

Pino Arlacchi

Translated from the Italian
by Marc Romano

William Morrow and Company, Inc.

New York

Library of Congress Cataloging-in-Publication Data

Calderone, Antonino, 1935–
    [Uomini del disonore. English]
    Men of dishonor   Inside the Sicilian Mafia / [interviewed by] Pino Arlacchi :
translated from the Italian by Marc Romano.
        p.   cm.
    Translation of: Gli uomini del disonore.
    ISBN 0-688-04574-X
    1. Mafia—Italy—Sicily.   2. Calcerone, Antonino. 1935–
I. Arlacchi, Pino, 1951–   II. Title.
HV6453.I83M3231713   1993
364.1'06'09458—dc20   93-15397
                                                                        CIP

Printed in the United States of America

First Edition

1 2 3 4 5 6 7 8 9 10

BOOK DESIGN BY SUSAN HOOD

PREFACE

During the 1980s it became obvious that the growth of organized crime in Italy had reached the point of national emergency. Mafia and organized crime families have come to control the greater part of the nation's illegal economy, as well as a significant percentage of the legal economy in large areas of southern Italy and in limited parts of northern Italy. According to figures compiled by the Ministry of the Interior, there are some five hundred mafia "families" whose collective membership totals more than fifteen thousand.

Italy's organized-crime problem is in some respects unique. True, there is a strong mafia in the United States, but its influence on the highest levels of the federal government cannot compare to the entrepreneurial Italian mafia's influence on the Italian political system. There are instances of careless management and illegal use of public resources in many Western countries, but nothing approaching recent developments in Sicily, where mafia or mafia-related enterprises have gained a monopoly over public investments from national and international sources. At the time of this writing, twenty-six hundred public administrators are indicted for corruption and other crimes; more than fifty town councils have been dissolved because they are heavily infiltrated by organized crime. Because of its economic muscle, its numerous affiliates, its ability to manipulate public institutions, and its complex, sophisticated structure, the mafia is the most powerful and dangerous criminal organization in Italy. Given its financial, political, and military resources (that is, its use of violence), the mafia is in a special position vis-à-vis other illegal networks and terrorist organizations. They too are insidious at the political and institutional level, but they do not command large autonomous funds or military forces. That notwithstanding, the mafia's actual power derives from the fact that it is not a single entity like a political party, a pressure group, a business, or an army. While at first glance it might seem apt to compare the mafia to such institutions, on closer examination the analogy proves to be flawed. The mafia is essentially protean.

In the early 1980s, new investigative tactics have resulted in an in-depth portrait of the mafia's organizational structure and activities, and composition. These new insights, however, have been immensely costly; investigators have had to pay with their lives for their contribution to the knowledge of the phenomenon.

As a result of this new information, we feel more assured of the accuracy of what we know about organized crime and are able to devise plans on how to fight it. It is the work of the Palermo investigative team headed by Giovanni Falcone from 1982 to 1991 that has drawn the distinction between the "mafia" and "Cosa Nostra." Thanks to Falcone, we have been able to unveil the secret architecture of Cosa Nostra and to uncover embarrassing links between it and Italian institutions.

The most important mafia repentants ("pentiti")—Tommaso Buscetta, Salvatore Contorno, Marino Mannoia, and especially Antonino Calderone—corroborate the anti-mafia forces' picture of a formal, secret association, with rigorous rules of conduct, decision-making bodies, specific functions, plans of action, and clearly defined admissions procedures.

The aim of Cosa Nostra is to protect and promote the legal and especially the illegal economic, political, and social interests of its members, as well as to regulate its own internal conflicts.

Cosa Nostra infiltrates the government by forming clandestine liaisons with officials and politicians by means of corruption, and even violence if need be. Other large organized crime syndicates— such as the *Camorra* of Naples and Campania, the *'Ndrangheta* of Calabria, and other Sicilian mafias that do not belong to the Cosa Nostra—also display a predilection toward violence and the manipulations of legal institutions. However, only the Cosa Nostra is capable of acting so relentlessly, systematically, and efficiently.

In addition to their more pronounced political infiltration, Cosa Nostra families are distinguished from groups more generically identified as "mafiosi" by the extremely selective criteria by which they recruit their members, who on the whole come either from mafia environments or from families that have belonged to the mafia for several generations, and by their great ability to control internal conflicts and their proclivity to use violence to subjugate smaller criminal groups that operate in their territories.

The Cosa Nostra recruits members by scrupulously checking the candidate's personal and family backgrounds. It rejects out of hand anyone with a father or close relative connected to the police; anyone born outside Sicily; militants or sympathizers of left-wing political parties; individuals not conforming to the canons of conventional family morality and sexual behavior (those with illegitimate children, homosexuals, divorcés, etc.); and relatives of Cosa Nostra victims.

These admission criteria have become even stricter since the judiciary offensive of the mid-1980s and the testimony of repentants like Antonino Calderone. Cosa Nostra responded to the indictments and arrests of its members by reorganizing into smaller and more tightly knit families and drawing even sharper distinctions between their own "men of honor" and those of other Sicilian mafia groups. In addition, the potential for violent internal conflicts is limited by the Cosa Nostra's own governing bodies, such as Palermo's Provincial Commission and the Regional Commissions, and by the discipline that the individual families impose on their own members.

Yet the firm control that the Cosa Nostra exercises over intra-mafia conflicts must not be confused with the exaggerated accounts of the mafia's "ability to guarantee law and order." Today's Cosa Nostra shows no interest toward repressing or containing other underworld elements. The families maintain tight control over their territories, but they tend to take a laissez-faire attitude toward petty crime; in part this can be explained by their need to have larger pools of criminals from which to recruit the "best."

The Cosa Nostra shares some features with other secret societies: initiation rites, selection procedures, rules of management, and specific roles for each member. As Calderone points out, however, it is not a static but an ever-evolving entity. Its internal affairs are regulated by a combination of two fundamental relationships. The first can be called "protective": the Cosa Nostra rigorously protects its members' economic interests while granting each man of honor a high degree of autonomy and freedom in his business dealings. The second relationship can be called "fealty"; the Cosa Nostra demands each affiliate's absolute loyalty and submission to the family and to its representative bodies. A man of honor acquires status through a commitment "for life," symbolically expressed in a blood oath.

Without these two interrelationships, the Cosa Nostra would not have the flexibility and economic power it does today. Each man of honor thus has complete independence in terms of his quota of legal and illegal activities (bars, restaurants, moneylending, gambling, construction, etc.). There are partnerships among members, but they are by no means required. The family can "regulate," tax, and, in extreme cases, even prohibit specific illegal activities (such as kidnapping in Sicily) for the sake of the general good, but each man of honor and each family has indisputable economic freedom.

Mafia families are business enterprises, and today's mafiosi are full-fledged entrepreneurs. But the true meaning of being a mafioso, a man of honor, cannot be identified solely with market forces. Cosa Nostra families are not only businesses; the Cosa Nostra Commission is not the board of directors of a huge criminal enterprise, and the mafia is not a multinational criminal corporation. Its administrative costs are minimal, because many crucial services are absorbed by the individual. For example, lawyers' fees, which are one of the greatest expenses for American mafia families, do not pose a big problem for the Italians, given the number of lawyers in Sicily who are men of honor.

The mafia's role in the international expansion of drug trafficking, for instance, is the product of decisions made by individuals and families who form partnerships on a case-by-case basis. At times, members of different families establish joint ventures or investment pools, especially when it comes to winning public contracts. In such cases the Commission may act as a regulatory board and as an arbiter, but these functions are not inherently necessary or fundamental to the Commission itself.

Naturally, all this does not prevent a substantial percentage of mafia profits from being invested in a coordinated, concentrated fashion, something that might lead us to imagine a guiding plan or strategy. But when we study the decision-making mechanism in depth, we realize that these decisions are simply collective reactions to new developments on the part of mafia entrepreneurs who intensely influence one another.

Today the newspapers are filled with revelations about ties between the Cosa Nostra and politics, Cosa Nostra and the judiciary, Cosa Nostra and secret services, Cosa Nostra and the Masons; but while these revelations are astounding, they are not especially new. What has emerged is that the network of relationships is much more solid and widespread than was previously suspected.

In other words, the number of men of honor holding important positions in public institutions and in the professions was and may still be much higher than any of us had imagined. This is a deduction based on my conversations with Antonino Calderone, on the recent testimony of repentants before the Antimafia Parliamentary Commission, and on information that has appeared in the news over the past few months.

Calderone spoke to me about four members of the national Parliament who were formally affiliated with Cosa Nostra, and about an unspecified but certainly significant number of regional deputies during the 1970s. Other more recent repentants have provided more details and names. As it stands now, about forty Sicilian politicians, including a former minister and six members of the national Parliament, have been indicted for mafia association and other crimes. There is thus reason to hypothesize the existence of widespread direct participation in the mafia by members of the elite corps of postwar Sicilian politicians.

Unless we imagine that these politicians from the immediate postwar period to the early 1970s had split personalities, we should conclude that, first, the traditional mafiosi and their political associates shared the same ideology and subculture of friendship and honor, and, second, that in the past Cosa Nostra was not by predisposition opposed to the state, to its offices, and to its representatives.

In more recent times, however, the relationship between the mafia and the politicians has deteriorated due to the state's effort to curtail the mafia's role in mediating political and social conflicts. After the institution of the first Antimafia Parliamentary Commission, and especially after the assassination of General Dalla Chiesa in 1982, the mafia lost much of its legitimacy. Politicians no longer flaunted their relationships with mafia bosses.

The expansion of the mafia's economic power in the 1970s also gave it greater political autonomy, which ultimately led to a complete rift between the Cosa Nostra and the state. The chain of high-level crimes that began in 1979 and culminated in the 1992 massacres of investigating magistrates Giovanni Falcone and Paolo Borsellino marked the beginning of serious public opposition to the Cosa Nostra; at the same time, mafia men became much more selective and secretive in their affiliations with politicians. Nevertheless, the Cosa Nostra continued to accept some unscrupulous politicians into its ranks, though they had become wary of these individuals who even by the Cosa Nostra's standards had become treacherous and inferior.

All of this probably contributed to a decrease in the number of politicians affiliated with the mafia. But this decrease was heavily offset by men of honor who decided to enter politics, especially in local Sicilian administrations, and by a greater involvement of politicians in economic partnerships with mafiosi, or in clandestine mutual associations such as Masonic lodges.

The picture I have drawn, based in part on Antonino Calderone's testimony, suggests the outline of a strategy for fighting the Cosa Nostra in the next few years. The difference between the mafia and the Cosa Nostra does not lie in their economic and social structure or in their cultural significance. The mafia is a great social, economic, and political problem in Italy, not to mention a probable future threat to a united Europe; the Cosa Nostra is an integral part of the mafia, the organized epitome of its power.

Our first objective then is to attack the secret society: We need to arrest the bosses, break up the leadership, confiscate their property, and identify and prosecute its protectors and partners in the political world. But the Cosa Nostra as a secret society is only one aspect of the mafia question. Once the Cosa Nostra has been destroyed, the mafia will still remain as an element of society and of culture in large areas of southern Italy, and it will not be quickly eliminated through arrests and convictions. The mafia is above all an aggregate of criminal families and enterprises, businesses, networks of power, and "clean" investments spread throughout developed Europe. To confront this problem in all its amplitude will take more than five years, and more than the resources of Italy alone. Calderone's vivid testimony makes that quite clear.

—PINO ARLACCHI
Rome
May 1993

ACKNOWLEDGMENTS

This writer has enjoyed one of the greatest privileges that a student of organized crime could have wished for: the possibility to meet with a first-rank mafia member who was willing to "talk," to do so at length and in utter freedom, and to be able to record this account. This has been made possible because of the special authorization granted by the head of the Italian police, Chief Prefect Vicenzo Parisi. My gratitude toward him is equal to the respect that I have for him as I watch him safeguard our country in this difficult moment of our history.

I also must thank the architect of my meetings with Calderone, Chief Gianni De Gennaro, director of the Anti-Mafia Investigative Agency, who has had confidence from the beginning that direct contact with a "repentant" on the part of someone outside of the investigative and judiciary branches would be useful in both the analysis and the fight to combat the mafia phenomenon. His collaboration and that of his staff, led by Dr. Antonio Manganelli and by Dr. Alessandro Pansa, were indispensable in bringing this project to its successful completion.

I would also like to thank Irene Benassi and Antonella Ruggieri, my students in applied sociology

Acknowledgments

in the political science department at the University of Florence. They have exhibited extreme promise as researchers in the far-from-easy task of deciphering and transcribing the conversations that have given life to this volume.

Finally, this book would not have been possible without the benevolent tolerance of my wife, Enza Trobia, to whom it is dedicated.

—PINO ARLACCHI

In such condition, there is no place for Industry; because the fruit thereof is uncertain: and consequently no Culture of the Earth, no Navigation . . . no Knowledge of the face of the Earth; no account of Time; no Arts; no Letters; no Society; and which is worst of all, continuall feare, and danger of violent death; And the life of man, solitary, poore, nasty, brutish, and short.

—THOMAS HOBBES, *Leviathan*

MEN
OF
DISHONOR

1

My name is Antonino Calderone; I'm fifty-six years old and have much to say about the mafia because I belonged to it. I have decided to trust in justice and to talk in the hopes that what I say will be listened to. It should be, since my statements will put my family in great peril. And I'm in danger too, because I'm telling the truth and not speaking just to hear myself talk.

Until I fled from Sicily I was a representative, a boss, of the Catania "family," as was my brother Giuseppe—Pippo. My brother was killed in September 1978, and after that everything fell apart. Or rather everything had already fallen apart. But we'll proceed in order and start with the story of the mafia in my city.

It's not true, first of all, that the mafia exists only in Palermo and Trapani. The mafia has been in the province of Catania since 1925. At first there was only one family in Catania. Then, around 1950–1955, a group of mafiosi from Palma di Montechiaro moved to Ramacca, a small town in the province, and asked the Catania family for permission to form a new family. Since then there have been two mafia families in Catania.

It would be best to explain from the outset that the "mafia" as such does not exist, at least not in our eyes. The mafia calls itself Cosa Nostra; we never use the word *mafia*. The Cosa Nostra is secret, an association of men of honor. Yet a member of the Cosa Nostra cannot tell anyone that he belongs to it, so one can imagine a situation in which two individuals suspect each other to be men of honor but can say nothing to each other. For them to find out if they are both members of the Cosa Nostra, a third individual needs to introduce them, a third man of honor who knows them both. In such a case he says: "This one is the same," or, "This one is Cosa Nostra," or even, "This one is like you and me." It should be added that the Corleonesi never introduce their own soldiers except to the few people who are close to them.

Many people speak of the mafia without knowing what they're talking about. There are also individuals who come to be called mafiosi but who don't belong to the Cosa Nostra and don't even know for sure that it exists. And then there are the common criminals, of whom there are plenty, and who in recent years have become legion. Not to speak of the outcasts—small-time hoods who run around in circles without knowing where they're going.

It's important to distinguish between the true mafiosi—those of the Cosa Nostra—and the others. Let's take the case of my arrest in 1986. I was arrested on May 9 on two warrants, one of which was from the procurator of Torino and dated from 1984. The warrant was for belonging to the mafia, that is, for criminal association. Some repentants had claimed to know that I belonged to what they called "the mafia." But they were speaking to hear themselves talk, because they weren't men of honor and couldn't have been part of the mafia. They were kids from Catania who had drifted up to Torino. They thought they knew that there was a certain organization, something they called the mafia, but they knew no concrete facts. In short, they were Catanian immigrants in Torino—common hoods and not mafiosi.

I apologize for the distinction I'm drawing between the mafia and common criminals, but it matters. It matters to all mafiosi. It's important: men like us are mafiosi, the others are whatever. We are men of honor. And not so much because we have taken an oath, but because we are the elite of the criminal world. We're vastly superior to common criminals. We're worse than everybody!

Every man of honor feels this way. He knows it, he repeats it to himself continually. He feels superior to all other criminals. When he sees kids from the common criminal world, he watches them carefully, cultivates them with the idea of bringing some of them in, but he always watches them from a certain distance because they are coarse and immature and are capable of doing things a man of honor would never do—making money off prostitution, for example, which the mafia doesn't tolerate.

The mafia does not organize prostitution; it's an unclean activity. Can you imagine a man of honor living on pimping, on the money he makes from women? Perhaps in America, where mafiosi have undertaken such activities, but the mafia in Sicily doesn't do it, period. Francesco Rinella, the brother of two men of honor and the son and nephew of men of honor, was never admitted into the Cosa Nostra precisely because it was said that he was a pimp.

Men of honor become such in large part through heredity, but not in the same way as the aristocracy, where the father leaves his title to his son. In the mafia it's more complicated. There's observation, a study of the best young men by the oldest ones. The most senior mafiosi—friends of the father, relatives of the mother—watch the young ones, some of whom come to stand out from the others. These are the new bosses, the new men of honor.

Let's take a convenient example: Palermo, where there are dozens and dozens of mafia families. There are more than fifty of them, at least one for each neighborhood. In other cities there's never this sort of concentration. Each family in Palermo is made up of a representative—a boss—and at least thirty or forty men of honor. All of these are married and have children, brothers, and relatives. And so we have a man of honor with two or three promising male children. These sons are watched by the whole group, and when one of them distinguishes himself because he's clever, determined, and ruthless, he is then cultivated, encouraged by adult men of honor who teach and guide him, and if he follows them they start to let him do a few things . . .

The boy then suddenly realizes—since he's clever—that his father is a member of the mafia, that his father's friends and brothers are mafiosi too, that they are part of a select circle. The mafia becomes everything to the young man. There aren't many outside influences in this environment; no one reads newspapers or books, even nowadays few go to school, and even fewer go to church.

There is a sense of identification, of imitation. Each boy tries to copy his older brother, his father, his uncle. He sees his reflection in them, and eventually he begins to feel and look like them. When one grows up in a mafia neighborhood, one understands, one senses it even if one doesn't know it.

In my time, for instance, no one knew what it was, this mafia that everyone talks about today. In Catania, stories were told about the "Black Hand." One absorbed the mafia mentality without knowing it. A young boy's imagination is stirred by certain images: someone arrives and kisses his father; someone else arrives and kisses him and his father.

Nowadays it's absolutely normal for two men who know each other well, who are close, to kiss on certain occasions. For example, when they meet, two men can kiss if they're good friends or relatives. But in my time, in Sicily, in Catania, in Palermo, and in every other city at the end of the 1950s, that never happened. When they met, two men would shake hands, bow, and smile at each other to show affection. But they wouldn't kiss, especially not in my city. When two men kissed, it had an ambiguous flavor; no one thought it was so—normal.

I began to know the mafia, to understand the mafia, when I saw Pippo, my older brother, who was a man of honor, kiss other men of honor. Men of honor always kissed each other when they met! They were the only ones who did it.

Pippo had other friends, young men like him, whom he had known all his life. They had been raised together, they had played together, they had worked together. Yet when they met as adults they didn't kiss. They waved. They would say, "*Ciao, ciao,* how are you?" They'd joke around and tease one another, but not kiss.

So, when I saw men kissing—I didn't know yet that they were men of honor—I stood there with my mouth open, wondering, puzzled.

I was born in Catania. In the worst part of it, among the worst people. I can't even say I was born in the San Cristoforo neighborhood. Worse: I was born on the very outskirts of the city, in the very last house in Catania; the place doesn't have a name of its own. It's a thinly settled area where houses end and the road to Syracuse begins, between the beach and the highway to Palermo.

There was never a lack of bread at my house, since my father always managed to scrape something together. He worked constantly. But next door there were people dying of hunger. One of my most vivid memories is of that family with so many small children and nothing to eat. They ate when my mother gave them food.

On Sundays, another woman in the neighborhood would do the following: since Sundays were feast days when all the families cooked meat and gravy and pasta sauce, this woman would put a pot on the coals and drop a little piece of fat into it, just so the neighbors and passersby would smell meat. But there wasn't any.

—

My father was a poor peasant who hired himself out by the day, and in his spare time farmed a tiny piece of land by the sea, near to the beach, almost in the sand itself. He had only two thousand vines, small ones, just enough to make wine for us. When he wasn't working for other people he would till his own vineyard, where he had also planted vegetables among the vines. My father was Catanian. My grandfather was from the province of Messina and he too was a farmer, but he was better off because he was a laborer with many sons working for him. But my grandfather himself never took much pleasure in work.

Even though laborers were quite well-respected individuals, my grandfather was never a mafioso, and my father's family had no notion of such things. My father wasn't a mafioso either, just a hard worker who didn't even have a criminal record, except for one charge for the illegal possession of a gun, the poor man—a gun he needed for his job. By day he tilled and worked, and by night he watched orange orchards for other people. For that he had a gun, but he never used it except to go hunting.

My mother's family is another story. As I said, the first mafia family in Catania was established in 1925. The founder was actually an uncle of mine, my mother's brother, who later disappeared.

My uncle Nino was a fugitive for many years; he had been accused of murder. The murder was somehow tied to a theft of livestock; I don't know the precise circumstances. While on the run he met many mafiosi, also outlaws, from the provinces of Palermo and Caltanissetta.

In those days a fugitive hid out for the greater part of the year in the Madonìe mountains, where there was no end of mafiosi and bandits and where it was very difficult to come looking for them. The Madonìe were very isolated, very tall. There were few roads through them, and few people knew their way over their paths and tracks, and those who knew certainly wouldn't tell the *sbirri,* as anyone from the state, the police, or the carabinieri came to be called. One would say now that the mafia "controlled the area."

Today this control is still essential for the very same reasons. The vital position in the Cosa Nostra occupied by Peppino Farinella, the vicious boss of the family from San Mauro Castelverde— a village in the Madonìe that lies at an altitude of more than two thousand feet—rests on his capacity to provide fugitives with a bewildering web of safe havens in the most inaccessible areas. The hiding places are under the jurisdiction of a number of men of honor who live in the populated areas below, and who are under Farinella's control.

The paths and tracks of the Madonìe have been in existence since antiquity, when they were first used to drive herds out of mountain pastures into the lowlands as the seasons changed. When winter came, even the most highly wanted fugitives would move to the lowlands and the hills—to Caltanissetta, Catania, and other places. They would travel by night, on horseback, through forests and gorges and along country paths. On one of these migrations my uncle's horse fell into a ravine. My uncle broke his leg and was arrested. He was tried, but was convicted for criminal association rather than murder.

In the meantime, he had been made a man of honor by the

mafiosi who were fugitives with him. Since in those days there was no family in Catania, he was made a man of honor in a family from Gangi.

I don't know how many years my uncle was sentenced to. Eventually he got out, but he was unlucky. The prefect Mori came to Sicily, and my uncle was sent to the Island [Pantelleria or Lampedusa, probably—P.A.]. Mussolini had sent everyone like him to the Island. But before going there my uncle had time to do something very important.

While he had been in prison, some mafiosi from Palermo arrived in Catania. Their name was Tagliavia, and they introduced clandestine gaming houses to Catania. In order to run them they needed local people. They took the initiative and set them up, but gambling houses can't flourish without people who know the environment well, who can find good clients and keep the underworld, which always gravitates around gambling, at bay. Thus, the Tagliavias had approached two or three reliable men, one Giuseppe Indelicato, one Tino Florio . . . They made them men of honor, later approached others, and so on.

When my uncle got out of prison toward the end of the 1920s, he found that a small group of Catanian men of honor had been formed, some ten to fifteen reliable men "brought out" by the Palermitans. My uncle formally belonged to a Palermo family, but he was Catanian, the city's first man of honor, and he had an excellent reputation because everyone knew of his record in the mafia. It was decided to bring him into the Catania family and to nominate him its representative.

My uncle quickly dedicated himself to the task. He increased the number of men of honor and made many astute decisions, leaving a mark that everyone remembers. He had started out as a farmer, but then had taken up smuggling between Malta and Sicily. Along with fish he imported coffee from Malta, where it was cheap, to Sicily, where it was expensive. A number of men of honor were involved in this activity, and from a business point of view the family prospered.

This is what he would do. He'd ask a man from the family: "What sort of work do you do? Good. Then do this . . ." If a man of honor worked in an orange warehouse, my uncle would find a way of having him open a small warehouse for himself. If another worked in, say, an ice house (there were many ice houses then, because there were no refrigerators and ice was in great demand), fine—my uncle would open a small ice house, put him in charge of it, and have other men of honor start working there. Then he would make the rounds of the bars in Catania and "suggest" that the owners buy ice from that house.

My uncle did the things they're doing now in the twenties, and for those days it was a small coup. He would protect his markets, encourage the businesses of men in the family. At the same time he involved everyone in smuggling coffee, which was a big deal back then, not unlike drug smuggling today. Coffee and saccharine would be brought in from Malta and resold in bars and refreshment stands, which were very numerous. In the twenties and thirties there were stands like that all over the city. It was a boom—not like now, when only a couple of them are left. The stands served very popular fizzy drinks based on citrus extracts; saccharine was added instead of sugar, which was much more expensive.

Given the great demand, the saccharine "trade" thrived, and my uncle controlled all of it. Business was good, the family was doing well, and people showed great respect for the men of honor, who were beginning to be known by the whole population. They were referred to as "those of the Black Hand," not as mafiosi.

Then Mori showed up and the troubles began. To tell the truth, these troubles didn't come about because of what was going on in Catania. Mori didn't consider Catania a mafia city, and at first he didn't pay much attention to it. What happened was that some American men of honor of Sicilian descent had started to hide out in Catania. They were fugitives from a mafia war in America. There was a Catanian man of honor who had lived in America for a while and was still in contact with the Sicilian families there. And they would say to him: "As soon as so-and-so shows up in Catania, make him disappear." Or: "Get such-and-such taken out of circulation. He just got there."

A number of Americans who landed in Catania thus disappeared—they were murdered. After a while Catanians started to vanish as well. Men would evaporate into thin air without warning: the famous "white *lupara*."* At one point nine people disappeared in just one week, something unheard-of in those days. It was very big news. And so all the men of honor in my uncle's family were arrested, but only on charges of criminal association.

As I've mentioned, the music changed and the mafioso's life became difficult. Many were sent off to the Island. There they were put in a sort of large barracks—a warehouse. Every morning the warehouse was opened and they went out to work. Most would go to the fields, and at night they were locked back up again. It would have been difficult to escape from the Island, since it's in the middle of the channel, where it's very windy. In the winter it's not cold, but the sea is almost always heavy.

It seems that at one point there was nearly a mutiny. The internees had rebelled and refused to go back into the barracks. So Mussolini sent a ship to anchor offshore, and through a loudspeaker they threatened to bombard the Island if the authorities weren't obeyed. This story is based on what I've been told by old men; my uncle himself didn't know anything about it.

The fact was that my uncle was in trouble. In those days Mussolini and Mori—who was the head of the Justice Department—did the following. They would sentence someone to five years on the Island, the maximum. When the five years were up, or even before, they would issue a decree and tack on another five.

Decreed! Five more years.

This had already happened before my uncle even set foot on the Island, and he didn't know anything about it. But soon afterward the additional five years were given to him too. "Oh, no, it's never going to end," my uncle thought.

I don't know the details, but a steamer came to the Island, my uncle took it, and it was all over. He ended up in Tunis. But before that, in 1935, the year I was born, he came to Catania as a fugitive

---

*In Sicilian dialect a *lupara* is a sawed-off shotgun. A "white *lupara*" is a clean, "bloodless" murder in which the victim's body is never found (translator's note).

and stayed for several days. Then he went away again, never to return. After he left, the coffee-smuggling business was taken over by another uncle of mine, Luigi Saitta.

My grandmother was sure that Uncle Nino was dead, and then all the relatives became sure of it too, because there was a mafia family in Tunis that had been formed in the thirties. You shouldn't be surprised if you haven't heard about it—no one who isn't an insider has heard about it. I learned about it only after I became a man of honor, when my brother started telling me, a bit at a time, everything that I had to know about the circumstances surrounding the mafia—the individuals who are part of it, about murders and those who had committed them.

Upon his arrival in Tunis my uncle set himself up in business, since he didn't think he'd be able to go home anytime soon. He acquired a large property on the outskirts of the city, but he didn't join the Tunis family, either because it didn't accept him or because he didn't want to be a part of it. At the time Tunis was a haven for many mafiosi fleeing from fascism. They came from Caltanissetta, Palermo, and other cities. They had formed a regular family with a representative.

Some men from the Tunis family and a few other mafia fugitives formed a close friendship with my uncle. Among the fugitives was Antonino Sorci, an important man of honor from Palermo, who was later killed, along with his son, in 1983. Family members complained to my uncle about their representative, saying that he made them carry out a whole stack of murders and didn't deserve to be in his position. Even fugitives who weren't part of the family were complaining. Sorci himself didn't trust the family boss but was compelled, for survival's sake, to commit murders and whatever else he was ordered to do. No one knew where Sorci slept because he was afraid that the representative was going to have him killed. Sometimes, so that people wouldn't know where he spent the night, he would sleep in a cemetery.

The case of the fugitives is worth a little elaboration. It was very useful to have them commit murders, since no one knew they were in Tunis. They were outside their territories and beyond the protection of their families. They were in the hands of other people, mafia people, to be sure, but dishonest and untrustworthy nevertheless—just like the Tunis representative, who used fugitives to carry out assassinations, stabbings, and anything dangerous. Everything would go off fine, only he would kill them afterward. He would justify their disappearances with lies that he passed on— if he even bothered—to the dead men's families.

So these Tunis mafiosi complained to my uncle about the representative. "Why keep going on about him?" my uncle replied. "Bring the man here to my property on some pretext. We'll arrange a big dinner, as though we're all going to enjoy ourselves, and we'll kill him." Everyone was enthusiastic about the idea. On the night in question the guests arrived, but—because the informant had gotten scared or had thought things over, who knows—someone told the representative. And so instead of killing him they killed my uncle. We haven't managed to find out anything more about it. There have been rumors and hints, but concrete facts have never turned up.

Many years later, after the war, someone from the province of Caltanissetta became representative of this Tunis family. After the governor of Tunis had driven the family out, this representative— his name was Calogero Giambarresi—returned home to his native town of Riesi. This was also the town of Giuseppe Di Cristina, the famous Di Cristina who was the Riesi family representative and the best man at my brother Pippo's wedding. They were the closest of friends.

When we heard about Giambarresi's return, my brother said to Di Cristina: "You should ask him who killed my uncle." Pippo already had a name in Sicily and wanted to carry out a vendetta.

Giambarresi didn't have a choice. He had to tell the truth because Di Cristina was his representative, and one of the cardinal rules of the Cosa Nostra is the duty to tell the truth to one's associates, and especially to one's superiors. He said, "I can't tell Pippo who murdered his uncle. If he wants I can go to Tunis to recover his uncle's bones for him, because I know where he was buried. But I can't tell him who murdered him." And in fact he couldn't say.

He knew, but he couldn't say it because Pippo had evil intentions. Pippo would have taken revenge, and Giambarresi would have had to pay for having told him.

Giambarresi realized that my brother was extremely angry with him, and he thought it best to leave the Riesi family. He joined the Caltanissetta family to put some distance between himself and Pippo and Di Cristina. I myself once ran into this Giambarresi in Caltanissetta. He was very frightened; he didn't know if he should offer me coffee or run away. He was scared that I would force him to tell me what he knew.

We wanted to know. But the only thing we managed to learn was that, many years before, my other uncle, Luigi, had been told that two brothers from Trapani, whose name was Di Stefano, had been involved in the murder. One of them had betrayed my uncle and informed the representative about the plan to kill him, but my uncle Luigi didn't know which one.

—

Let's turn to the story of the mafia in Catania, which is also the story of my mother's family. My uncle Antonino was succeeded, as I said, by my uncle Luigi Saitta, a very prominent man in the Cosa Nostra. Pippo held him in enormous esteem. He had always defended him from his critics, and in fact fought like a lion for him. Some men of honor didn't think much of Uncle Luigi because his family situation was messy. His wife had cheated on him, left him, and run off with another man, with whom she had other children. My uncle should have killed her but he didn't; he couldn't bring himself to. But these men's condemnation was hollow, a pretext, because my uncle had been made a man of honor when the situation with his wife already existed, and everyone knew about it.

There was another reason for the discontent. By the end of the fifties the Catania family had grown. The representative in those days was a longtime mafioso, Vincenzo Palermo, a very old man who had only one arm. The other had been shot off. Palermo was a tough man of the old school who had lived the life of a fugitive and was used to shooting and murdering without much of a fuss. My uncle Luigi was of that school too.

But when it came to naming my uncle vice-representative, a group of men of honor in the Catania family began to raise objections. They were weak men, often in trouble, and in reality they were scared of my uncle. They didn't want him as a boss because he could shoot well and was capable of personally killing anyone who committed a few big blunders.

Nevertheless, these individuals dredged up the pretext of his family situation and opposed him. My brother defended Uncle Luigi by saying, "My uncle is already in the family. According to you he's worthy of being a part of it. Didn't you yourselves make him a man of honor? Someone who has been admitted into a family can hold any position inside it. You can't come here today and say that he can't be elected vice-representative. In that case, you shouldn't have made him a man of honor."

The matter became more and more serious, and the controversy developed into an internal war in the Catania family. On one side was a group that stood with my uncle, and on the other were those who maintained that he couldn't become vice-representative. Unfortunately, not many stood by him. A break occurred, and the others formed a family of their own.

Agatino Florio, one of the first men of honor in Catania and formerly the family vice-representative (who now became representative), my brother, and a very few others remained with my uncle. A large number defected, and as their representative they named the very same Vincenzo Palermo who had once been so close to my uncle.

2

The nomination of a family boss takes place through regular elections, with everyone having the right to vote. If there are, for example, thirty or forty men of honor in one family, everything is very simple. I've participated in elections in my family, which has never numbered more than forty men. To elect a boss, a meeting is arranged, a secretary is appointed to preside, and he is the first to propose a name. The secretary says: "I see X as representative. Who agrees?" And then everyone declares himself, in public, by holding up his hand.

All this is fine if the family is small. In big families—those numbering 150 to 200 men—things are done differently. Each *decina* boss gathers and polls his men, then reports their feelings, since a family of 200 can't be gathered together. There are no suitable places and it's too dangerous: a large group in one place is too easy a target for the police or enemies.

A family's hierarchy begins with the men of honor, the "soldiers." In Palermo they're called *picciotti.** We've called them soldiers for a long time, even before the film *The Godfather.* Above them are the *decina* bosses, that is, the heads of groups of five, ten, twenty, or even thirty men of honor. There's no fixed number; it depends on the size of the family. Above them are the vice-representative and the representative.

*"Boys" in dialect (translator's note).

In my family, the vice-representative has no right to vote at all. If the representative is absent, he is the one who decides, but if the representative is present, the vice-representative counts for little or nothing. The members of the council don't even have to call him in when they meet. The council is made up of representatives and *consiglieri*. If there's only one *decina* boss, or two at the maximum, they are also called in to council meetings. When there are many *decina* bosses—four, five, or even up to ten—they are not called in.

If a problem concerning a specific *decina* has to be discussed, the boss of that group is often called in and officially asked for explanations and clarifications of the matter in question. Otherwise, it's the council that decides.

The *consiglieri* have nothing to do with the *decina* bosses. They are entities unto themselves. A *consigliere* is an ordinary man of honor who at some point is chosen for the role. He is a truly important figure. In some cases he is as important as his representative, since he is very close to him, influences him, informs him, and presents things to him in a certain light.

The *decina* boss is different. He has specific duties: he commands men and follows orders; he has to "take care" of his *decina;* he's the channel between the representative and the men of honor. The representative, for example, can say to a *decina* boss: "Pass on to your *decina,* to someone in your *decina,* that this specific operation needs to be carried out [murder, extortion, blackmail, etc.]. Pick one of your men and let him do it. If you need to, ask this other *decina* for another man." And that's all. Or rather, that was how everything was until a short time ago. No one went over his superiors' heads. If a man of honor had to ask for authorization from the head of the family, he would turn to his *decina* boss, who would forward the request to the representative, who would approve it or turn it down.

At one time the hierarchy inside a family was more formal. The representative would not give direct orders, nor would he himself speak to men of honor. Orders would always come from the *decina* boss. Today the arrangements are often different. There are representatives who have direct contact with some men of honor, either because they're closer to him or because he considers them more trustworthy.

But let's turn to the *consigliere*. As I've said, the *consigliere* has no relations with the *decina* boss or with the vice-representative, who is named by the representative immediately after his own election and is the person the representative most trusts, who is ready to substitute for him in case of arrest, accident, or absence. In the past there have been many cases, however, in which the vice-representative was also elected and played an important role in all the family's business.

The *consigliere* is always elected by the family's men of honor, and his duty is to stand beside and even to control the representative. If the representative's head swells and he becomes a despot and starts to give absurd orders, making mistakes that affect the whole family, it's the duty of the *consigliere* to slow him down, to make him see reason.

The *consigliere* must tell the truth and present things to the representative as they are. That novel, the film that was made from it, *The Godfather,* I mean, was well researched. I've read the book and seen the film (as has everyone else in my family, in fact). Granted, like anything that gets novelized it goes beyond reality, but in certain respects it's accurate. The *consigliere* really is a *consigliere,* someone who offers his honest views to the boss, and the boss is presented as someone who needs to hear another opinion.

A family is autonomous in its own territory. The power of the representative and *consigliere* is autonomous too, but not in every case—the decision to kill someone, for instance.

If a man in the family's territory has to be killed as punishment for a standard error, business as usual, like a *sbirritudine* [being a police informant—P.A.], the representative makes the decision, the *decina* boss has it carried out, and the man is no more. The representative's only responsibility is to report to the district boss— the boss of a territory that encompasses three families. The representative tells him: "Listen, you should know—what happened yesterday [or the day before yesterday, or last week, etc.], I had it done." In his turn, the district boss mentions it when he sees the provincial representative, and everything ends there.

The important thing is precise information. Accurate, exact information must circulate in the mafia. Otherwise nothing can be certain and everything becomes a big mess. Around 1975 my brother was in danger of being killed by a group of Catanians who had fled to Milan after an encounter with the Pillera gang, because the boss of the Catanians had become convinced, completely erroneously, that Pippo had become the Pillera boss. Three of them left from Milan expressly to kill him, and if it hadn't been for Gerlando Alberti—who pretended to go along with the plan, but had two of the killers disappear during their stopover in Naples—I don't know what would have happened. Lack of information could have cost a man his life.

If it isn't known who committed a murder, or if it's known but the information is wrong, then no one can be sure of anything, not even of his own safety. And this is the game that those diabolical, dishonest Corleonesi played. They lied about the murders they committed! And they fucked everyone! But let's drop the Corleonesi for the time being and move on.

If, on the other hand, an important man has to be hit—a politician or policeman or judge—the decision has to come from above, from the highest level, namely from the regional commission, which I'll talk about more thoroughly later. This is logical. A murder of this kind can cause harm to everyone. True, the killing is done in a given territory, but its consequences will be paid later by everyone.

And then there are particular instances in which the commission, or even the provincial representative, can decide—even for ordinary killings—that it's better to remain calm. Because a verdict is being waited for, or because countermeasures are in the air, or because it's a moment in which the government is making threatening gestures (it will pass . . . best to wait for a while). In these instances, even if someone denounces someone else's misbehavior—"So-and-so did this"; "Such-and-such did that, we have to step in!"—the answer from the summit is: "It's all right. Patience. There's no need to act today. We'll wait a while longer."

There's only one case in which these strictures are suspended:

that of a mafioso who unexpectedly goes into hiding, who vanishes with the object of contacting the carabinieri to inform them of something serious, to collaborate with them. In such circumstances the alarm is immediately sounded. The order, in fact the obligation, for every man of honor is to look for that individual and to kill him on the spot, wherever he is and at any time. Any man of honor can and should kill him under any circumstances and without waiting for the approval of anyone, even if there are police around or if trials are still pending.

But if another kind of matter is involved—if the decision can be postponed—one tries to take one's time so that the newspapers won't write about it and there won't be a public uproar. There's always time. There's no danger of things being forgotten with the passage of days and months. The mafia doesn't leave things unfinished, half-done. The mafia is serious. It's useless to fool oneself: if it has made a decision, it will carry it out to the finish—except in cases where there's been a change of command, and even then only if it's a limited infraction that doesn't break all the rules of the association.

I'll explain myself better. One shouldn't forget that the mafia is an organization of people who have taken an oath—an organization that has specific rules. But still it's comprised of men, and men have their own preferences, their own enmities, and their own antipathies, even when they hold high positions. If Michele Greco has the commission approve a decision of his that has to be carried out in a month—or in two months, or three—and when the time comes to carry it out he's no longer the boss of the commission, then there's a chance that nothing will be done about it. In the eyes of the mafia members the decision could be perceived as too personal, something that one *would* carry out even if one wasn't entirely convinced by it, but that one would also let slide if Greco was no longer in the same position of leadership.

But if it's a decision that concerns everyone, that has a bearing on the interests of everyone, then there's no choice. There's no appeal. Were it decided that every repentant must be killed, from the first to the last, there's no turning aside. Even if the leadership changes, even if so much time passes that the men who come to form the commission no longer know me or the other repentants, there's no fooling oneself. They will not forget.

The men of the mafia never forget. They always take revenge. Think of my brother: in the 1970s, thirty-five or forty years after my uncle's death, there he was, trying to find out how my uncle was murdered, and he was ready to kill those responsible who were still alive! The old mafia was like that. And the "new mafia," as it's called in the newspapers, is in this respect exactly the same as the old.

In 1969, immediately after he was named provincial representative from Palermo, a mafioso like Gaetano Badalamenti (there's no sense in calling someone like him "new" or "old") ordered Salvatore Zaza, a Neapolitan camorrista affiliated with the Cosa Nostra, to kill a man. Why? Because many years before, toward the end of the 1950s, at the Agnano horse track, the man had slapped Lucky Luciano, who had just appeared from America. The killing was carried out, and Badalamenti was proud to have it immediately known in the United States that the offense had been washed away with blood, even if after some delay.

—

The shrewdness of the Cosa Nostra has always lain in the fact that, although it is an association of men of honor, secret and for the few, at the same time it has remained connected with normal life, with the professions and ordinary businesses. Except for judges and the police, there are all kinds of people from every segment of society inside the mafia. The mafioso is like a spider— he builds webs of friends, of acquaintances, of obligations. Today money has taken over and everything has degenerated, no one spends the time to cultivate friendships, but until recently there were still people like my brother Pippo, who fully lived the life of the mafioso.

And there are many entrepreneurs in the Cosa Nostra. In fact, the majority is made up of businessmen: people who own shops, firms, enterprises; people who make deals, come up with ideas; people on the go from morning till night; restless men who enjoy the active life, who love new things, who have endless connections in every sphere; entrepreneurs on the alert twenty-four hours a day. By day they run their affairs like everyone else, and they work hard. And at night, instead of going to sleep, they're likely to go out stealing, like the representative from the Catania family who had a thriving trucking business that serviced innumerable small businesses in the city. He was a respected and well-known figure, but at night he would go out stealing with the uncle of Nitto Santapaola.

Luciano Liggio knew how to farm, as did all the Grecos and Corleonesi. The Bontades were citrus traders. There have always been many citrus traders and exporters in the Cosa Nostra, and today there is an infinite number of builders and building contractors. Cavataio was a small builder. Rosario Spatola was a major contractor, one of the biggest in Palermo. One of the Vernengos had an ice house. Badalamenti kept cows and sold cheese. Many others were involved in trucking, used-car dealing, butcher shops, livestock trading, fishing, fruit products. Nitto Santapaola started off as a traveling shoe salesman and ended up with the Catania Renault concession, which was inaugurated in the presence of the prefect and highest authorities, while his brother Salvatore had a rotisserie. The Ferreras sold mineral water and had gambling houses. Later on, with money from smuggling and drugs, many bought hotels, farmland, and a great number of apartment houses. The Santapaolas bought themselves a whole section of the *via* Vincenzo Giaffruga neighborhood in Palermo.

There are priests as well—like Father Agostino Coppola, who officiated at the marriage between Totò Riina and the Bagarella woman while Riina was a fugitive—and doctors and lawyers. Mafia bosses have a weakness for the law. They send their sons to university and make sure they study law. Giovanni Bontade was an attorney-at-law, and he was called "the lawyer." The lawyer Chiaracane was a man of honor in the Misilmeri family as well as the son and nephew of mafia bosses.

The respect a mafioso enjoys within the Cosa Nostra is not dependent, however, on his profession or academic degrees. Though he was a great man of honor, a real leader capable of commanding and ruling a family, sure of himself, elegant, Stefano Bontade had a very modest education. He was the complete opposite of his brother Giovanni, who had a university degree but was a more lackluster and indecisive person, and was considered very much inferior to Stefano both inside and outside the family. All the more so since he would run off crying to Michele Greco whenever Stefano or someone else mistreated him.

The Corleone bosses were not educated at all, but they were cunning and diabolical. They were also sharp and ferocious, a rare combination in the Cosa Nostra. Totò Riina was unbelievably ignorant, but he had intuition and intelligence and was difficult to fathom and very hard to predict. And at the same time he was savage. His philosophy was that if someone's finger hurt, it was better to cut off his whole arm just to make sure. Bino Provenzano was nicknamed *"u viddano,"* "the Peasant," because of the cunning of his methods. My brother called him *"u tratturi,"* "the Tractor," because of his capacity for slaughter and his effects on a problem or an individual.

One of the best men of honor I've known is without a doubt Totò Greco "Cicchitedu."* He was a mesmerizer gifted with great charisma. And he was very different from that sham, his cousin Michele, a nobody who was kept in mothballs until 1975, when his other cousin, Totò Greco "the Engineer," made him a provincial representative and district boss.

Nor is it a given that a man of honor's reputation and notoriety outside the Cosa Nostra coincides with his real position inside the organization. Everyone knows Calogero Vizzini, "Don Calò," and everyone has heard of Genco Russo. They were renowned, the newspapers talked about them all the time. Yet Vizzini was never a representative inside Sicily. The boss of the regional commission at the time (in the fifties) was actually Andrea Fazio, a mafioso from Trapani whom no one knew. And Genco Russo was only the representative from the province of Caltanissetta. The notoriety of Russo and Vizzini was not viewed with pleasure inside the Cosa Nostra. They were too much in the limelight, gave interviews,

*"Little bird" in dialect (translator's note).

even allowed themselves to be photographed. They became household names, like singers and ballerinas. They were talked about very ironically in the Cosa Nostra in those days. Totò Minore used to say about Genco Russo, "Did you see him in the newspaper today, that Gina Lollobrigida?"

The great men of honor were little known. They were people who shielded themselves from publicity, like the aged Giovannino Mongiovino, whom my brother once offered the position of regional representative. He begged him to take it because his authority was enough to guarantee the respect of every family. But Mongiovino refused, saying that he wouldn't hear of representing people who didn't deserve to be in the Cosa Nostra.

—

I was in school until the sixth grade. I went to elementary school until the beginning of the war, then I stopped; I only started again after the arrival of the Americans. When I enrolled in school again I was twelve years old and still couldn't read or write, so my brother sent me to take private lessons with a woman tutor who came from a rich family in the neighborhood. I went to her for one or two years, I don't remember exactly, and then I took the seventh-grade exams. My tutor's father had been Pippo's godfather (confirmation godfather, nothing to do with the mafia). He was not a man of honor. He was a normal person, a merchant, and had several large grain warehouses. As a child I saw those warehouses often. They seemed absolutely enormous to me, with high walls all around and an immense interior courtyard surrounded by concrete silos filled to the ceiling with fine grain.

Two of my maternal uncles, Vincenzo and Luigi Saitta, were finding themselves in troubled waters economically. Both of them were doing the best they could to make ends meet. Luigi, you'll remember, was a mafioso of some rank. Vincenzo wasn't a mafioso, but he was no less a rascal than Luigi. Two men like that were having financial problems because fascism had left the mafiosi impoverished. There was nearly no mafia left after the war. The Sicilian families had been shut down by the prefect Mori. The mafia was a plant no longer being tended. My uncle Luigi, a boss, a power, had been reduced to pickpocketing to earn his bread, to survive.

Then the reorganization began. There was talk of tobacco. My uncle Vincenzo in particular, an intelligent man well endowed with talents and friendships, knew some people in Puglia, from the Lecce area, who had a government contract permitting them to acquire sacks of powdered-tobacco fertilizer. These sacks were produced by a state enterprise and were being sold for paltry sums to farmers. My uncle got himself into the same contract and would show up in front of the factory with a convoy of trucks. After being paid a bribe, the factory director would have the trucks loaded with uncut tobacco, the good kind used for cigarettes. The trucks would leave for Catania and cross the strait of Messina without a problem. In those days the passage of ferryboats between Italy and Sicily was closely controlled by the customs service, since salt in Sicily cost much less than it did on the continent and there was a thriving contraband trade. But my uncle knew a functionary in the railway service who had enough rank to allow him to avoid inspections. My uncle's trucks, and the train cars he sometimes used instead, would cross the strait in complete tranquillity.

It wasn't necessary to have a large amount of capital. The fertilizer cost very little, and the bribes were something between friends, between people who respected each other. They would be paid after the sale of the shipments. There was no need to lay out large sums of cash. Friendship substituted for money and banks.

The loads of tobacco would be dropped off near my house, in the grain warehouses that had been emptied out expressly for this purpose—mountains and mountains of tobacco bags that we children would play on top of. The bags were all the same size and had originally been filled with almonds—a hundred kilograms of almonds each. At the end of every workday my uncles would fill a bag with the money they had taken in and begin to count it. But it was the money of the time, the "Am-lira" of the American occupation, which was worth little. The partnership was made up of my uncles and another person, who in reality directed it all.

Pippo would take part too, as a trusted collaborator, but he wasn't a full partner and was paid less.

The most fascinating sight for us children was that of the grain (that is, tobacco) warehouse's courtyard immediately after the arrival of a large shipment. On these occasions a colorful crowd would assemble in the open space—two, three hundred people of every type. Poor people and ruffians came from every quarter of Catania, from villages in the provinces, from places even farther away. And I would enjoy the scene from the window of my tutor's house, which had a view of the courtyard. I'd ask for permission to get a drink and go mingle in the crowd. They were good-humored people who would play with me. They were happy because there was money to be made. Each of them would buy a bag or two of tobacco. They would go home and resell it, in paper parcels weighing a kilo or two, to retailers, who in their turn would sell it to smokers in little packets of thirty to fifty grams. No one in those days bought ready-made cigarettes. One would go to a tobacconist to buy tobacco and papers to roll it in. But it was easier to restock on the street. Naturally, those who bought the bags would earn more money than the retailers, and they'd make more friends too, since they knew where to get tobacco, and where to get it without danger.

Let's not forget that there was nothing at all legal in this business, even if customs was entirely aware of it. In fact, my uncles' secret partner, the one who had organized everything, who had introduced my uncle Vincenzo to the tobacco manufacturer and the railway functionary, was himself a major in the Finance Guard.* A crony of my uncle Luigi, he was later promoted to colonel and died, the poor man, of a heart attack while he was at the wheel of his car here in Catania.

It was a profitable business that allowed my uncles to reestablish themselves after the terrible times under Mori and during the war. Then, like he often does, at a certain point the devil stuck his tail

---

*The Finance Guard (the *Guardia Finanza*) is the armed-police branch of the Italian customs and internal revenue services; depending on context, it is rendered as either customs or the Finance Guard (translator's note).

into things. But before explaining how, I have to relate one incident.

One of the wholesale buyers who came to restock at my uncles' warehouse, Natale Di Raimondo, had declared a little while before that customs had confiscated two bags from him. But it wasn't true. My uncle Luigi had ways of knowing for sure that it wasn't true. He didn't lack the means since the most important partner in the enterprise was the chief of the Finance Guard in Catania himself. Thus it was obvious that Di Raimondo was lying in the hopes of not paying. Di Raimondo was one of those who didn't pay on the spot, but only after he'd sold the merchandise—on his word, as is done between honest people. Everyone would pay sooner or later. There was trust. But there was also fear of the consequences of a possible falling out with uncle Luigi, who was a very well-known mafioso. My uncle said to him, patiently and politely: "Natale, don't insist. Look, I know that customs has nothing to do with this at all. If you don't have the money to settle your account, it's no problem. But don't keep on with this story about customs, because it isn't true."

"I'm not paying, because customs took the two bags from me," Di Raimondo retorted.

Sometime after this discussion, the usual crowd gathered in the warehouse courtyard to wait for the arrival of a shipment. There were many people, especially since weeks had passed since the last consignment. The customers were fidgety because they were dying for a smoke, prices had gone up, and the wait was tense. It was a summer afternoon. My uncle Vincenzo was in the courtyard, his hands in his pockets, talking with the buyers and saying that there was a delay, urging them to be patient.

Then this Di Raimondo arrived and asked: "Isn't there any tobacco for me?"

"There isn't any tobacco for anybody. We're standing here waiting for it to come at any moment. As soon as it's here there'll be tobacco for everybody," my uncle replied. But Di Raimondo figured that it was a setup—can you imagine?—against him, expressly arranged to not sell him tobacco because he had missed some payments. To think that my uncles would have canceled the sale of a great quantity of goods to two hundred people simply because he hadn't paid!

But there's little one can do, alas, about idiots. Di Raimondo threw a punch at my uncle, who was standing there with his hands in his pockets. My uncle fell, hit his head, and was knocked unconscious. My other uncle, Luigi, the mafioso, wasn't there. He was asleep in his house, which was a little way off. Pippo, however, was in the courtyard talking with a few people when he heard voices and saw my uncle on the ground, with Di Raimondo pulling out a knife to stab him. This Di Raimondo was not a mafioso. He was just a small-time Catania hoodlum. He might also have been a police informant. So Pippo drew his pistol and shot at Di Raimondo, who tried to defend himself by pulling a bundle out of his pocket. It was a handkerchief wrapped around something. Everyone thought it was probably a hand grenade, because Di Raimondo had a brother who had fought as a partisan in the North (it was a peculiar family), and they all scattered.

My brother kept on shooting, but it was, unfortunately, an automatic pistol that jammed almost immediately. He was forced to take cover, and he hid behind some barrels that happened to be in the courtyard. What Di Raimondo actually had was a pistol, and he started shooting at Pippo. In the meantime, Pippo cleared his pistol and hit Di Raimondo, who fell to the ground. Everyone yelled: "He's killed him! He's killed him."

I was in school at the time, that is, in the house of my tutor, who lived on the second floor, overlooking the warehouse. I had heard the shots and the yelling, and I immediately thought of Pippo. I ran out of the house and saw him washing up and getting ready to run off to hide.

Di Raimondo wasn't dead. A man of honor at the scene—a certain Ferrera, who was nicknamed "Cavadduzzu" and was the father of the celebrated Ferrera brothers—helped him and brought him to a doctor. Di Raimondo was treated, and, after a couple of days of being in critical danger, recovered.

My family took care of the matter after that. They went to speak with the chief of police and everything ended there. The incident was closed. They knew everything at the police department. More than three hundred people had been in the courtyard, and half of them were small-time smugglers who every few days would go in and tell the police what they knew (and even, sometimes, what they didn't know, because they made up nonexistent facts either to make themselves look good or to feel important). In any case, the matter was resolved in the following way: Di Raimondo had to declare that he had pulled a small knife, although with no violent intent, and my brother had to declare that he had misread the gesture and reacted by shooting out of justified self-defense. I don't think anyone went to trial.

But the smuggling had to stop. They had to wait until the furor raised by the episode died down, and Pippo went into hiding for a while. In the meantime, the demand for contraband tobacco lessened because the factories had started producing again and there were no longer shortages at the tobacconists'.

After the tobacco trade dried up, Pippo and my uncle Vincenzo opened a fabric store. My brother had experience selling fabric because for ten years he had worked as a clerk at a wholesaler's on the Piazza Bicocca in Catania. The new business opened in 1948, and that was when my brother was made a man of honor.

■

I've already talked about the split that occurred in the Catania family in the fifties, after the outcry against naming my uncle Luigi vice-representative. The members of the family that was created after the split would meet in another neighborhood, San Cristoforo, while my uncle, Pippo, and the remnants of the old family met on the Corso d'Italia. No division of territories had taken place. There has never been a real division by neighborhood in Catania because the single-family tradition made for one unified territory.

The Palermo families had contacts with both my uncle's group and its rivals. They tried to reconcile the divided family, but they didn't succeed because neither my uncle Luigi nor Pippo wanted to hear of going back to being part of the family as it had been, with the same members. Thus the split endured for many years to come.

These were very sad years for me. I was very fond of my uncle Luigi, who developed a terrible cancer of the nose. He was operated on in Milan, but the operation went badly. I even quit my job at the Agricultural Commission so that I could be near him and care for him.

Pippo got engaged during this period. He saw a girl, he liked her, and he followed her to see where she lived: that was how it was done in those days. The girl lived in a palazzo that belonged to a man of honor whom Pippo knew well. He was in fact nothing less than the nephew of Giuseppe Indelicato, the representative of the rival family. My brother had met this man of honor a number of times, since he was one of the more receptive of our rivals, a person who could be talked to and reasoned with.

Pippo slowly began to realize that he liked the girl quite seriously, and the decision ripened in him to marry her. He started by telling this nephew of Indelicato, who was none other than her brother. He stopped him in the street and communicated his intentions toward his sister. The man of honor was happy with the news, because notwithstanding the rift between the families, he held Pippo in great esteem. Thus a course of diplomacy began. The marriage smoothed the quarrels, people calmed down, and the Catania family reunited. People from all over Sicily had tried to resolve the conflict, and they had come up with nothing. A marriage, however, settled everything.

At one point a delegation went to my uncle Luigi and officially proposed to make him the provincial representative—no longer the vice-representative of a single family, which he was before the split, but a much higher position. But my uncle didn't accept: "I'm dying now, and I can't work anymore. Keep me, if you want, as a soldier." And he suggested nominating Giuseppe Indelicato, Pippo's new uncle, as provincial representative, because he was capable of uniting the discordant family by proving himself greater than small quarrels and vendettas.

—

True, the division inside the family had never been total or irreversible. Even if people had become enemies for clan reasons, for reasons of power, not every bridge had been burned. There were still principles that outweighed the differences. Let's take the friendship, the respect, between two strong men: my uncle Luigi and Vincenzo Palermo. It had never ended, not even after they found themselves on opposing sides.

The proof is in the following episode, which took place after the split. Vincenzo Palermo was protecting some Catanian landowners. One of them had started falling victim to acts of outrage on his land: thefts, arson. He was also getting anonymous letters. He turned to Palermo, who went to the countryside and tracked down the author of these annoyances, a certain Catarinella, a fugitive who was too big for his britches.

Palermo had a little talk with him to put him in his place. But Catarinella drew a gun and shot him. The unfortunate Palermo had no gun and was even missing an arm. But he was a sly old-timer, and when he saw the gun aimed at him he turned sideways to present a smaller target and protect his chest. In so doing, however, he was hit in the other arm and fell to the ground. Palermo's driver was Salvatore Santapaola, Nitto's brother. He picked Palermo up and brought him to a hospital.

When my uncle learned of the incident he immediately went off to find his old friend, notwithstanding that they hadn't been able to speak to each other since the split. While embracing him he asked him: "Who was it?"

"Catarinella," Palermo answered. Five or six days later, three corpses were found in the countryside controlled by Catarinella—all fugitives, all members of his gang. Catarinella got the picture. He ran to the police and asked to be arrested as guilty in the shooting of Vincenzo Palermo.

A trial was set and the two were confronted face-to-face. Catarinella repeated his confession, but Palermo refuted it: "Listen, you can say all the nonsense that comes into your head, but I don't know you. I've never seen you before. It wasn't you." And Catarinella was acquitted.

When Palermo recovered, he went to my uncle and said to him:

"Luigi, I'll be with you to my dying day. If one day you find out that I've lied to you or betrayed you, shoot me because it'll mean that I've gone insane."

Fine. That was what friendship once was. My uncle had them all killed, including Catarinella, the trial notwithstanding, because my uncle respected and admired Vincenzo Palermo.

3

The family was revitalized. And, as one would expect, after having resolved its internal woes, it began to focus on its external problems. It was a good time to enlarge the family. There were several promising young men to "make," to bring into the group of men of honor.

Among these young men were individuals who would become important in the years to come. There was the son of Salvatore Ferrera, the nephew of Cavadduzzu—a person of my own age, Franco Ferrera. There were two other nephews of Cavadduzzu, Nitto Santapaola and his brother Natale. Nitto's older brother Salvatore was already a man of honor. We were thus four young men of about twenty-two to twenty-four years of age. Other than us there were several bright kids to be drafted as soon as possible: Natale Ercolano, another nephew of Ferrera's, and a few others. Eight of us in total.

But we young men were in the dark about these plans, or at least I knew nothing about them. While I was in Milan to look after my uncle, who had just been operated on, my brother arrived and asked me to leave the room because he had to talk to him in private. I had the feeling that they might have been talking about me, but they didn't tell me anything and Pippo went back to Catania.

I was anxious to find something out, but I didn't know how to go about it. I wasn't exactly on familiar terms with my uncle Luigi, an old-fashioned man who commanded awe and who held everyone at a distance. I would address him with the formal "you" (as I did, in fact, all my uncles). I would never have dared tell him that I didn't have money, or that I was hungry, or that I needed cigarettes.

On the other hand, as far as money was concerned, it would have been useless to bother. My uncle never parted with money. He was a terrible miser who wouldn't even give someone a cigarette. He didn't ask for anything and didn't offer anything. He was upright. One day he said to me: "Listen, today we have to go down to Catania. There someone will call on you, make some propositions. Don't accept. I've already lived through those speeches. And I lost a brother. Look at what I'm reduced to. I have no money and I'm dying." He was speaking with difficulty. They had removed his whole nose. He was disfigured. "Tell them no. You don't know how nice it is at night to go home, or maybe to the movies. Where it's quiet. Without anyone coming to look for you. And then later you can to to bed and be sure that no one will come knocking on your door, neither the carabinieri nor anyone else.

"And no matter if you don't have money to have fun or even to buy cigarettes. You'll be able to walk down a street quietly, looking at the people and thinking how strange and funny life is. Tell them no. Remember that the thing they'll talk to you about when we get back is like a rose: it's nice to look at, but if you touch it you'll get hurt."

This my uncle said to me in 1962, immediately before I joined the Cosa Nostra. Sometimes I think about those words. To tell the truth, right now, thirty years later, I'm not sure if the advice he gave me was frank and impartial or if it had other motives. But these are very intimate and personal musings about which I don't want to talk.

—

The money from the smuggling operations had been invested badly. The shop my uncle Vincenzo had opened with my brother didn't work out and they had to close it down. They opened another one later on, with new partners—a big store for shoes, fabric, and other goods, where I worked as well. But after a year and a half that undertaking also failed, and we found ourselves, Pippo and I, without jobs, penniless, forced to live on what my father managed to bring home.

We were very poor. My father was working in a warehouse but wasn't earning much. I'll never forget it. One time, while we were at the table, I was deeply affected because I suddenly came to realize how badly off we were, how bad things were. Pippo was disturbed at the sight of me crying. I was only fifteen or sixteen years old.

Several days later Pippo went to see a rich guy, a man from Palermo who had an olive-packing business that also produced salted anchovies, salted olives, artichokes in oil, and other things. He said to him: "Listen, you must give my brother work! We want him to work!"

And so I was taken on. I'd stand at the door and keep track of the workers, which was no small task. There were 100 to 150 women, and they came from all over Catania.

I worked there from 1952 to 1957, when I went into the service. It has to be made clear that at the time Pippo was already a noted man of honor, and that the rich man from Palermo had arrived in Catania with the recommendation of the mafia. My brother's request had been a truly small thing, because the gentleman was very wealthy, and until then no one had asked him for anything.

━━

At the time the mafia had no money. We mafiosi, all of us, were in dire economic straits. But the idea of wholesale extortion never entered our heads. The only instance I remember was an extortion that took place in the late fifties or early sixties against the Rendos, who had the largest construction firm in Catania. The goal was to do the Costanzo brothers a favor. A bomb was placed in the chimney of the Rendo offices; after that, the usual phone call asking for money was made. But this was small potatoes. No one went around to shopkeepers asking for a cut. We didn't even dream of setting up rackets. We didn't have the right mentality for that yet.

Life in the fifties and most of the sixties was tough—a little business, a little smuggling, pilfering, buying and selling stolen goods. We thought small. We didn't dare defy the law more than that.

We would go to landowners and tell them to employ someone and give him a fixed pay—the so-called "guardianship." It wasn't extortion, because afterward the property would be protected in earnest. The duke of Castelbianco, for instance, a very rich man, was paying off the vice-representative of the Catania family, a person called Salvatore Torrisi. Torrisi would receive his stipend and nothing would ever happen on the duke's land. If the duke needed Torrisi he'd telephone him. He would ask him to come to his property with him, to protect him from possible kidnapping (of which there were a few every now and then in the Sicily of the fifties), and that was it.

Of course, a few times Torrisi went to the duke and said to him, "Look, your lordship, I have so-and-so, a fugitive, out there. See if you can give him something." And the duke would provide it. It was the old rural mafia that lived on the margins of the law and did more good than harm, and didn't need much to be happy. It was glad to be associated with the duke of Castelbianco in exchange for measly pay.

The rural mafia had traditions that no one thought could be translated to the city, to shops and factories. It wasn't by any means a question of being afraid of the police. Some say that the police was better then, more organized, more capable of finding things out and making arrests. Apart from the fact that the police has always been a step behind the criminal world, the truth is that we ourselves never thought about extorting from shopkeepers, about the thousands of lire to be squeezed out of grocers.

We didn't reason that way. If we had to think about extortion, we'd think about the big landowners, about the rich and not the small. But since there weren't many large landowners—there were no industrialists, no businessmen yet because the economy was still agrarian—and they were all protected, we didn't go near them. It wasn't worth it.

4

I worked in the anchovy and packed-olive business until 1957. I left for the military on July 2 of that year. I was stationed first in Avellino, then near Eboli, where I was taught to drive tanks. I finished up my military service in Civitavecchia, and in 1958 I returned to Catania.

There I set myself up in business for a while. From a young man who owned a jewelry shop, I learned to silver mirrors. But I couldn't earn enough money, and I left to take a job at the Agricultural Commission. My uncle knew the director.

At the Agricultural Commission I met my future wife, who worked there. Then my uncle fell ill and I quit my job to take care of him, as I've said. Then I teamed up with Pippo, who was a partner in a small building-contracting business with my uncle. It was 1960, and my brother knew a lot of people in the region of Palermo who would assign public-works contracts through private negotiations. We won three commissions in the province of Messina; Pippo and I spent almost a year working with our laborers.

These jobs then came to an end and the business became shaky, especially given the illness of my uncle, who ceded his shares to Pippo. It was about to collapse when Pippo had the good fortune of coming into contact, through Concetto Gallo, with the right politicians. I forgot to mention that one of the partners in the business from my uncle's days had been this Gallo, one of the heads of the Sicilian separatist movement, a former national deputy who was also a man of honor in the Catania family. He had even held the position of *consigliere,* but later had been demoted. With Gallo's help, my brother at last succeeded in obtaining contracts worth almost three billion lire. Almost three billion in 1962! Keep in mind that gasoline cost ninety-two lire per liter at the time, compared to fifteen hundred today. Their business was called Sidexport and built a number of motels in various Sicilian cities by using prefabricated components made in the Tyrol.

There was more good news the next year. Along with Pippo's brother-in-law we started a company that sold petroleum products. We would acquire coal and heating oil that we subsequently resold to apartment buildings, to private individuals, and to small businesses. Pippo's brother-in-law knew coal, and I was familiar with heating oil because I had worked in the oil-products department at the Agricultural Commission. We had even leased a large depot, but then we fell into disagreement with Pippo's brother-in-law.

Meanwhile, I had met Graziano Verzotto, the secretary of the Christian Democrat party in Sicily. He was a power, the close friend and right arm of Enrico Mattei, the director of the ENI.* My brother, especially, knew Verzotto very well. They were close, as Giuseppe Di Cristina was with Pippo too.

One day Pippo asked Verzotto if he could get Agip† to give me a gas station, since I knew so much about fuels. Verzotto answered that there was an opportunity. In a square on the outskirts of Catania, an area that has become part of the city center today, there were some empty Agip storage tanks that hadn't been dug in yet since the municipality had denied authorization to do so.

"Permission isn't a problem," Pippo said. "I'll get the municipality to give it to you immediately." Pippo knew Nino Succi, who was vice-mayor and commissioner of public works. He wasn't a mafioso, but he was very close to my brother. He grew up in Catania, where he owned some hotels. He's dead now.

"If they give the authorization, the service station is yours,"

---

*Ente Nazionale Idrocarburi, the giant state-owned energy conglomerate (translator's note).
†Agencia Generale Italia Petroli, an Italian gasoline company (translator's note).

Verzotto promised. And he told Pippo to speak with the man who held the Agip concession in Catania, one Vanzetti, who confirmed Verzotto's okay but said he was sure we'd never get permission. It was an important square that had been slated to become a public park.

Pippo went to his friend Succi and had to insist a bit because Succi was reluctant. In the end the vice-mayor told him: "Listen, Pippo, I'll give you the authorization, but you know that Agip will never give you the distributorship."

When the time came, the Agip people sent for me and said: "Mr. Calderone, try to understand. There's this poor fellow, Mr. Noci, who's been in line for this concession a very long time. You have to give it up. We will, however, commit ourselves to giving you a large service station on the outskirts of Catania that will generate a lot of business for you."

It was true. The service station was on the road to the Catania airport. It was perfect. I'd already made all the arrangements. All the permits had been filed and all the advertising was ready to go. We were excited about opening at any moment, when one evening the Agip regional director came to my house.

"You see, Mr. Calderone, you must give all the papers back to me. I'm sorry, but you no longer have the concession. The director has given it to a friend of his. What's more, he has given him five distributorships."

What happened was that Mattei had died in an airplane crash, and now a purge was taking place in Agip: all of Mattei's men were being thrown out. Like that—boom. And in Rome they had named another director who had a friend in Catania to whom every new distributorship that opened up in the area had to be given (five, to be precise).

I had prepared all the papers and secured all sorts of permits. All I was waiting for was for them to turn the business over to me. I was ready. I was even insured.

"I won't give up the distributorship," I said.

"You realize that they'll fire me," replied the functionary, whose name was Tagliaferri.

"What are you saying? I've been waiting two years for my service station. I've earned it. And I have your letter, Agip's letter, signed by you, conceding it. And you come here to tell me that you'll be fired."

"Listen. You know what they're going to do? So they don't have to give you the distributorship, they're going to let me go. They'll be able to claim that the grant letter isn't valid anymore."

"How does that affect me? When you wrote the letter you were regional director."

In any case, Agip insisted. At all costs they wanted me to return that letter, but there was absolutely nothing they could do to force me. I didn't have the least intention of capitulating to this outrage.

Our lawyer at the time was Laterza, the fascist member of the Socialist party. Pippo knew him well because he had given him money for some public-works contracts. "Let's ask them for a hundred million in damages," my brother fired off to the lawyer. A hundred million in 1963! Laterza wanted to start a parliamentary inquiry as well.

The matter began to get bigger. In the end the director of Agip sent me a telegram urgently calling me in to see him. Not the regional director, you understand, who in the meantime had been recalled from Sicily. I'm talking about the Agip general director for all of Italy, the one sitting in his skyscraper in Rome. His name was Bartolotta.

Pippo and I went immediately. We went to the skyscraper facing the pond, and went up to the fifteenth floor. We had barely arrived when the director said to us, "What simply incredible characters you are! So stubborn!" And he pressed a button. In came a tall, distinguished-looking man with a handsome face.

"Look, gentlemen. This is Solaro del Burgo. [I'm not sure of the name. It was as long as he was tall.] He's from Turin. He's sly and polite. You remember when Garibaldi came to your parts? Garibaldi was in front with his gun, ready. Behind him came the Turinese with their guns. If Garibaldi missed they'd have killed him. That's what the Turinese are like." And he burst out into loud laughter.

Then he became serious and said to me: "Give me back that

letter, the grant for the distributorship. And have Laterza's accusation withdrawn as well. I'll give you at least three gasoline distributorships. I promise you." And he added, "Do you believe me?"

He was the director general. And he had called me, Antonino Calderone, all the way to Rome.

"Sir, I believe you," I replied.

"I'll give you one of them right now. It belonged to a fellow who went bankrupt. I'll give you the other ones afterward. You can return to Catania in peace, Mr. Calderone, because I've seen that you . . ." And so on.

The director had calculated well. He understood that the matter had grown large, and he was afraid of the scandal and its legal repercussions. And he had seen too that Pippo and I knew what to do with the distributorship, that we'd hold on to it, and that we would manage it well. He probably didn't know we were mafiosi. He probably didn't care.

I received the first distributorship immediately. It was very small and located on the *via* 6 Aprile. After a couple of years I got another, in Giarre. It was a huge service station with three car washes, but it was in bad shape because Giarre's little mafia kept threatening the manager, who was operating at a loss. He was forced to sell a citrus orchard to cover some of his debts. It wasn't that money was being extorted from him; the local mafiosi wanted to run him off so that Agip would assign the distributorship to someone else, one of them.

How did they go about it? Four or five of them would loiter in the service station's café, by the door. Clients didn't dare come inside. Three or four others would line up at the pumps, and each would ask for a hundred lire's worth of gas, then for a complete checkup—oil, tires, water, everything. Three quarters of an hour apiece. And that was how almost all the distributorship's customers disappeared. No one wanted to go there anymore. They destroyed that man completely.

The Agip directors in Catania called me in and said: "Here's a distributorship. Do you want it?"

"Of course I want it."

"There is, however, five million in debt to pay off."

"What? I won't pay that."

"No. You'll pay. We'll do it like this. We'll give you a supplemental agreement, a kind of authorization in which you'll pay off a part of the debt with every fill-up, every sale."

And that's how it was. I was freed of the debt without even noticing it, and the service station ran under full steam.

The little local mafiosi were no problem. I knew them very well. It was a tiny gang. They weren't men of honor, just a small-time camorra of the kind found in the province of Messina. I was polite and correct with them. I went to visit them—the way it's done between people who respect one another—to inform them that I had taken over management of the service station, and they replied that they were pleased, that they were all for it, and that if I ever needed anything . . .

The boss was named Leone, and he had dozens of tractor-trailer trucks. He had become the de facto owner of the service station recently, but with me that was no longer possible. We reasoned the problem out peacefully, and we concluded that he would become the customer and I the manager.

The mafiosi from Giarre never showed their faces. Or if they did come for gas, they'd shell out for it like everyone else; they'd even come to pay their respects to me. Sure, there were those who were still in the habit of loitering around the café, but I told them: "Boys, stay out of the way. If you want to visit me, you're welcome to. But you'll have to sit over in that little corner and stay there."

They knew that they couldn't stand up to us. Later (such is life), a few of them ended up being killed. But apart from the fact that it wouldn't have done them any good to clash with us, it had to be kept in mind that we were friends. They made themselves available as friends. The mafia had nothing to do with it.

■

Later, in 1970, I married. In 1971 my brother Pippo was arrested. At that point I had a large number of interests. I had distributorships. I even sold fuel and lubricants wholesale. After my brother's arrest I had to give up some of these enterprises because I was often in Palermo with lawyers or for other reasons. I had my cousin

Marchese, who was also a man of honor, take over management of the largest service station. In time he outgrew the position, started smuggling, and never worked again.

But it's time to talk about one of the most important events in my life: my official induction—the ceremony through which I joined the Cosa Nostra.

5

Let's return for a moment to my uncle Luigi Saitta, the mafioso. We would see a lot of each other, even after our return from Milan. He'd take me to the movies, tell me about his life, warn me about dangerous people and duplicitous behavior. He advised me to always think before acting. I'd feel flattered by his attention. I was a boy, and I was deeply affected by the trust that such a reserved and old-fashioned man would place in me.

One day he said to me: "You know, Nino, one night this week we're going to go out for a good meal." I understood what he was talking about, but I was happy to play the game. And I was thinking too that before "making" me they'd put me to the test: they were going to study me a bit more, then they would ask me to do something difficult, and after that they would make me a man of honor. In point of fact, they had already examined me because they had me drive a car that belonged to a radiologist friend of my uncle's who had been the victim of an attempted extortion. My presence at the wheel of the car must have signaled that the doctor was under my family's protection.

I knew that candidates for the Cosa Nostra were usually made to do much more difficult things. Shootings, stabbings. To test the mettle of men of action, and to compromise them in such a way that they could never pull back out.

But all they asked me to do was what I've told you. Maybe it was because I was a blood member of a family that had proven mafia traditions. I don't know what I would have done had they asked me to murder someone. I would probably have ducked out of it, as I tried to do for the whole rest of my tenure in the Cosa Nostra, even when I had become a vice-representative.

This has always been my weak point, or my strength—it depends on how one looks at things. Nitto Santapaola accused me several times—in later years, when I already ranked very high in the family—of never taking part in any shooting.

He was right, the monster. I always tried to slip out of it, in effect, every time someone had to be killed. I'd come up with excuses, or I'd arrange things so I couldn't be found when it became necessary to operate that way. In 1976, 1977, and 1978 I disappeared from Catania precisely because I foresaw the coming shootouts. I ran away with my family to Palermo, to the Naples area, to Gioiosa Marina. Even Pippo's family came with us a few times. But let's not lose the thread; we'll return to the spring of 1962.

One night they brought me to a little village at the foot of Mount Etna. In the car were Pippo, another uncle of mine, and Pippo's uncle-in-law, Peppino Indelicato. We pulled into the courtyard of a little country house. The owner was a member of the family, obviously. His name was Santo and he made gravestones.

Inside the house I met many people I'd seen before. But I knew them in normal life as people who had other occupations, and I was already acquainted with some of them. I had imagined, for example, that the family's representative, Orazio Nicotra, was a man of honor. But many of the others I hadn't suspected in the slightest. Then there were some who I was sure must have belonged to the group but who weren't present—the cousin of Professor Navarra Di Corleone, for instance, who had hidden out in Catania for so long because Luciano Liggio was out looking to kill him, and who my uncle had sheltered. Well, I was positive he was a man of honor, and yet he wasn't, while a completely peaceable man like a certain Caradonna—the owner of a trucking business about whom one could think anything except that he was a man of honor—was.

And then there were us kids—eight in all, among them Nitto and Natale Santapaola, Francisco Ferrera Cavadduzzu, Giuseppe

Ferlito, the uncle of Alfio, later killed in Palermo, and others. We were looking at one another, some of us nodded to each other, and we were all very excited.

At the very moment we were about to move into a larger room, I noticed Pippo. He was upset. He was talking to some of the older men with great animation. He wanted to call the ceremony off because there was an extra person to initiate who had not been agreed upon—a person he didn't like, who shouldn't have been there. They had investigated for months, choosing the ablest and rejecting the dubious ones. They had even studied all the details for this day. They had made a decision everyone was bound to, and at the last moment someone was introduced who didn't belong there. Instead of seven of us, there were eight.

The extra person was Natale Ercolano, a boy who later turned out to be the best of us. But my brother and my uncle weren't objecting simply because Ercolano hadn't been expected and because he had shown up there as a result of some behind-the-scenes machinations. They didn't want him, above all, because he was a Cavadduzzu. Of the eight boys to be initiated, four belonged to the Cavadduzzi: the two Santapaola brothers (sons of the family boss Salvatore Ferrera's sister), Franco Ferrera, and Natale Ercolano.

They were all closely related, the Cavadduzzi, a real clan—a very dangerous thing to have inside a family like ours. My brother and uncle were looking at the long term and thinking: "These Cavadduzzi are bringing four of their men into the family at once. Young people, clever and determined, like Nitto Santapaola. They're a menace to the future because they'll end up laying down the law. The rest of the family—we, that is—will be overwhelmed."

Pippo told the older men present that nothing would take place that night because the rules had been broken. Then all the elders retired into another room and talked it over at length. We boys were confused. We didn't know what was happening and we had no idea of what to do. At a certain point Peppino Indelicato, who was the provincial representative, came out and, pointing to one side of the room, said, "You boys go over there."

He began: "My dear young men, do you know why we're here tonight?"

Someone who knew, who thought he knew, answered yes. The others said nothing.

"We're here tonight because we're going to give you a great gift. Tonight we're going to make you . . . Do you know about the mafia? You've heard it mentioned, you have some idea what it is, this mafia everyone talks about?"

"Yes, yes, of course," a few said.

"Good. Well, then, tonight . . ." The representative fell silent. He was going too quickly. "But you must realize that the real mafia isn't the mafia the others talk about. This is the Cosa Nostra. It's called the Cosa Nostra!"

When he said it he raised his voice as though it were an official pronouncement. It seemed as if he were letting something heavy fall from him. I was astonished. It was the first time I had heard the name. Or rather, I had heard it before, during the days of Valachi, the American repentant. I had read it in the newspaper but had thought "Cosa Nostra" meant the American one. "Ours is called the mafia," I had said to myself.

Instead the representative kept on repeating it, enunciating the words to make sure they would be imprinted on our minds: "This is the Cosa Nostra. Co-sa Nos-tra! Understood? And the Cosa Nostra is not the mafia. The mafia is what the *sbirri* and the newspapers call it.

"And now I'll tell you how the Cosa Nostra was born. It was born in the time of the Sicilian Vespers. When the people rose up and the Beati Paoli were born too. The men of honor took revenge against the Beati Paoli. We arise from events that took place in Palermo."

I knew these things, but the others, it seemed to me, didn't at all. They had absolutely no idea who the Beati Paoli were. I don't want to brag, but I had read those books—even *Coriolano of the Woods, Talvano the Bastard,* and the others. I was well informed.

The representative went on for a while explaining the significance of those stories. Then he said:

"Now, here are the rules. First of all, wherever you come across a man of honor who's a fugitive, you must remember that another man of honor's duty is to take care of him, even to hide him in his own house if necessary. But woe to whoever takes another man's daughter or wife. If he does, he's a dead man. As soon as you learn that a man of honor has touched another's wife, that man must die.

"Second, whatever happens, never go to the *sbirri,* never betray anyone. Whoever does will be killed.

"Third, stealing is forbidden."

At this point Natale Ercolano, the Ferrera candidate objected to by my brother, leaped to his feet and shouted: "Stop! Hold everything! I can't accept that! I don't agree!"

Ercolano was a thief. He was always stealing. Otherwise, how could the poor fellow have managed to get by? And almost all the young would-be men of honor present in the room stole. I was probably the only one who had no experience in the matter. There was a moment of general consternation.

Uncle Peppino smiled, amused. "You, sit down! Be quiet—later I'll explain how it is that we don't steal," he said to Ercolano, who in any event remained perplexed for the remainder of the ceremony.

Uncle Peppino continued his explanation of the other commandments: making money off prostitution wasn't permitted; quarrels with other men of honor were to be avoided; silence about the Cosa Nostra was to be maintained with outsiders; sober behavior was to be encouraged; boasting and showing off were not condoned; and, as I said before, under no circumstances was one to introduce oneself to other men of honor.

So many fine words! So many fine principles! And so many times over the ensuing years did I find myself confronted by a lack of respect for these rules—by deceit, betrayal, murder committed precisely to exploit the good faith of those who believed in them. At last I had to conclude that the real Cosa Nostra was very different from the one I was presented with on this occasion.

But that night everything seemed beautiful and extraordinary. I was entering a new world, a world of exceptional people ready to risk their lives to help their colleagues, capable of avenging wrongs, more powerful than one could even imagine.

After explaining the rules, the representative paused and then said: "Now you know what the score is. So, do you or do you not want to be in the Cosa Nostra? If you don't want to be in it you still have time. You can go, even though we've revealed ourselves. Nothing will happen to you. If you decide to come in, there's one thing you have to realize clearly: one goes in and comes out of the Cosa Nostra with blood! One cannot leave, one cannot resign from the Cosa Nostra. You'll see for yourselves, in a little while, how one enters with blood. And if you leave, you'll leave with blood because you'll be killed. One cannot abandon, cannot betray, the Cosa Nostra, because it's above everything. It comes before your father and your mother. And before your wife and your children."

The representative's speech went on for a long time. Pippo and the older men of honor broke in too, straightening out concepts, giving examples, clarifying problems.

The ceremony was well done, complete, the old-fashioned way. There were to be many more in the years that followed, and we "made" a great many men of honor. I myself, as the family vice-representative, organized a number of initiations. But I can't recall one as correct, as special, as this one. Or maybe it just seemed that way to me; I felt it to be that way because I was a boy and hadn't yet become disillusioned. The other young men were like me too. We were all more innocent. We hadn't yet shot and killed. Not one of us eight that evening had murdered anyone. In those days one didn't kill so easily. Not even Nitto Santapaola had killed yet. He committed his first murder the following year, in 1963, and he wasn't even charged for it. They accused Franco Ferrera, who was defended by the lawyer Leone, the president of the Republic.

The kids we "made" in the ensuing years were all kids who could shoot, who had shot before, and who already knew everything there was to know about the Cosa Nostra. There was no need for long explanations. The ceremony didn't impress them.

Uncle Peppino continued: "Now, each of you choose a god-father." Usually the godfather an initiate chooses is the person who has followed him, has "taken care" of him in terms of introducing him into the Cosa Nostra. He's a man of honor who has assumed the responsibility of presenting the candidate to the family. In my case it was Uncle Peppino who had brought me in, and thus I chose him as my godfather.

At this point Uncle Peppino picked up a needle and asked me: "Which hand do you shoot with?"

"With this one," I answered.

Then he pricked one of my fingers and squeezed out a little blood, which he dripped onto a sacred image. I looked at it. It was the Madonna of the Annunciation, the patron saint of the Cosa Nostra, whose feast day falls on March 25.

Uncle Peppino lit a match, touched it to a corner of the little image, and asked me to take it in my hand and hold it until it burned entirely. I cupped my hands—I was quite affected, and was sweating—and watched the little image turn to ashes. In the meantime, Uncle Peppino asked me to recite the oath with him. According to the formula, if an associate breaks the commandments of the Cosa Nostra he will burn like the little image of the Annunciation.

The oath over, everyone came up to kiss me. I had become a man of honor. The representative went on to repeat the ritual with the other young men, and before closing the ceremony he turned to all the new Cosa Nostra members and described the Catania family hierarchy, the situation in the provinces, and that of the Cosa Nostra all over Sicily. He dwelt in particular on the role of the *decina* boss—the direct superior of each of us young ones.

—

Over the ensuing years I participated in many ceremonies, as I have said. And I could see how some rituals changed according to local custom. In some families an orange thorn would be used to prick the candidate's finger. The Riesi family would use a gold brooch pin reserved exclusively for that purpose.

In emergencies, inductions would take place more quickly. The presence of at least three men of honor was enough, even if they belonged to different families or even families from different provinces.

Take the induction of Antonino Madonia, who belonged to the Resuttana family, which took place inside the Ucciardone prison.

Or that of Nello Pernice, of which I was one of the organizers. Pernice's godfather was Luciano Liggio of the Corleone family. There was also, apart from me, Francesco Madonia of the Valle-lunga family. There were thus three men of honor who belonged to three families from three different provinces.

Nello Pernice's case is a bit complicated, but it serves to clarify the rules of initiation. He was supposed to be a part of the Valle-lunga family, but Liggio wanted him as his right-hand man in Milan. Liggio needed him desperately in Milan and had to move fast, all the more so to avoid the likely protests of the Catania family.

It probably would have been more correct, in truth, for the induction to have taken place in the latter family, since Pernice, who came from a former Italian colony in Africa, was living in Catania at the time. But on this occasion (one of very, very few), Liggio acted properly. He informed both the then-representative, Orazio Nicotra, and my brother, the provincial representative, who were in custody awaiting the Trial of the Hundred-Fourteen.

■

The ceremony was over. But there was one question that had been left unresolved. Natale Ercolino, the thief, had raised a problem that actually was of interest to everyone. Uncle Peppino came up to him and said, in a loud voice so that everyone could hear: "Natale, try to understand me clearly. It's not that you can never steal. Sure, it's better that you don't, because that's a Cosa Nostra rule. But one needs to know how to understand the rules. You have to live, and if you have to steal in order to live, then so be it. As the provincial representative I can't support you. I can't give you a stipend that would allow you to live well and not go out stealing. I don't have the money, and, then again, it doesn't work that way. The family doesn't function like that. So, steal, by all means. But be careful who you steal from. You always have to know who you're stealing from. You can't steal from a man of honor or his relatives. From anyone else, yes."

Everything was clear now. We could move on to the celebration. We popped I don't know how many bottles of spumante. I don't know how many roast chickens we ate. It was an event on a grand scale. I'll never forget that night.

—

Not even two weeks had passed since my induction into the Cosa Nostra before the requests started. I was waiting to be given the concession for the Agip service station when my *decina* boss sent for me.

"Listen," he said, "I've heard that you're waiting for that concession. Do you intend to run it on your own? Wouldn't it be better to take on a partner?"

"I'm not on my own. I have Pippo for a partner," I answered quickly. Then I went to Pippo and asked him:

"Maybe I don't understand this right. Joining the Cosa Nostra means sharing one's own property with others. What is this? Some sort of communism?"

And he answered that legitimate businesses were something entirely personal and unrestricted. The family couldn't interfere in such questions. Private property was recognized, and everyone was free to do what he wanted with it. But illegitimate business was different: before doing anything, one had to inform one's superiors, to ask their permission, at least for most things. It was forbidden to engage in anything illegitimate completely on the sly.

6

Until the end of the sixties, my life in the mafia was, all told, normal—because the mafia itself was normal, and because I was living in Catania, in a family that never grew larger than forty men, a hobby-shop size compared to the Palermo families. There had been, granted, the Palermo mafia war of 1962–1964, but all that reached us were echoes, reports, refugees. It all seemed distant and far away. Our activities consisted of asking for favors, smuggling, fencing. We weren't aiming for great wealth. We didn't think about the big time.

Until 1962 Pippo and I lived in my parents' house. We left after my brother's engagement and moved into another house; it too was very poor, miserable, with two little rooms. It was located in the south end of San Cristoforo. Think about it for a moment: Sicily and Catania are in the south of Italy, and we were living in the south end of Catania's poorest quarter.

But we stayed there only for a few months. After having secured those contracts in the area, Pippo became a builder and we moved into the center of Catania, into a very big house—the first big house I ever lived in, where I even had a room all to myself.

One day a lot of people came to the house. Pippo introduced me to them: Totò Greco Cicchiteddu, Antonio Salomone, Nino Geraci of Partinico, Gianni La Licata, who was later murdered by Pippo Calò, and others. There were seven or eight men of honor, all fugitives.

We threw mattresses down on the attic floor, which could ac-
commodate them comfortably—that says something about how big
the house was. Every now and then I would bring them coffee. A
few days later the Catania representative arrived, and animated
discussions followed. They went on for a long time. Even Gerlando
Alberti, who lived in Milan, had come down for the occasion, and
for only one day.

I was dying of curiosity. Pippo finally explained to me why these
people were in our house and told me the reason for the meeting.
Gerlando Alberti had come because someone had informed him
that Angelo La Barbera was going to be arriving in Catania from
Milan, by plane, and was going to stay at the Central Corona hotel
on the *via* Etnea, which in those days was the best in the city. And
there he was to be killed.

Along with his brother, Angelo La Barbera headed the family
of central Palermo, and he had found himself at war with the Greco
family of Ciaculli and with the whole Palermo Cosa Nostra. In
June 1963 there were a series of attacks against and murders of
prominent mafia figures; a couple of Alfa Romeo Giuliettas packed
with dynamite had been blown up, one of which resulted in the
Ciaculli massacre.

Both the mafia and the police thought that the La Barbera brothers were responsible for the massacre and everything else, and
everybody was looking for them.

But before explaining how the mafia bosses, who thought they
knew everything, were in fact being hoodwinked by a single man
a bit more cunning than them, I have to tell the story of Angelo
Bruno.

I met Bruno, the representative of the Philadelphia family, in
1962. He was the first important person I met after having been
made a man of honor. He was a quiet, self-possessed man—a
personality. He slept at the Excelsior and was a man of great power
in America. We had always looked at America as a colossus, as
much for the mafia as for money and other things.

In those days there were seven families in America. Five were
in New York and two were outside it, one in New Jersey and one
in Philadelphia. There were seven representatives and Bruno was

one of them—one of the biggest. Pippo told me he was a member of the grand jury, the commission of seven that ran everything in America.

The Philadelphia vice-representative was called Testa. Bruno had learned about the state of the Cosa Nostra while he had been in the village of Testa's father, Calatabiano, which lies on the border between the provinces of Catania and Messina. He asked me to find out if there was a family in Calatabiano, but there wasn't any in those days. Now they're killing each other in droves there.

Angelo Bruno was a native of Vallelunga, in the province of Caltanissetta. When he came to America he was eighteen months old and wasn't called Bruno, but Andaloro. He changed his name later on.

He had come to Sicily because he wanted to find out about his own roots—to meet his relatives, to visit the village of his birth. He was seventy-five years old, give or take, and spoke Sicilian. His wife didn't. She was Italian, or rather, Italian-American. He was introduced to us by the Vallelunga representative, at the time one Calogero Sinagra, also a cousin of Bruno. Bruno had been particularly pleased to come to Sicily and find out that in his native village his cousin was a representative, just like him.

At the end of his visit Angelo Bruno said to Sinagra: "You should come with me. I'd very much like you to stay with me in America for a while."

And he did bring him there. He paid for everything. He kept him for four or five months, and he had him tour the length and breadth of America, paying for all the best hotels. It drove Calogero Sinagra crazy. Sinagra wasn't rich. He was just a livestock trader in a village of five thousand people lost in the middle of Sicily. And ignorant to boot. Illiterate. His life had been spent around stables, marketplaces, carts (and among the rules of the Cosa Nostra at the time, naturally). What he saw in the America of the sixties—such a huge world, so many new things, so futuristic—really drove him crazy.

On the occasion of his visit to Sicily, Angelo Bruno wanted to buy a casino in Italy. He knew gambling very well—he was an expert. When he had been a simple man of honor, he said, he had owned, in partnership with a few others, a casino in Cuba. He told us that because before coming to Catania he had made a tour of all the Italian casinos, and he was disturbed by what he had seen.

"Those are gambling dens, not casinos," he told us. "Our casino in Cuba was completely different. It was something of quality. If we knew that a player liked a certain type of fish, and it couldn't be found there, an airplane would immediately be dispatched to get it. In Italian casinos they even ask for a cover charge. Over there . . . he liked a given brand of whiskey? He liked something else? . . . There it was. In the restaurant, for example. What, a player paying? No way he'll pay in the restaurant! He doesn't pay, and that's it. We would give him anything he wanted."

Angelo Bruno had been in Cuba when that man before Castro was there, Batista. Fidel Castro had barely shown his face when Batista's men sent for Angelo Bruno and asked him if he could kill Castro.

"To kill Castro in those days," Bruno told us, "would have been the simplest thing in the world. A snap." He informed his *decina* boss, but the man was an ignoramus who couldn't see past his own nose. All he could see was the Cosa Nostra. As far as family work went he was a fox, but he didn't understand anything about business, about the bigger world outside. He couldn't see them at all, those things.

"I couldn't talk to the representative directly because I was a soldier and compelled to go through the *decina* boss. And this is what I said to him: 'Listen, Batista wants us to kill Fidel Castro. Can you imagine what could happen if we do Batista a favor like that? We'll be the bosses here. We'll build a paradise—a huge property, a palace—with all the money we'll make.'

" 'We won't do any such thing. We won't do anything political. We won't get involved like that,' the imbecile replied.

"It was the fifties. Castro was still very, very small. And now Cuba is his. All of it! And we can't even get near it anymore!" exclaimed Angelo Bruno, who was still bitter. "The problem is the people who don't understand. It's the same thing here, these casinos with those idiots running them who make people pay to come in."

And after convincing himself that the situation here really was different, he stayed a little while longer and then went back to America.

But he returned. And while he was with his wife and a relative in the Catania train station on the way to his village, he bought an English newspaper and read that there was a summons out for him—a warrant for his arrest.

"It doesn't look like I'm going anywhere," he said to his relative. "First I have to see how things stand. We can't go to a hotel because they'll arrest me immediately. Find me a solution."

And he came to our house accompanied by his cousin. He called the United States and learned that it had something to do with a loan-sharking operation. There was someone, a woman, who had ratted on him because . . . a black man was involved . . . I don't know the details very well. Bruno had tried to reconcile them, but the woman was maintaining that it was he, Bruno, who was the loan shark. Then the black man was found dead. It was a serious mess.

Next he telephoned a lawyer in Catania, decided to turn himself in, and reached an agreement with the American authorities. They would wait for him at the Rome airport to take him into custody. And, in fact, they got him and took him away.

Bruno and his wife stayed with us only for one night. His wife slept; he didn't. He started talking to me and Pippo. He told us the story of Cuba and Castro, spoke to us about his life and the American Cosa Nostra. These were clearly unusual circumstances. He usually spoke little. He was a great man, reserved, but my impression was that he was a good man. He predicted pleasant things out of my very recent induction, kissed me, and said to me: "Good luck." But he said it to me from the heart, in the Sicilian-American way.

I was twenty-eight years old. He was the first great man I met. Later on, around 1980 I think, I heard that his house had been blown up and that he was dead.

I've told the Angelo Bruno episode not just because I experienced it directly and was affected by it, but also to show how far away the Americans were from us. When I read about an Italian-American Cosa Nostra—both Italian and American, that is—as though it were one single organization, I have to laugh. We've never had a relationship between organizations. Our Cosa Nostra is autonomous. The regional commission decides things on its own.

Many of us knew American men of honor. We would exchange favors. We would hide a few fugitives or send them some of ours. We would also recognize the validity of their oath to the Cosa Nostra. The title of "man of honor" meant as much here as it did there. But that was all.

They were more attached to business, to money, than we were. And sometimes the welcome they extended to Sicilian men of honor on the run or just visiting was not the best.

7

Let's return, then, to the decision to kill Angelo La Barbera during his sojourn in Catania. The illustrious mafiosi who were staying at my house wanted to kill him because they hadn't yet realized that the dynamite-filled Giuliettas had not been placed by either him or his brother, but by Michele Cavataio.

Who was Cavataio? He was the representative of the Palermo district of Acquasanta, and he had formed a group of his own—today it would be called a "back-room" group—with a few old bosses from other families. These bosses had been dethroned, but they hadn't accepted the situation and had formed a secret coalition with Cavataio.

They weren't many, but they were daring and very dangerous, since they were experienced men of honor, they knew everyone, and they were in a position to know the moves of everyone else and weren't the objects of suspicion themselves.

At the root of everything was Cavataio's resentment of the Cosa Nostra elite. A friend of Cavataio's had been murdered by Antonio Salomone, the representative of the San Giuseppe Iato family, because he had cut into one of their wine distributorships. Since the bosses of the Palermo Cosa Nostra had approved the killing, Cavataio went ahead and killed Calcedonio Di Pisa. But he killed him in such a way that blame fell back on the La Barberas.

Then a series of car bombings broke out near the houses of the most important mafiosi, each of which began to fuel everyone's suspicions about everyone else. In a world as complicated as the Cosa Nostra's, where even small wrongs are remembered for years and there are thousands of tangled relationships, grounds for suspicions and hypotheses are never lacking.

Everyone had some motive for revenge, recent or long-standing, hidden or overt, against everyone else. Cavataio's bombs had sown chaos inside the mafia because no one admitted to having placed them and because they focused police and press attention on the victims. This is how Bernardo Diana, the vice-representative of Bontade's family, was killed; even the sister of Salvatore Greco Cicchiteddu was threatened in one attack. The Giulietta blown up in Ciaculli killed seven policemen and carabinieri, and the damage to the Cosa Nostra it caused would last through the seventies.

Cavataio was merciless and vindictive. To eliminate one adversary he was capable of razing a whole building without qualm for the innocent lives he claimed. His plan was to incriminate everyone, weakening them through internal strife and police arrests so that in the end he himself would remain the lone boss of the Palermo mafia.

But those geniuses in the Palermo Cosa Nostra didn't understand anything and blamed the La Barberas for all the damage. A meeting of the provincial commission made up of all the district bosses was called, and Salvatore Greco asked Angelo La Barbera how on earth it was that Angelo's brother Totò, who had been charged with looking into the murder, hadn't come up with anything. La Barbera's explanations were considered inadequate, and suspicions of the La Barberas increased.

Salvatore Greco then accused Totò La Barbera of having been the assassin himself, and in the course of the meeting Totò was strangled by the district bosses. Afterward Salvatore Greco assigned the task of burying the body to Gigino Pizzuto, who told me all of this several years later, around 1972.

But Angelo La Barbera managed to escape from the meeting, and Cavataio claimed this fact as proof of his involvement not only in the Di Pisa matter but also in the bombings and attacks carried out against the commission bosses. And since the disruptions continued after Angelo La Barbera's escape—though, as always, at

Cavataio's hands—the entire Cosa Nostra united in a search for the culprit.

The order was to take him at any cost, to kill him on sight. But Angelo La Barbera was looking for them too, because he wanted to explain himself, to talk it over, to convince them that he had had nothing to do with it, that he too was looking for the man behind the attacks.

In the end La Barbera succeeded in establishing contact with a few bosses, and after very long negotiations they set a date and place for a meeting to clear things up. La Barbera brought Stefano Giaconia, one of his most trusted men, to the meeting with him. It's said (I'm not sure if it's true) that Giaconia showed up wrapped in dynamite. He looked like a salami with a fuse in its hand.

"If anything suspicious happens here, I'll light the fuse and blow us all sky-high," he announced as soon as he came to the meeting. One of the men present then made, probably without meaning to, some sort of signal. Angelo La Barbera ordered Giaconia to escape, and any hope of reaching some sort of resolution vanished. La Barbera became convinced that it was pointless to try to explain anything. They would have killed him anyway. The hunt intensified.

That was why all those people had come to Catania. They quickly got organized, going to the various hotels to see if La Barbera was staying there, dividing tasks among themselves. Gerlando Alberti was waiting for someone in Milan to send him the code words "The train car has left" to indicate that La Barbera was on his way. But La Barbera didn't arrive. Or he arrived and didn't stay the night in Catania but went on to Messina by car. It was never known. Angelo La Barbera was later stabbed to death in prison, but for unrelated reasons.

—

From 1962 to 1969, the year of the massacre on the *viale* Lazio, great confusion reigned in the Palermo mafia. Many died in the mafia war and more than a hundred were arrested. The biggest bosses were jailed, and then there was the Catanzaro trial. The Ciaculli "Giulietta" attack against the Greco family in 1963 caused the greatest damage. The government convened the Antimafia Commission. The Cosa Nostra no longer existed in Palermo after 1963. It was K.O.'ed.

The mafia was on the verge of disintegrating and seemed to be falling apart. It's enough to say that the boss of the Palermo provincial commission, Totò Greco Cicchiteddu, abandoned his post and emigrated to Venezuela. He was a fugitive and had already been sentenced.

The families were broken up. The absolute minimum of activities was undertaken. There were almost no killings. There were still some ordinary murders, the sort where the culprit is immediately found, but there were no mafia murders. Not even cuts were being paid anymore in Palermo.

But the mafia was still in charge in other cities. As I've said, there were no particular problems in Catania. We were calm and there were no murders. No one in the city thought about the mafia. They were all thinking about development: at the time Catania was the most industrious city in Sicily.

Cavataio's game was uncovered at a certain point, but too late. The arrests had already been made and there was no longer anything to be done. Everyone was forced to wait until the release of the biggest bosses in 1968–1969, after the Catanzaro trial.

Before any reorganization, any thought of the future, it was absolutely imperative to resolve the Cavataio problem. Two lines of thought were forming inside the Cosa Nostra: make peace with him or destroy him. The two lines were not fixed. They changed from moment to moment, and according, above all, to how Cavataio's strength was perceived.

At the beginning it was thought that Cavataio had large forces behind him and that he had infiltrators inside every family. And for that reason many negotiations to come to terms with him were begun.

How strange the Cosa Nostra is at times! How practical and accommodating it had become. Everybody had been hurt, betrayed, insulted. Everybody loathed Cavataio for the people he'd killed, for the underhanded way in which he acted, but it was his strength that had the last word. If he was strong, peace had to be made with him.

In the end, Cavataio's strength was revealed to be a bluff. After all was said and done, he didn't have any. But before everyone realized that, how much time was spent on making contacts, coming to agreements, making trips and embassies! And how many precautions in talking, in conversations inside the families themselves.

The watchword was to stay alert and talk as little as possible because there was the risk of Cavataio's plants going off to inform him of our movements and secret plans. Exceptional safety measures had been adopted because we no longer knew from which side the attacks were coming. The young men, the ones who did the shooting, were ordered not to get into a car alone with anyone, not to go to any appointment without being accompanied by someone else who would be waiting in the car outside, and to tell the *decina* boss or someone else in case of any gathering on the part of other families.

The events of the first years of the sixties presented a lesson to bear in mind. Even a respected and important boss like Pietro Torretta would play games of deceit with Cavataio. Totò Greco thought that Torretta was his man, and instead Torretta would run off to tell Cavataio everything. In the end, the decisive evidence against Cavataio was provided by Pietro Torretta himself.

One day a soldier had to go to an appointment with "Uncle Pietro" and brought another man of honor, Gianni La Licata, along with him. The latter waited for him down in the street while the other went up to Torretta's apartment. They immediately tried to kill him. The soldier reacted quickly. He pulled out his gun, started to shoot, and threw himself out onto the balcony shouting: "Gianni! Gianni! Gianni!"

But he hit the ground dead because the men in Torretta's house had shot him while he was running out to the balcony. Gianni La Licata managed to get away, however, and related the episode to the commission, which realized the mistake it had made imputing the massacres and everything else to the La Barberas, and understood that the involvement of Pietro Torretta meant that the finger was pointing another way. And Cavataio was quickly settled on.

Let's return now to the beginning of the story, in the wake of the Catanzaro trial, when it was believed that Cavataio was strong and that peace with him and his people would have to be made. At this point three mediators appeared, all of them Palermo outsiders either because they had been born elsewhere or because, like Gerlando Alberti, they hadn't been living in Palermo for very long and did not directly participate in the dealings of the Palermo families.

In addition to Alberti, the mediators were Pippo Calderone and Giuseppe Di Cristina. News of their intention to bring about peace started to spread. There were official meetings with spokesmen from the larger families and with the Palermo district bosses. The opinion of representatives from the other provinces were heard, until Ciccio Occhialino, representative from Palermo's Giardino Inglese family and a Cavataio man, let Pippo know that the latter wanted to meet with him to discuss the situation.

My brother and Cavataio saw each other a couple of times. In one of these meetings—Nino Sorci was present as well—Cavataio declared himself open to peace and laid down his conditions. But my brother's mouth fell open when he saw Cavataio becoming excited in the course of the talk, slipping his hand into his sock, and pulling out a piece of paper. It was a map of Palermo with as many circles as there were mafia neighborhoods, and with the names of the families, the representatives, and all the known men of honor written down. Cavataio put the map on the table and started to say: "This district boss has to go here, that family boss there, we'll put this one over here, move that one away from there . . ." He was laying down his conditions, in short. He was diagramming the system, something the president of the United States would do. Like Bush.

Unbelievable stuff. Pippo's astonishment arose from the absolute proof—"blunt" proof, as certain mafia lawyers say—that Cavataio was crazy, a megalomaniac. No one can treat the Cosa Nostra families like that, as though they were pawns in a chess game. But it arose from another consideration too. How was it possible for a man as cunning as Cavataio not to realize the danger that the very existence of such a document represented?

Perhaps Cavataio wasn't all that smart. Or maybe Liggio had been right when he'd said, referring to the mental capacities of Cavataio's counterparts, "In the country of the blind a one-eyed man is king." The fact is that Cavataio is dead precisely because of that map, which he'd shown to other people too, the clever fellow.

Apart from the absolute prohibition—it still holds in the mafia today—against committing to paper anything that refers to the Cosa Nostra, in those days there was still a practical reason why that map was extremely dangerous. The police knew nothing about the real structure of the mafia. As yet there had not been any repentants to describe its hierarchy and to name names. Judges would make piles of errors when they investigated murders. And many people thought that the mafia, that is, the Cosa Nostra, didn't exist at all.

The mediators of the controversy nevertheless decided to call a meeting. They had to communicate the results of their talks to the Cosa Nostra bosses, and they had to pass on to Totò Greco—who in his capacity as secretary of the Palermo commission was the boss with the most weight—Cavataio's willingness for peace. The meeting took place in Switzerland, in a Zurich hotel, and was arranged under the greatest secrecy. My brother and Di Cristina were informed of the site of the meeting only once they'd arrived at the Rome airport. The Palermo Cosa Nostra bosses didn't trust them or Gerlando Alberti because they'd had too many contacts with the diabolical Cavataio.

The meeting (Tommaso Buscetta was there too) opened with a show of pleasant words. "Peace, peace, peace! Enough murders. Let's forget everything and move on," the mediators recommended, and they received the assent of many.

But Totò Greco Cicchiteddu sat there silently the whole time, and at the end he declared: "Fine. Fine. Make peace. Do what you want. You're in the majority." He did it in a way that showed he was not, in fact, in agreement.

Then he called Pippo aside and said to him: "I can't agree. I want Cavataio dead."

"If so, dear Totò, let's stop this now. We'll begin the discussions again," Pippo replied.

"No. No one must know my intentions. You all should behave as if you were making peace. We'll leave here with the decision to make peace. But we have to kill him."

"I know we have to kill him. But if we officially decide to make peace now and later on we murder him instead, we'll be going against the whole Cosa Nostra in Sicily. They'll accuse us of being like Cavataio, of not respecting pacts, of doing things in secret, illegally," Pippo insisted.

Cicchiteddu cut him short. "I'll kill him on my own. There's no need for you to be involved."

Pippo knew that it would be useless to keep trying to convince him. "Listen, Totò. I accept what you're saying. You're right. They put that bomb under your house and were on the point of killing you and your sister too. But tell me how I, who represent other interests, can maintain this double talk the way you want me to? If I must, I at least need some men of honor to be in on it, who'll take responsibility for it too. I can't run around in circles like an idiot repeating 'peace, peace, peace' when it isn't true simply because you told me to. I have to tell someone else that it's a trick, that there isn't peace. And that person has to become involved, to be equally responsible in the deception. Tell me who I can tell."

"You can tell Stefano Bontade. And then Stefano, and only him, should decide if he'll tell Gaetano Badalamenti."

"And Di Cristina?"

"You can tell him too."

The phony peace began upon their return to Sicily. Bontade and Di Cristina were informed, then Badalamenti, Liggio, and other high-level spokesmen who were gravitating toward Palermo. There was talk of reconciliation and of a life so quiet that it verged on being boring. The rest of the Sicilian families ended up convincing themselves that an era of harmony had begun. (The Palermo men wanted harmony too, but after Cavataio was dead.)

It wasn't easy, however, to flush Cavataio out. He was sent messages of peace. He was invited to negotiate. Everyone declared themselves ready to discuss his map. But he had gone into hiding and wasn't taking the bait.

The only ones who had a channel to him were Pippo and Di Cristina. Neither of their positions with respect to Cavataio was completely insincere. They hadn't yet given up, once and for all, the idea that later, even if it was extremely unlikely, some other solution might be found.

Cavataio didn't trust the declarations of peace emanating from the Zurich meeting. For him, true peace could come only from a pledge signed at a general summit of representatives from every Sicilian family, something on a grand scale that had never been done before. If that sort of mafia "parliament" was not called, he would never come out from underground.

And in the meantime he was becoming more and more intractable. During a meeting with Di Cristina he refused to budge on one question, and when Di Cristina asked him to be reasonable his only answer was to say that if his proposals weren't accepted, within an hour Salvatore Scaglione, nicknamed "the Fighter," would be killed. And to show that he wasn't joking, he told Di Cristina where Scaglione could be found within an hour. The poor Di Cristina begged him to let it drop, and Cavataio made a magnanimous gesture: he picked up the phone and stopped the killer, who was just setting out.

This event frightened the Cosa Nostra bosses, who were still hesitating about the need to get rid of Cavataio, and compounded the map incident and the many other events.

At last a concrete plan for the elimination of Cavataio was settled upon. At first the thought was to exploit a fact known by very, very few people. Every now and then Cavataio would go to Acireale, near Catania, where his children were in school. It would have been possible to mount a successful attack along the way. But then it was decided to do nothing.

Nevertheless, Stefano Bontade, Gaetano Badalamenti, and Di Cristina secretly agreed among themselves to kill him right there, in the province of Catania, without saying anything to Pippo, even though he was the province's leading man of honor. This was a grave impropriety.

It was Giuseppe Di Cristina, one of my brother's dearest friends, who suggested that they neither warn him nor get him involved. There wasn't any real reason, just jealousy and envy, since Pippo was becoming more and more prominent and was earning the trust of ever more men of honor.

A team was formed, a group of gunmen. Badalamenti provided two of his men working in Catania, the Sciacca brothers, and Natale Rimi. One day when they were waiting for Cavataio to come by so that they could shoot him—to no avail, because for the time being Cavataio wasn't going to Acireale—they stopped by my gas station to get some coffee. The manager was the cousin I've already mentioned, Marchese, who recognized and greeted them. Later he told Pippo that he'd seen them.

The next time my brother saw one of the Sciaccas he asked him why on earth they and Rimi had been in the neighborhood but hadn't dropped by to say hello.

"We couldn't go off looking for you, dear Uncle Pippo," was the answer. "How could we? We were waiting to kill Cavataio. You didn't know?"

Pippo flew into a rage and rushed to Palermo to see Bontade and Badalamenti. He dissociated himself from the operation against Cavataio, accused them of treachery, and threatened terrible reprisals against the men working illegally in his territory.

But his anger didn't last long. He was a good man, and in reality he was very fond of Stefano Bontade and Gaetano Badalamenti. He believed in the rules of the Cosa Nostra and trusted his friends. It was because of this that he died.

—

The December 10, 1969, *viale* Lazio massacre that brought Cavataio's life to an end took place without the knowledge of my brother, who learned of it from the newspapers and was later filled in on it by the Palermo bosses.

So many inaccuracies have been written on the subject. According to what Pippo told me, five men from three separate families took part in the operation: one of the Grado brothers and Emanuele D'Agostino, both provided by Bontade; Bernardo Provenzano and a brother of Leoluca Bagarella, who were sent by Gaetano Badalamenti; and Damiano Caruso, who was considered the ablest soldier in Di Cristina's family (just imagine what the others were like, given the messes Caruso made of this and other jobs).

The soldiers arrived at the offices of the builder Moncada in several cars. Caruso and the others were disguised as policemen. Some other cars were circling around to keep an eye on the situation. In one of them was Salvatore Riina, who was directing the operation.

Caruso didn't rise to the occasion. The disguise trick was blown immediately, because instead of waiting until everyone was in position, like the police does, Caruso began to shoot wildly, without hitting anyone, and thus allowed Cavataio to take cover behind a desk and start returning the fire. Cold and precise, Cavataio killed Bagarella with a hit in the middle of his chest. He shot at Provenzano and wounded him slightly in the hand. Cavataio was unusually skillful. Caruso himself was hit in the arm, again by Cavataio, who then hid under a table and played dead. He thought his attackers would run off without making sure of their work.

But Provenzano and the others had been ordered to kill everyone there and then to burn the place down to get rid of Cavataio's famous map of the Cosa Nostra. To that end they had brought a few cans of gasoline with them, which they weren't able to use because of Caruso's rashness and Cavataio's deadly reaction. They had to think of their own dead and wounded. They didn't have time to set fire to anything.

A surreal silence had fallen in the room. Cars could be heard passing by on the avenue. Provenzano paused for a moment, cleared his head, and then thought of Cavataio's socks, which he figured might still contain the map. He started to pull Cavataio out from under the table by his feet when he detected an odd resistance and realized that he was still alive. Cavataio was ready and fired a shot into his face—or rather, tried to shoot, since his pistol was empty.

Provenzano pulled on the trigger of his machine gun, which jammed, and he couldn't clear it because of his wounded finger. So he hit Cavataio in the head with the butt of his gun and tried to kick him into unconsciousness; at last he managed to pull out his pistol and kill him. But he didn't find the map. Perhaps he didn't have enough time. The operation had lasted three minutes and had left five dead and two wounded, not counting Caruso and Provenzano himself.

The killers fled by car, with Caruso driving even though he was wounded. Bagarella's corpse was put in the trunk and was later buried in someone else's grave at the cemetery in Corleone. As a reward, Caruso was sent to America to recover from his wounds.

Bagarella's participation in the *viale* Lazio massacre, and his death, have remained unknown to investigators and to many people in the Cosa Nostra itself. It was Pippo and Totò Riina who told me about it. The latter was very unhappy because at the time he was engaged to Bagarella's sister, a young teacher from Corleone, and I remember that for some time after the massacre he wore a black tie in Bagarella's memory.

The massacre caused a chorus of protest against the Palermo men on the part of all the Sicilian families, who accused them of having informed no one and of having lied about their intentions for peace with Cavataio.

For some time Pippo was afraid both of how Cavataio's remaining supporters would react—especially the ones who were hidden, undeclared—and of protests from the many people who could have demanded justice for such an unexpected and violent act on the part of the men supposedly mediating the Palermo conflict. We closed up the house in Catania and dropped out of circulation for a couple of weeks. But nothing happened. No one protested against us. Even the remonstrances against the Palermo men died down quickly. The families wanted to close the books on the past. They were tired of conspiracies and wars. An era was over, and before them lay a decade of promise.

8

The Catanzaro trial turned out well for the mafia. Many defendants were released from jail, and the Palermo families began to reorganize. The provincial structure was not reestablished immediately, because the districts still weren't working in a satisfactory way. Instabilities and headaches remained. When Salvatore Greco Cicchiteddu, the boss of the Palermo province (in Palermo the province boss is called secretary), left for South America, he entrusted his post to Antonino Sorci, who was a district boss at the time, but Sorci was arrested and we had to start all over again.

After Catanzaro, in any event, a provisional government was organized in Palermo—it seems to have been called a regency, as the judges who interrogated me defined it—made up of Gaetano Badalamenti, Luciano Liggio, and Stefano Bontade.

Sometime after the *viale* Lazio massacre, Badalamenti sent for Pippo, Calogero Conti (who was then vice-representative of the Catania province), and me. He invited us to Cinisi, his village, and over dinner he asked us if we could harbor his friend Luciano Liggio, who was a fugitive there but who could no longer stay with him.

While we were at the table a priest showed up. He was introduced to us as a man of honor from the Partinico family. His name was Agostino Coppola. (He was the one who later collected the ransom in the Cassina kidnapping.) During the trip back, my brother and I joked about this priest who was a part of the mafia.

We accepted Badalamenti's proposal willingly. Di Cristina took care of finding forged papers and a house for Liggio, who arrived a few days later. Before settling down in the place Di Cristina had found, Liggio stayed in a country house on Calogero Conti's property. One night the convoy of four or five cars escorting him had shown up there. Luciano Liggio climbed out of a blue Mercedes driven by Stefano Bontade. His bearing was proud and distinguished, like . . . I don't know—that of a president of the Supreme Appellate Court. He was elegant, in an expensive double-breasted jacket and a light hat. He sat down right there, on a milestone on that country road. And all of us looked at this Liggio, fascinated, as if who knows who had just shown up.

On the other hand, it's pointless to deny that Liggio was already a personality at the time. He was number one in Sicily—the big cheese.

He stayed only a few days in Conti's house. He wanted to leave because he said he was cold. He was as capricious as a child and full of demands. He made us run around a couple of provinces to find him Ferrarelle mineral water because he wouldn't drink any other kind. In fact, he was forced to drink tap water, which made him sick (he said) because he'd had an operation on his prostate.

He drove us crazy. He changed places a couple of times more until we managed to find him a small house just out in the countryside, in the hills, in San Giovanni La Punta, a pretty place where he remained for almost two years. He was joined by Bernardo Provenzano, who was a fugitive too. They passed themselves off in the village as two meat traders, two butchers. Liggio would say that he'd been ill and had come there because he needed fresh air.

The house was rented under the names of Antonio and Giuseppe Farruggia, with forged papers provided by Di Cristina. They were the very same papers found on Liggio when he was arrested in Milan, and Di Cristina griped to Pippo about Liggio's carelessness in still using the papers after so much time had passed.

Hiding a prominent fugitive is no small thing. One has to protect him, keep the area he's in under surveillance, forestall the unexpected, bring him food and drink. We brought Luciano Liggio everything. He was in our care. We would even put money in his pocket, given that, his repute notwithstanding, in 1969 he didn't have a lira.

Nor did we have great resources in those days. When Pippo had no money to give Liggio, he would go to the contractor Costanzo and ask him for it. Gino Costanzo knew that we were harboring Liggio and wouldn't refuse, in the same way that the others we turned to wouldn't refuse. Some defrayment of the costs came from illegal gambling dens, some from a sort of self-taxation on the part of the people who managed them, and some help came from Palermo too.

When I say that there wasn't any money in those years, that the mafia had no money, I'm not just saying it to exaggerate. After the arrests of 1962–1963 and the Catanzaro trial of 1968, everybody's money had run out. It had gone to lawyers, prison fees, and the like. There was a collection of funds that produced twenty or thirty million lire, handed over to Totò Riina as the Palermo regent, which served to maintain whoever needed money urgently or found himself facing an emergency.

Toward 1971 we went as far as organizing a series of kidnappings. The kidnapping of Pino Vassalo—the son of Don Ciccio, a builder who had grown rich through his friendships with the Cosa Nostra bosses—was an act of necessity. The proceeds, four hundred million lire, were distributed among the neediest families in Palermo.

Naturally the Corleonesi quickly took advantage of this, and a couple of months later, without telling anyone, they pulled off the Cassina kidnapping. It's pointless to add that the proceeds from this initiative were not distributed among interned or money-troubled men of honor from other families.

Even Stefano Bontade found himself in deep trouble. Fortunately he had a right to a portion of the earnings of Tommaso Spadaro, the cigarette smuggler, who was bragging about paying Bontade wages. When they began to leave prison around 1968, the Cosa Nostra bosses were almost all starving. Luciano Liggio probably owned a few houses or properties, but he wouldn't sell them.

I tell you—Totò Riina cried when he told me that his mother couldn't come visit him in prison in 1966 or 1967 because she couldn't pay for the train ticket.

The only exception were the Grecos. They'd been well off for ages. But when I talk about the Grecos in this case, I mean the other branch of the Grecos, the one that later became confused with that of Michele Greco.

Then we all became millionaires. Suddenly, within a couple of years. Thanks to drugs.

Let's return to Liggio the fugitive. The house in San Giovanni La Punta had a little terrace overlooking the inland-facing side, where there were no other buildings. One fine day Liggio stripped naked and lay out in the sun. Why not? No one could see him. But some distance away an apartment building was under construction, and it was almost completed.

Since the builder wanted to sell the apartments, he often accompanied prospective buyers to see the place. And whenever the clients saw the naked man sunbathing next door, they would get a bad impression and refuse to buy.

Eventually the builder went to the carabinieri to protest the presence of this naked man who was preventing him from selling anything. So the next thing that happened was that the carabinieri came knocking on Liggio's door. He was in his underwear when he saw them approach.

"Hmm, carabinieri. What do I do now?" he thought. He couldn't escape, and he was alone in the house because Provenzano had gone out. There was no choice but to open the door. "Good morning," he said to the militiamen.

"Good morning. The inspector would like to see you."

"Right now?" Liggio replied courteously. "Look, I can't come right now." And he lowered his shorts. "As you can see, I have a catheter." It was true, because he really did have a prostate problem. "I'm waiting for the doctor to come take it out. Right after that I'll come see the inspector."

"No problem. You can even come in the afternoon," the carabinieri answered. As soon as they left, Liggio got dressed and ran to the telephone to call Pippo's office. I happened to be there.

"Come quick," he said to me.

"What's the matter? What happened?"

"Come immediately, I tell you. And don't come to the house. Come to the bus stop."

I went right away. "You want to tell me what happened?" I asked Liggio.

"The carabinieri came. They want to talk to me. The inspector wants to talk to me."

"But if the carabinieri came, why are you still here? Why haven't you run away?"

"Because they didn't seem to suspect anything. They didn't recognize me."

We decided to go to the city to discuss what happened with Pippo, who said: "Listen, professor . . ." He called him "professor" instead of Luciano. Liggio liked it. After all, many in our circle considered him a sort of professor. "They didn't come because they knew you were there. They wouldn't have shown up like that, casually knocking on the door. And I'm also sure that if they had shown up any other way they wouldn't be alive now," said my brother, alluding to the reputation for ferocity and alertness that the "professor" already had by then.

"What if they do figure it out? If they start having suspicions? What should I do?" asked Liggio, who was worried by the prospect of having to leave a hideout he had grown to like. He was happy with the house, happy with the village. He had even found two women, two sisters. He was attracted to one of them, and he had asked my cousin to get a sleeping pill to knock out the other sister so that she couldn't see . . . But I don't know if he was fucking them.

"Look, they didn't recognize you. And up to now they haven't had a single suspicion. I don't know if they won't have any in the future, or if they won't develop any from the fact that you won't go see the inspector."

"All right," Liggio said pensively. "You know what? I'm going. I'm going to the carabinieri."

In the meantime, Bino Provenzano had arrived from Palermo. He had come by train to be surer of not being seen, and because he didn't know how to drive a car, even if he did have a well-made fake license. He'd go around telling everyone that because he had a license he could drive too. But he couldn't, and all of us who had good cars made damn sure he didn't touch them.

Provenzano was told everything, and it was decided to send him to the inspector instead of Liggio, under the pretext that Liggio was feeling ill. From the carabinieri's reaction it would become clear what the real reason for the summons was, and whether they had any serious suspicions.

We drove Provenzano to the main square of San Giovanni La Punta, where the carabinieri barracks were. We waited a long time. Liggio was becoming nervous. He was swearing and saying that he had done the wrong thing, that he shouldn't have sent him in his place. And he kept swearing until Provenzano came out. Looking calm, he walked by the car and said: "It went well."

We followed him a little ways and then had him climb into the car. "What did they say to you?"

"Nothing. Someone who's building next door complained to the inspector because he's always seeing a man lying around naked," said Provenzano, feigning annoyance.

We looked at Liggio, scandalized. Liggio played along and pretended to be insulted. "Who's this son of a bitch who says I go around naked? It's not true. I don't run around naked." In truth he was relieved.

Provenzano said: "I told the inspector that you were ill, that you'd been operated on and needed sun. He replied that he understood, that he was aware we were here because you were convalescing, and that all you had to do was wear swimming trunks, have some clothes on, that's all."

Liggio thought for a bit and then burst out: "I never have to leave! We're home free. We're no longer fugitives. The carabinieri know we're here. They don't suspect anything and they'll never come looking for us."

Liggio remained a fugitive in Catania until July 1971, the date of Pippo's arrest on a charge before the Palermo Tribunal during the Trial of the Hundred Fourteen. He left Catania because it became too risky to live in a territory controlled by Pippo, who was now the focus of police searches and surveillance. They could have found him by following my brother.

He hated to leave. He had begun to feel at home, and he had met some people, among them Nino "Big Heart," a young man of honor whom he liked a lot because he didn't talk much but "did things." Big Heart would often go see him in the San Giovanni house and accompany him on expeditions in search of the investigator Angelo Mangano, Liggio's worst enemy.

Liggio loathed Mangano because at the beginning of the sixties he had arrested him in Corleone, but above all because of a number of cruelties Mangano had inflicted on his sister. Liggio knew that Mangano was a native of Riposto, a coastal village north of Catania, and he thought that during the summer he would almost certainly return there to go swimming. "Nothing better than to kill him," Liggio was always saying. Every morning in August he would leave San Giovanni La Punta with his faithful Big Heart for the beaches around Riposto in order to track down Mangano. They would blithely head off in a Fiat 500, pistols in hand, but with a big knife too. Liggio didn't intend to shoot Mangano once he'd found him. He wanted to quarter him with his own two hands.

He didn't find Mangano in Sicily, but he found him some years later in Rome, in 1973, and tried to kill him. You remember the famous attack on the investigator Angelo Mangano that the newspapers wrote so much about? Well, I'm in a position to tell you how the events went. One of the plotters of the attack was Liggio; the other participants weren't Sicilian, but Neapolitans. I learned of the circumstances from a number of people, among them Pippo, who said to Stefano Bontade, "Fortunately, not a single Palermitan was involved in something so badly botched."

The Neapolitans who were in on the operation with Liggio were Ciro Mazzarella and Michele Zaza, both smugglers. Mazzarella was driving the car, which he pulled up near the door to Mangano's house. Liggio got out of the car to shoot Mangano in the head at close range so that he wouldn't miss. However, either because of a defect in the gun or because of a defect in the bullets or for some other reason, Mangano was not mortally wounded. Moreover, at the very moment of the action a disagreement had arisen between Liggio and Zaza that made them lose precious time. Nello Pernice told me that Liggio never forgave himself for that failure.

Liggio was bloodthirsty. He liked to kill. He had a way of looking at people that could frighten anyone, even us mafiosi. The smallest thing set him off, and then a strange light would appear in his eyes that created silence all around him. When you were in his company you had to be careful about how you spoke. The wrong tone of voice, a misconstrued word, and all of a sudden that sudden silence. Everything would instantly be hushed, uneasy, and you could smell death in the air.

One time during his stay in Catania, I allowed myself to tell him he was crazy. Yes—I, Antonino Calderone, once told Luciano Liggio that in my opinion he was crazy, insane. Liggio had a woman in Taranto. He had met her during his convalescence in a hospital in the area, and he wanted to go see her. When he told me about it I quickly replied: "Professor, that's crazy. You want to go see a woman who knows your identity, who knows who you are. Don't you realize how dangerous that would be?" That was exactly what I said to him. Spontaneously, without thinking about it much.

Then the talk turned to the investigator Mangano. Liggio pulled out a big knife and began to wave it around as though he were about to kill Mangano. "See how I want to do it? I want to cut him like that, and that."

Immediately afterward my cousin said to me: "How could you have dared say those things? To speak like that to Luciano Liggio? You're a fool. Didn't you see how he was looking at you? How his face turned ugly when he was waving that knife in front of you?"

While he was in Catania, Liggio began to have it in for another person too—the journalist Giuseppe Fava, who was murdered by the mafia many years later, in 1984. Fava's sin was to have insulted him. He had allowed himself to write an article in which he made fun of Luciano Liggio's eyes. Liggio asked Pippo to find out Fava's address and daily routine. He intended to "give him a present." Pippo objected to the request and answered that there was no reason for Liggio to worry about a man of that stature.

He killed for fun, out of sheer brutality. One day he said to a young man, Giuseppe Madonia: "I don't think you're capable of killing a carabiniere." And they went off in a car to look for anyone in a carabiniere uniform, who luckily they didn't come across. The episode was recounted to me by Madonia's father, who was shuddering at the memory of it. His son was still a boy, inexperienced and easily influenced.

After Pippo's arrest, Liggio went to Milan and began to organize kidnappings. He needed money, and was also dealing drugs along with Nello Pernice. But he didn't sever his ties to Catania completely. Francesco Madonia told me that every so often Liggio would come to Catania, but I never saw him again except for one occasion, when, in the company of Nello Pernice, he came to see me at my service station to make a very unusual proposal. He told me that he knew about my close friendship with the Costanzos, who, he also knew, would periodically withdraw one or two hundred million lire from the bank to pay their workers. The money—in cash—was transferred to the company's offices under a carabinieri escort. Liggio asked me to watch the Costanzos to find out the date and time of the withdrawals so that he could stage an armed robbery at his convenience. It wouldn't be a problem if the escort responded with force—the robbers would have answered more than adequately. And the Costanzos wouldn't have lost anything, since the money's transportation was the responsibility of the bank.

The proposal was strange, even somewhat provocative. Liggio was planning to hit people under my protection—my friends—and in addition was taking it for granted that he could operate in an area under my jurisdiction.

On the same occasion I noticed something else that was strange about Liggio's behavior. He wasn't calling me *"tu"* anymore, like in the past, but *"Lei."* I asked him why and he replied that it was because I hadn't complied with his request not to hire a defense lawyer for my brother in the Trial of the Hundred Fourteen. He had been charged in that trial as well, and as a sign of protest he hadn't hired a defense lawyer; he expected the other defendants to follow his example. I justified myself by saying that I couldn't leave Pippo without a defense, but he kept on calling me *"Lei."* When afterward I told him determinedly that I wouldn't do anything that would allow him to pull off the robbery, he leaped up and went away. It was the last time I saw him.

Liggio's behavior had worried me. I told Francesco Madonia about it and I went to see Pippo in jail to discuss what had happened. Both agreed that Liggio's requests were so outrageous that there had to be another motive behind them. After a while Pippo shook his head and concluded: "It's without a doubt an excuse to break off relations with us, seeing that we helped him and thus that he has contracted debts toward the Calderones. Everyone knows that that's what Liggio does. He turns against people who help him because he doesn't want to owe debts of gratitude to anyone. He also behaved that way toward Gaetano Badalamenti, who hid him for a long time."

Liggio's resentment toward Badalamenti (and the many Palermo families allied with him) was, in truth, based on other factors took, and was shared by the other Corleonesi. The accusation against Badalamenti was that he had grown rich from drugs at a time when many families were finding themselves in serious financial trouble and many men of honor were practically starving.

9

While Liggio was hiding out in Catania he was visited by two bosses of the Palermo Cosa Nostra—Salvatore Greco Cicchiteddu and Tommaso Buscetta—who had to discuss a question of considerable importance with him: the mafia's participation in a coup d'état, the so-called *"golpe Borghese"* of 1970. To receive these guests, Liggio went into the city center, to Pippo's house on the *via* Etnea, where I was living too. I was thus there when they arrived. My brother was waiting for them on the balcony, and at a certain point he came in and said: "They're coming. Tommaso's here too."

Liggio flew into a rage: "What's he doing to me, coming here with that dishonored man? Instead of shooting him in the head a few times he's running around with him." Pippo was walking down the stairs to meet them and didn't hear Liggio's comment. But I asked him why he was so hostile toward Buscetta. Liggio answered that Buscetta had a "pimping" past, but he collected himself quickly because the guest had come into the house, and he greeted Buscetta cordially.

The topic quickly turned to Prince Junio Valerio Borghese. The name wasn't completely unknown to me. I thought he had been the leader of the MAs or the NAs* or whatever. You must forgive

*Calderone's confusion is about the name of the MAs, the *Motoscafi armati* or "armed speedboats" section of the Italian navy in World War Two. The prince had led this very successful PT-boat group throughout the war (translator's note).

101

me. I've never been what you might call well educated, but I've learned something from reading the newspaper every day, and a lot from *Settimana Enigmistica.**

I had no idea what those MAs were. I had seen them in *Settimana Enigmistica.* When I first heard people talk about Prince Borghese and the MAs, it didn't make any particular impression on me. I thought of the MAs of the *Settimana Enigmistica.*

They were talking, in essence, about joining a military coup that was to begin in Rome and radiate out over the rest of the country. The role of the mafia was to have consisted in participating in the Sicilian operations. At a prearranged time the mafia was to have accompanied people into the various prefectures and substituted them for the prefect. The channel to the coup plotters was a Palermo mafioso I knew, Carlo Morana, a somewhat unbalanced man who was good friends with Di Cristina.

There was a long discussion. Opinions were divergent. Greco and Buscetta stayed some twenty days at my brother's house, talking with Liggio—who had no particular objections to taking part in the coup d'état—and with other mafia bosses. There were many meetings, but not too many. It was the world soccer championships and few mafiosi wanted to miss the matches.

The inducement the coup plotters were offering the mafia was the reversal of a series of already concluded trials, among them that of the Rimi family from Alcamo and Liggio's for the killing of the physician Navarra from Corleone. But the mafia was very suspicious because the coup plotters were fascists, and there was the precedent of the prefect Mori. "We'll help them seize power, and then they'll arrest us, especially since they'll have learned who we are," a number of mafia bosses were thinking. Others were proposing to ask for a reversal of all mafia trials, a sort of general amnesty for everyone.

They decided to join the so-called coup d'état, but without making a real commitment. Almost to make fun of it.

Pippo went to Rome to meet the prince. He was picked up at a

---

*A popular Italian crossword weekly (translator's note).

predetermined point on the bank of the Tiber by a man whose identifying mark was a black bag and a copy of the *Messaggero*. He asked if my brother was "Pippo from Catania," then accompanied him to Valerio Borghese. Borghese told my brother that he wanted some men to take over the Sicilian prefectures and install new prefects. If anyone resisted, the mafiosi—who were to wear identifying armbands on the occasion—were to arrest him immediately.

Pippo heard out the terms of the plan patiently, but he jumped when the prince started talking about arrests: "Arrest who? We mafiosi, make arrests? Listen, we don't do police work! We won't arrest anyone," my brother said, shocked. "If we have to kill someone, fine. We'll kill him. But we don't do the work of the police."

Valerio Borghese agreed that the men of honor wouldn't have to carry out arrests. They were to provide support for whatever acts of violence were necessary and in general help out the young fascists from Catania, Palermo, and other cities, who already knew what they had to do. In Rome they were to occupy the RAI* and the Ministry of the Interior. From there the prefectures would be taken under control.

Then Borghese promised to overturn the trials, and Pippo said: "Dear prince, we're agreed. But afterward you won't play any tricks and repeat the story of Mussolini and the prefect Mori?"

"No, no, don't worry. If you help us, we won't hurt you. We'll respect our pacts. But you must understand that if there are murders after we take over the government, the magistracy and the police won't be able to just stand by. They will have to carry out their duty."

"Logical, logical. One can't ask to commit murders and go unpunished. No. The agreement is to look at all these things with another eye."

But it was the whole plan that in reality convinced no one. Liggio and others had said they were in agreement, or they were pre-

*Radio Autodiffuzione Italiano, the Italian government broadcasting service (translator's note).

tending to be. Many others didn't agree and said so. In my view the mafia was bluffing in order to help get some of its people out of prison and to "adjust" a couple of trials.

After talking it over, we came to the conclusion that it made sense to say yes to the coup plotters. If the coup d'état was pulled off and won with our help, something could be hoped for. If they won without us, they would certainly fight us. They would send us all to the Island, like under fascism. We would be wiped out. So we agreed to say that we were with them, but without giving them any kind of list. They wanted a register of all mafiosi. Pippo told them that we had two thousand men at our disposal but that a list of them was out of the question.

At the appointed time, the conspirators would be told to turn to a given person in a given village, a given neighborhood, and they would know only his identity. And then afterward we would recommend people to be rewarded or placed in new positions. But no list. We weren't idiots. What if those fascists later took all the people on the list and sent them God knows where?

—

But then nothing happened. They told us that on day X they wanted one of our people in Rome with a handful of men. Natale Rimi went. They gave him machine guns, and shots were heard that night. Rimi was meant to fly back to Catania the next morning to tell us what to do, if we should send other men, etc. Pippo went to pick him up at the airport and Rimi said that nothing had come of it.

Later on we learned that a carabiniere general in Naples had pulled out at the last moment. But we had always had our doubts, as I've indicated to you, about the feasibility of the whole business. The following year, at the Trial of the Hundred Fourteen in Palermo, an anonymous letter surfaced that described the whole episode.

A funny story linked to the failed coup involved my brother. It was still 1971. He was arrested in Catania and brought to Palermo, where he was held for two days in a carabinieri barracks. The first person to interrogate him was Captain Russo, who was later killed in 1977. Russo asked him: "What do they call you at home?"

"What do you mean, what do they call me?"

"Your relatives, your friends, what do they call you?"

"They call me Pippo."

"There! It's him! It's Pippo from Catania," the captain shouted, leaping up and running off to call the commander. "It's him, it's him!"

My brother was baffled. "That man is crazy. Certifiable. Who is he? [Captain Russo was in civilian clothes.] I tell him my name and he starts screaming like a madman."

—

After the fortunate outcome (for the mafia) of the great Catanzaro trial and the killing of Cavataio, Gaetano Badalamenti became the most powerful individual in the Cosa Nostra. One of his first moves was to organize a series of attacks in Sicily to show everyone that the mafia had returned, stronger than ever. "We must take Sicily back. We must make our presence felt. Every last carabiniere must be thrown into the sea," Badalamenti said. Thus disorder and chaos had to be sown, and judges, politicians, and journalists murdered.

I don't know if political targets were part of the mafia plan. I do know that at this point Francesco Madonia, from the Resuttana family, was told to place a series of bombs in various public offices and to hit a number of prominent men. Because of an error in their preparation, many of the bombs didn't go off.

Another bomb was brought to Catania by Madonia himself and another man. The device was handed to my brother, who hid it for my cousin, who in turn, at the request of Luciano Liggio, set it off in the Palace of Justice, behind the entryway into the Court of Assizes. A trial for armed robbery was being held for a certain Mirabello and others, and the attack was credited to outside accomplices of theirs. Mirabello was condemned to the penitentiary.

The attacks on public figures were more successful than the bombs. I don't have more precise facts, but Pippo told me that the disappearance of the journalist Mauro De Mauro in 1970 and the murder of the Republic of Palermo procurator Pietro Scaglione the following year were parts of the mafia strategy.

Those first years of the 1970s were a time of great unity. There was no friction. Tano Badalamenti was coddling Luciano Liggio; Riina and Provenzano were on the rise and bowing down before "Don Tano" as though he were their father.

It was also necessary to kill the parliament deputy Nicosia, the fascist, and the president of the Sicilian Region, Giuseppe D'Angelo. Nicosia survived only because of the inexperience of his would-be killer, once again Damiano Caruso, who managed only to wound him, while the deputy D'Angelo's life was saved by the veto of the family boss who had jurisdiction over the area. D'Angelo was in great danger of being murdered because the Cosa Nostra accused him of having loudly demanded the establishment of the Antimafia Commission after the Ciaculli massacre. Years had passed since 1963, but the damages inflicted by the commission were still being felt. But Giovanni Mongiovì, the representative of Enna province—where Calascibetta, D'Angelo's native town, was located—was against the murder, and certainly not for fear of retaliation.

10

I was married on December 14, 1970. A bit late for someone born in Sicily: I was thirty-five years old. I was married in Catania, to a girl who worked at the Agricultural Commission and who has since stuck by me through all the ups and downs of my strange life. I have always tried not to tell her anything about my pledge to the mafia, to keep her removed from its problems, hatreds, and fears. I pretended, as much as it was possible, to lead a normal, quiet, comfortable life. I did the same thing with my children. They understood anyway, since they're intelligent, but pretending helps.

The best men at my wedding were Francesco Cinardo and Gino Costanzo, who was Pippo's best man too and the baptismal god-father of his son Salvatore. In those days our relationship with the Costanzos had become much closer, especially since Pippo's contracting business had failed and we were managing the Costanzos' interests in various parts of Sicily.

The honeymoon was brief. It was before Christmas. First we went to Naples, where Stefano Bontade and Stefano Giaconia organized a nice dinner at the restaurant Giuseppone a Mare in Mergellina. Later, through a man who was very close to the Cosa Nostra—the actor Franco Franchi—they booked us a room at the Massimo d'Azeglio hotel in Rome, where we all stayed, and we had another party at a restaurant in the historic center. Then we went on to Milan, where we were invited out by Giuseppe Bono—

the major drug trafficker—and Antonio Salomone. While we were there Pippo called me to say that Salvatore Ferrera, who was also in Milan at the time, had been hit in the head by a pistol shot. I immediately went to visit him in the hospital. Ferrera told me that he'd been shot by a certain Arena because of something about a division of profits from the sale of stolen furs. Then we returned to Catania, even if my wife was somewhat reluctant.

From 1971 to 1973 I felt almost at home in Palermo. Every week I would go to see Pippo in the Ucciardone prison, and there I met various men of honor. I saw a lot of a friend of mine, Salvatore Rinella, who had been introduced to me a few years before by Francesco Di Noto, a member of the Palermo family of the Corso dei Mille. Through the Costanzos I had found Rinella and his brother a small shop in the Catania area to use for a dairy business, and they were grateful.

The Rinellas and I would see each other almost every week, and we spoke about many things even though Salvatore Rinella wasn't a man of honor. It was a real friendship. When my time as a fugitive began in 1976, Rinella put me up in a villa he leased in Casteldaccia, near Palermo. I felt terrible when I read the account of his murder in the newspapers in 1987, while I was in France.

Gaetano Badalamenti was often there during my talks in prison with my brother; he had arranged for his visiting hours to coincide with Pippo's. At these meetings I would pass on to Badalamenti messages sent to him by Totò Riina, and vice versa. One time Badalamenti told me to inform Riina that he needed to "put a necktie on" one of the Silvestri brothers. These were four or five brothers, not men of honor, who had committed the great folly of falling out with the Costa Nostra: they had punched a man of honor inside the Ucciardone prison. The fight went no further because an associate of the Porta Nuova family stepped in and separated the combatants. But the verdict was quickly handed down: death.

In this period I would often meet Riina, who told me how he had organized the Cassina kidnapping. Kidnappings were the order of the day in Palermo at the time. One day the brothers Antonino and Gaetano Grado, men of honor from Stefano Bontade's family, told me about another one. We were in a restaurant, and the moment I started speaking well of Pippo Gambino, an inseparable friend of Totò Riina, Gaetano Grado contradicted me and said that Gambino had, along with Grado's brother Salvatore, tried to kidnap someone in the center of Palermo, in the area of *via* Ruggero Settimo. Because the victim had dared to resist, Pippo Gambino had shot and killed him.

In the same period—we're still in the opening years of the seventies—Totò Riina proposed that I invest with him in drug trafficking. Riina and his group were just getting into the business. They didn't have enough capital, especially since they hadn't yet collected the Cassina ransom. Totò asked me to pledge the greatest amount I could collect from the Catania family. After consulting my brother, I pulled together five million lire. Bino Provenzano joined in with three million, but he had to borrow it from Nitto Santapaola because he had no funds. The money was handed over from Nitto to Bino in my presence in Palermo, at an antique shop run by a small, fat fellow named Enea.

I waited for a good long time, but the profit on my investment wasn't to be seen. As soon as I could I asked Pippo Gambino about my money's fate, but he answered that he had no idea, and he suggested that I talk about it with Totò Riina directly.

I asked Riina what had happened, and he apologized, telling me that problems had cropped up because of the poor quality of the drugs, and that he had therefore been forced to sell them at a low price. When everything was tallied up he managed to recoup four and a half million lire for me. He added half a million to this sum—from his own pocket, he said—because he hadn't given me a wedding present yet. In fact, I had earned exactly what I had anticipated—nothing at all.

In didn't believe Riina's excuse. In reality he wanted to punish me because I had passed on to Pippo—against Riina's wishes—what Riina had told me about the Cassina kidnapping and the drug trafficking that Badalamenti had launched into without Riina's knowledge. But it wasn't quite like that. Riina had authorized me to tell Pippo about the Cassina kidnapping, but not about the drug dealing that Badalamenti had started without the knowledge of the other mafia bosses, who were in grave economic difficulties.

You could ask, at this point, how Riina came to know about Badalamenti's covert activity, and why he kept it secret. Didn't it break the Cosa Nostra rules to undertake illicit activities without at least letting the members of one's own family know? Or did that just hold for the soldiers and *decina* bosses, while the family bosses could do what they pleased?

The question isn't easy to answer. The Cosa Nostra has its rules, but then there are special cases with their own shadings and complications. There are those who follow the rules, and there are the exceptions and abuses. There are those who are tolerated, those who are made examples of, those who come to be punished. Many mafia bosses feel that they can allow themselves abuses. They consider it a mark of power. Liggio, Riina, and the Corleonesi were maestros of abuse. And of deceit.

Gaetano Badalamenti should have made it known, at least to his peers, that he had started to traffic in drugs. That is, *if* he had chosen to abide by the rules of the Cosa Nostra. He should have then, according to the rules of courtesy, invited other family bosses to go into partnership with him. But he didn't.

He could have justified himself by saying that it wasn't a question of a set rule, and that since men of honor had complete freedom in legitimate business, the same principle ought to apply to illicit business that doesn't prejudice the security of the family. Or he could have invoked the Cosa Nostra's practice of not talking about the drug business because of the large number of requests for participation that arise when someone mentions it. Or he could have raised the territory question, maintaining that he was exporting great quantities of heroin to the United States, and that since his activities were being carried out at the Punta Raisi airport, which was in Cinisi territory—his territory—he wasn't under any obligation to inform anyone.

But who had told Riina that Badalamenti was getting rich like that, on the QT? My suspicions fell on Domenico Coppola, a relative of the famous Frank Coppola, nicknamed "Three Fingers," and a brother of Father Agostino of the Partinico family, which was intimate with Badalamenti but closely linked with Riina too.

I remember, in fact, that Totò Riina passed by my service station once and asked me the favor of going to the airport to pick up Domenico Coppola and Nello Pernice. I did, and immediately afterward arranged a dinner at my brother's country house in Montorosso Etneo. Various men of honor came, among them, naturally, Totò Riina. During dinner it dawned on me, from a series of hints, that it wasn't by chance that the encounter between Riina and the others was taking place in Catania. It was, in fact, a prearranged meeting because some important pieces of information had to be exchanged far away from Palermo. Domenico Coppola began by congratulating everyone present for the positive outcome of the massacre on the *viale* Lazio, and at the same time railed against a declaration made by Antonio Minore, the Trapani mafia boss who, while in the United States, had criticized the action against Cavataio, claiming that it hadn't been right to kill him after the Palermo families had led everyone to believe they wanted to make peace with him. Minore was in the United States because he had escaped from internal exile in Sommariva Bosco, in Liguria, after the Social Democrat parliamentary deputy Lupis obtained a passport for him.

The dinner lasted a long time, and at one point Coppola and Riina went off and conferred together for a while. When Badalamenti later learned of the meeting, he became extremely angry with Coppola and even wanted to take steps against him.

It was useless, in the end, to find out who was right and who was wrong. Riina reacted quickly as soon as he learned about Badalamenti and the drugs. He started trafficking too, and he said nothing about it to Badalamenti. The second great mafia war arose from this, among many other reasons.

Power, for instance. Or rather, the excessive power that went to the head of Badalamenti, who at a certain point toward the end of 1973 proclaimed himself representative of the Palermo province, making Luciano Liggio provincial *consigliere* and Stefano Bontade his vice-representative. Badalamenti wanted to crush everyone with his weight, with his strength. And instead the others crushed him.

Was it even possible? Does it seem realistic to you, does it make sense that Luciano Liggio—someone who never took his hat off to anyone, not even when he went to church—would bow to Badalamenti simply because he made himself (or had himself named, it doesn't matter) provincial representative?

In fact, at the first meeting they held—toward the beginning of 1974, to decide whether to reestablish the system of provincial commissions made up of district bosses that had been in effect before 1962—Liggio left the group and dissociated himself from everything with the words, "You created this commission. Fine, you can keep it! I won't be second to anyone." And the troubles started.

There's no need, in any case, to mention this incident in order to express what Liggio thought of the pacts, rules, and customs of the Cosa Nostra world. I've already told you the story of the planned Costanzo robbery. Well, here's another.

Between the end of 1972 and the beginning of 1973, during Pippo's imprisonment, my cousin Salvatore Marchese told me that Calogero Conti, the vice-representative of the Catania family, had asked him on Liggio's behalf to identify a rich person who could be kidnapped. The choice had come down to two names: the publisher Ciancio, who owned the newspaper *La Sicilia,* and the textile trader Pavia. Marchese also told me that the choice had fallen on Pavia because the hours of the trader's comings and goings had been determined through one of his employees. The employee had even introduced Marchese to Pavia himself.

It was unheard of. Pippo had a position and influence much greater than those of Calogero Conti. The kidnapping was meant to take place in the center of Catania, in the very heart of our territory, and no one had consulted us. There hadn't been the slightest discussion inside the family, and yet everything was ready to be carried out.

I berated my cousin for the slight this represented toward me and my brother. He tried to defend himself by arguing that the division of territories in Catania wasn't as strict and binding as it was in Palermo and other places. That was true, but he couldn't have been unaware that a kidnapping was something too serious not to at least discuss with the local authorities in the Cosa Nostra. Marchese also told me that he had been bound to keep it secret from everyone, that he had violated that secrecy because of his loyalty toward us, and that he was running a risk of grave reprisals. I confronted Calogero Conti too, who gave me the same sort of answer.

I forced Marchese to tell me the day and time planned for the kidnapping—when, I decided, I would set myself up directly in front of Pavia's store. On the opposite side of the street was a clothes shop where I could happen to be under the pretext of buying clothes for Pippo. When I arrived there at the appointed hour I almost ran into Totò Riina and another person who was with him (Gino Martello or Pippo Gambino, probably). From the corner of my eye I also made out, at a certain distance, Nino Badalamenti and Nello Pernice, who were trying not to be seen by me. We all pretended to have been there by coincidence, we greeted one another, embarrassed, and the kidnapping didn't take place.

Afterward I asked Calogero Conti why the kidnapping he'd mentioned hadn't come off, and he replied that, daylight savings time having come into effect, the external circumstances had changed. There was too much light. It was an off-the-cuff answer, but I pretended to believe it.

11

These gentlemen were also taking advantage of the fact that Pippo was in jail. I did what I could to run the family in his stead, to make his presence felt, but it wasn't the same thing.

Speaking of Pippo's absence, another episode comes to mind that happened around 1971 or 1972, when Pippo was in the Ucciardone prison. It was a curious and funny incident that I haven't talked about before now. It concerns Franco Franchi. As I've said, Franchi was friends with many mafiosi and probably was himself made a man of honor after 1978. He was very close to Stefano Bontade. Franchi's right-hand man in Rome, a sort of chauffeur and factotum named Gregorio, belonged to the family of Santa Maria del Gesù and thus to that family's *decina* in Rome, whose boss was Uncle Angelino.

Pippo and I were also very close to Franco Franchi, whose real name is Franco Benenato. There was a party whenever Franchi came to Catania. We were often together. While Pippo was in jail, Franchi came to Catania, to Acireale, to shoot the film *The Godfather's Godson,* a parody of *The Godfather*. I was there every night. I've always loved the cinema. I was the friend of an important actor, and would chat with the cast and watch them shoot scenes. My presence was welcomed; they would even ask me if a given scene was working or not, if it was funny enough.

After every shoot we would go to the hotel and have dinner together. Franchi was an extroverted type. He liked to play the piano and sing. One night he wanted to come to my house, and I introduced him to my wife, my sister-in-law, and my nephew. They were happy to meet such a famous person, but the atmosphere wasn't precisely carefree: my sister-in-law's husband was in jail. Franchi immediately understood the situation. He empathized with this young woman and her son, so he sang the ballad "Papa, How Much Does Freedom Cost" to my nephew, a child of ten whose father was in jail. He was very moved, two tears welled up, and the rest of us were moved as well. Franchi had everyone crying. Then, to lighten things up a bit, he sang "I'm the Last Lover," a ballad he had presented at the festival of San Remo.

He was a sensitive man, an artist. When he left my house that night, we all went out onto the balcony and kept waving to him even as his car was heading off toward the highway.

Several days later, in the evening after the day's shoot was over, Franchi said to me: "Listen, Nino, the film's finishing up here. Then we'll have to go. I need a favor."

"What is it?"

"The equipment truck could be set fire to. New equipment couldn't get here before two or three weeks. That way I could stay here longer and not have anything to do."

Franchi was staying at the Hotel Maugeri in Acireale, a good hotel with a large staff. So I hired a couple of kids to do the job. That cretin Nino Condorelli showed up at the hotel for a quick look around before torching the van. He went into the hotel, allowed himself (with his hangdog look, and dressed like a starving man) to be spotted in the lobby, then left. A waiter noticed him and followed him until Condolleri got near the truck. Thinking he was about to steal it, the waiter raised the alarm. But Condolleri was a professional, or thought he was. He managed to set fire to the van, more or less, and to damage the equipment before running away.

Since it took a couple of weeks to fix everything up and in those days film work was paid per diem, Franco Franchi had a little holiday in the country at the expense of the production company.

Another memorable evening took place in the summer of 1973. Pippo was fresh out of jail and had also just undergone a terrible operation. It was the first time we'd been out together for fun in a long while. Franco Franchi was doing a show in Enna and we went to see him.

With him was the singer Minnie Minoprio. After the performance we all went to a restaurant. It was a big, big party. We stayed the whole night. Franchi got drunk, and in a short time my brother, who never drank, followed suit. But it was a special night. He had survived a difficult procedure. A tumor had been removed from his throat and he had to speak through a device he pressed against his neck. And so he was drinking, drinking, drinking along with everyone else. No one wanted the night to end. At one point Pippo took off Minnie Minoprio's shoe and began to drink from it. He put the shoe on the table, filled it with wine or champagne, and then drank to her. Minoprio was pretty, fun, and game. I don't think she was aware of what was going on. She didn't realize who she was drinking with, or perhaps she did and was excited precisely because of it.

Some years later, after Pippo's death, when I no longer saw anyone, someone came to me who knew about my acquaintance with Franco Franchi, a certain Romeo, the director of a private television station in Catania. He asked me if I could help him get in touch with Franchi in Rome. He wanted to offer him a contract for a commercial.

I telephoned Franchi: "*Ciao,* Franco. It's Nino, from Catania, the brother of . . . "

"Oh, yes, yes! What can I do for you?"

"I have a friend here who wants to ask if you might do a piece for his television station."

"Listen, I have to come to Catania because, as you know, I have an appointment with some friends." He assumed that I had been told about his visit, but I hadn't heard a word about it. He thought that I was still in the inner circle, in the sphere of men of honor who counted, and thus that I knew things. "I'm coming to Catania to do some things with friends. And so we'll see each other. You'll surely be there with them."

I asked Nitto Santapaola and a few others about Franchi's imminent visit. They told me that the occasion was the premiere of the movie *Paprika, Chocolate, and Hot Peppers,* which was by Michele Greco's son, a man of honor and a film director. His father wanted to, as they say, "launch" him. (But why wasn't he simply launched off a balcony? He was worthless. He was just the son of Michele Greco.) It appeared, however, that he didn't get along with his father. He put on artistocratic airs and was in business with some members of the Palermo nobility. They had a Honda dealership next to the chamber of commerce building.

I recommended that Franchi meet this Romeo, and I told Romeo to go to dinner with the group after the screening, although I myself wouldn't be going with them. Romeo was astonished and asked me why. I couldn't answer. How could I tell him that for a long time now I hadn't been going out at night with those people? How could I tell him that it was too dangerous, that I was scared they'd kill me?

They went to a very good restaurant, La Costa Azzurra. Nitto Santapaola was there, and Cavadduzzu, and the others. In short, the cream of the Catanian mafia. The victors.

12

In the 1970s there were many kidnappings, much extortion, and, above all, much smuggling—a huge amount of smuggling. The mafia's prosperity began during this time. Before then we had scraped by with small-time, legal activities. Everyone had some sort of trade or shop or small factory, and the fact that one was a mafioso helped out a bit in one's dealings with suppliers, clients, even competitors. But there were no special advantages. There was no credit at the banks. Contracts were awarded to the large enterprises, to those closely tied to politics, and to those with the money to pay off bureaucrats. My brother, who was able to get a construction company going as early as the 1960s, was an exception.

But not even in the seventies or later were the Catania men of honor able to break into the world of contracts successfully. There was a handful of big businessmen who already controlled everything. They knew how to run their affairs. They were much better and cleverer than we were when it came to money. Banks were hostile to us. Pippo's company went under precisely because he had tried to settle a disagreement between the Costanzos and the Banca Nazionale del Lavoro; his involvement was a favor to the director of the Catania branch, a relative of his partner Concetto Gallo. Since then all my brother's property has been registered in my name, because after Pippo's bankruptcy there was a risk that everything he had would be taken away from him. This legal fact aside, there was never a distinction between the property of Pippo and his family and that of mine and my family. And we've always done everything together, whether legal or illegal.

Only in the 1970s did illegal activities grow large enough for mafiosi to live off them. In the past there were very few wealthy men of honor. Apart from the Grecos and the Salvos—and the La Barberas, who grew rich in the construction industry—the economic condition of most mafiosi was wretched. Just imagine—a well-off mafioso was so rare that Nino Sorci (the man of honor who was with my uncle in Tunisia, and who slept in cemeteries to avoid being killed) had come to be called *"Ninu u riccu."** *

Today many are rich. The Santapaolas are all rich, and it's obvious. Others are rich, too, but it's not obvious because they hide their money. They don't want to come to the attention of the police because they're afraid of the law that allows money and property to be confiscated. Some time ago I read in the newspaper that five hundred million lire in cash was found during a police search of the house of Francesco Ferrera's wife (or his mistress). It was in a bedside table. Well, if they hadn't found it they wouldn't have known it existed.

The black market in cigarettes was the biggest thing in the 1970s. It started in the decade's opening years and by 1974–1975 it had become fairly large. There was an agreement that lasted until 1978 among the bosses of the Sicilian and Neapolitan Cosa Nostras— Zaza, Nuvoletta, and others—to close the Naples market to outsiders and to establish rotations and quotas for the participants.

The rotations were for cargo space in boats. One turn would fall to the Neapolitans, the next to the Sicilians living in Naples, the one after that to the Sicilians from Palermo and elsewhere. Every two months, I believe, a boat would come to Sicily. Its load of cigarettes would be divided among the Cosa Nostra families. So, one to two thousand cartons were for Michele Greco, a thousand went to the Corleonesi, two thousand belonged to the Bontades, one thousand to the Di Cristinas, and so forth. With each shipment some twenty to twenty-five thousand cartons would be divided up.

*"Nino the rich" in dialect (translator's note).

Totò Inzerillo and Francesco Scaglione would take care of unloading them. They had gangs to do the work. They would also take inventory and deliver the figures to Gaetano Badalamenti, who would then divide up the shipment among everyone. The rest of us did nothing. It was very convenient, but it didn't produce enormous sums, like drugs did.

It would earn well enough, however—on the order of ten to fifteen million lire every two or three months for every thousand cartons of cigarettes. One couldn't increase one's quota beyond a certain limit—about two thousand to twenty-five hundred cartons—because there was a maximum load a boat could carry on each run, and any increase in one's own quota meant a decrease for someone else. Also, Pippo didn't have the heart of a speculator. His quota was a thousand cartons, as befitted an important boss. But when the ten million lire in profit arrived, two or three million would immediately end up as presents—subsidies for the family's needier men of honor.

Sure, one could have taken a boat for oneself alone and earned a lot more. But who had all that capital to invest? And what about the risks? And the right connections? The Neapolitans controlled the port and had contacts outside, with the tobacco manufacturers and the captains and crews of smuggling ships. Some of us Sicilians had good contacts too, but never enough money. There had been attempts, however, to do things on a larger scale.

In those days various partnerships between men of honor were being established, even within the same family. There was competition too. Nitto Santapaola, my brother, and Francesco Mangion, for example, were partners in a smuggling enterprise.

I myself tried my hand at it in 1975. I organized a gang of my own, which worked like a dream and brought in a lot because the whole setup was well thought out. I hired men of honor who were very young but smart and eager, who worked hard and didn't ask for that much. The expenses were very few. Not much had to be invested, since Giovanni Bontade would give me the merchandise on trust. The price was 100,000 lire per carton; I would resell at 160,000 to 170,000.

My men acquitted themselves well with the shops in the Catania market. We would earn 60,000 to 70,000 lire per carton. That meant 120 to 140 million lire for every 2,000 cartons. We had 20 million lire in expenses and 100 to 120 million lire of net profit to divide among 10 people. In 1975, 10 million each wasn't exactly a sum to sneeze at!

The first job went off like clockwork. The payment was punctual, and our supplier's trust in us grew. Without capital and at minimal cost I managed to get the cigarettes to Catania and earn us more than a nice pile of money. We invested all the profits in a second shipment, but something unforeseen ruined everything. To explain this stumbling block I have to tell you about a problem. Nothing in particular—the usual problem that crops up in the Cosa Nostra.

Nitto was jealous of the money we were making. He criticized me incessantly. He complained to Pippo because his men weren't able to make as much as us. To keep his complaints at a minimum I even took his elder brother on as a partner. The result was that the two Santapaola brothers began to quarrel bitterly. My salesman and Nitto's would run into one another at the marketplaces and compare profits.

"How much did you all make per carton?"

"Seventy thousand lire."

"So how come we only got forty thousand?"

It was obvious that something wasn't working out somewhere. I knew that very well because their whole system was wrong. Francesco Mangion, the gang boss, would waste huge amounts of money on expenses. He would go off to Greece for two or three months, the big spender, to contact captains and find "crates" to smuggle the goods in. He would throw money around and put everything on the gang's account. Or he'd go straight to Rotterdam or Brussels, to the representatives of the cigarette manufacturers, and buy at 90,000 lire per carton. He and a few others would have gone ahead of time to set up the deal. They'd stay in the best hotels for months at a time. They'd live the good life, going to the best restaurants, buying the most expensive clothes, and making the enterprise pay for everything. Their expenses were enormous. And thus a carton would come to cost them 120,000 lire rather than 85,000 to 90,000.

Instead I would go to Palermo and ask, "Giovanni, when is the ship due?" "It's coming on such-and-such a day. Send the fishing boat to such-and-such a place." We had bought a fishing boat for some twelve to fifteen million lire. That was our entire fixed capital. My expenses consisted of the trip to Palermo, talking with Giovanni Bontade, and the trip back. Then we would hire men for the fishing boat: a captain nicknamed *"Nick u capitanu,"* a mate, and a few others because they would have to pretend to fish at the prearranged spot until the ship arrived. There would be a few other expenses for storing the cartons, but not a single unnecessary outlay.

On the second voyage our fishing boat caught fire. It was coming back to Catania with our shipment in its hold when, according to what the captain said, a gas canister fell from its holder while they were cooking and set the boat alight. NATO navy forces on exercise came to help and towed the boat to Syracuse, where the captain and his mate were arrested for smuggling. I've always suspected that the fire was set by the captain. Perhaps he had been paid to burn the boat.

We weren't set back too badly because we had financed this second trip with proceeds from the first, but from then on I gave up smuggling.

I made a number of other trips to Naples to take care of some logistical aspects of smuggling common to all the families in Sicily. During one of my stays in Naples, Giovanni Bontade, who was called "the Lawyer" and who was the brother and rival of Stefano, confided to me that he had just committed a double murder. He had had a falling out with two smugglers who came from or operated in the North. During a business argument one of them had been foolish enough to lay hands on Giovanni and yank on his necktie.

Bontade had waited until the pair's next appearance in Naples to take his revenge. He had a man of honor from Palermo bring them to Peppe Sciorio's house in Giugliano under some pretext. There he strangled them with the help of the man from Palermo and the owner of the house. He almost certainly had the help of other people too, because strangling isn't an easy thing to do. It's hard and requires a lot of strength.

I remember Bontade criticizing Sciorio—a man held in great esteem by Stefano Bontade—for losing control of himself after the deed was over. Bontade himself brought the bodies to the Marano property of the Nuvoletta family, which was happy to get rid of them.

The cigarette-smuggling agreement between the Sicilians and Neapolitans didn't last long. Too many conflicts had arisen. It had become impossible to make sure everyone stuck to the agreed-upon prices. The Neapolitans, as usual, played their tricks. Each time it was their turn they tried to unload many more cartons than was their due. This was 1979, and drugs were also attracting the attention of the more powerful men of honor.

13

My brother's role as architect of peace inside the Cosa Nostra began in 1973–1974. The Trial of the Hundred Fourteen was over. Riina's regency was superseded by the usual Cosa Nostra structure, even if the overwhelming strength of Gaetano Badalamenti, who had installed himself as Palermo's provincial representative, was worrying many. Liggio, as I said before, reacted promptly and declared himself unbound by the decisions of the regional commission, which replaced him with Totò Riina and Bernardo Provenanzo as *consiglieri*; they were to alternate every two years.

Pippo was the only person to have intuited how much fire was smoldering under the powerful Badalamenti, and how tenuous was the structure of the Cosa Nostra reconstituted after Cavataio and the Trial of the Hundred Fourteen. He had realized it even before Di Cristina did, and he would talk to me about it all the time. Very slowly, a plan formed in his mind.

It was something very daring and new—a system to put an end to the betrayals, misunderstandings, jealousies, and controversies that were poisoning the relationships among men of honor and causing so much trouble and so many deaths. It was a way to bring about permanent peace, to avoid shedding blood every time someone thought someone else had made a mistake.

Very late one winter night, Pippo telephoned me at home and asked me to come see him immediately. He needed, once again, to talk about his ideas for the Cosa Nostra. He made me sit down in an armchair and kept me there for hours while he spoke. He started with the facts.

"Look, Nino. In the Cosa Nostra the principle is that men of honor have to tell the truth to each other. You know that very well. We have to know who has committed a murder or a theft, who has ordered a kidnapping, who is protecting whom. If we don't, everything collapses. Then men like Cavataio appear, men who sow discord and make us kill one another. But the truth isn't always black and white. There are many complicated situations that cause endless discussion. And there are other times in which the truth is plain. And then there are pieces of the truth that can confuse the real things and make them appear in another light.

"Situations inside one family are easier to resolve because there's the representative, the *consiglieri,* and everyone knows one another. People live in the same area and work together. We watch one another without being aware of it. It's harder to have secrets or confuse things.

"But there are much larger questions that crop up outside individual families and no one knows how to handle them. There are the strongmen who stretch the rules and operate in other families' territories. They kidnap or murder someone on their own authority, without saying anything, so that no one can ever prove they did a given thing. And if proof is found, to whom can one complain? No one. Sure, if a family is harmed it can react on its own, with its own men. But that means the second family will respond, and everyone else has to stand aside and wait to see who wins, or to look for a way to bring about peace after the shit has come down.

"So why don't we establish a commission for the whole of Sicily, a place where any question can be discussed as soon as it arises, or even before it arises? Where every important matter is resolved, like murders and whom to support in elections, where those who make mistakes are punished, where the whole Cosa Nostra can be spoken for instead of the usual Greco, Liggio, and others from Palermo? It's been tried before, this regional commission, in the fifties. The regional representative was Andrea Fazio from Trapani.

We have to put it back on its feet, Nino. And it has to be stronger than before.

"And why don't we write down laws, statutes for the Cosa Nostra that everyone has to respect without playing games and without calling out all one's forces every time the law isn't convenient anymore? We don't put things in writing, I know. But we don't need to write down names or make a map like that madman Cavataio. We need only write: these are the rules and everyone is bound to them."

I was looking at him with admiration. Once more it was confirmed to me why my brother Pippo was so often consulted, listened to, and respected by individuals much more powerful than him, bosses of families with hundreds of men who did not, however, have his intelligence, his ability to look far ahead. His plan was impressive and convincing. And it was the only one that could save us from the disasters and conflicts looming over us.

In the following months Pippo dedicated a lot of time to the realization of his plan. Throughout 1974 he traveled all over Sicily. He obtained the consent of the most prominent families, above all the ones outside Palermo. The regional commission was established in 1975, as were the statutes, which were written down in my brother's hand.

The statutes were an instrument to bring order to an ever-more confusing situation. They applied to the families. They weren't a code of conduct for the individual man of honor. A Cosa Nostra mafioso already knows what the rules are; there's no need for a code. He knows that he has to do the right things, that he has to be honest, that he has to tell the truth to other men of honor, that he has to be "pure" and shouldn't look at other men's wives, and so on and so on. These rules are fine, but a utopia. They're a bauble that everyone pretends to admire while running drugs, murdering, stealing, and doing as one pleases. The mafiosi have a whole lot of rules that, in effect, they violate continually.

The statutes—and the regional commission, obviously—were to regulate the behavior of families, to prevent rifts and the breakdowns that could have been caused by another Cavataio or in another time of terrible government repression, like the sixties. One of the most important rules worked out by Pippo was the one according to which there couldn't be more than two brothers in the same family, and two brothers or blood relatives couldn't both be at the top of one family or of a provincial organization. Under this rule, for example, Pippo and I had become mutually exclusive, because he was representative of the Catania province and I was the vice-representative. According to Pippo this rule was indispensable because it would prevent power from being concentrated in blood families. The Cosa Nostra had become, he thought, something increasingly more private, clannish, of limited interests that would ultimately, sooner or later, come into conflict with one another.

"You remember how angry I was that night so many years ago, when we made you and Nitto and the others men of honor? The Cavadduzzi brought in four of their young men that day. Now they're a force, a danger that can hardly be held in check. Four Cavadduzzi in 1962 already. Then Turi and Nino Santapaola were added, and they were six. Then came Pippo, Sabastiano, and Aldo Ercolano: nine! And finally Vincenzo Santapaola: ten! One single clan that's almost as big as a mafia family! And that very nearly destroyed the family!

"Wasn't I right not to want too many brothers, too many cousins, and too many close relatives inside the family? It always ends with them wanting to be in control. The blood tie becomes more important than anything else. And it's blood that doesn't see reason, that destroys whoever stands in its way.

"If we create a law by which only one brother can be at the top, and by which no more than two brothers can be in the same family, from that moment on we'll have to replace those who are in such situations, or else we wait for the expiration of each term—in Palermo it's five years—and the men will slowly be replaced.

"If we go on like this, we'll go backward instead of forward. Don't you see how those fools, those Cavadduzzi, are trying to breed sons like some sort of medieval barbarians? Don't you see that a half-wit like Salvatore Ferrera—who we used to laugh at— has become strong and respected because he has four sons? Francesco, Natale, Pippo, and Nino are all thugs, and yet Pippo is a top man in the province. Who was Salvatore Ferrera before having all these sons? He was nothing."

After Pippo's death I tried, in vain, to track down those statutes among his papers.

■

The newspapers called it the "Cupola," but to us it was simply the "Region"*: a committee of six people, each of whom represented a Sicilian mafia province (thus the provinces of Messina, Syracuse, and Regusa were excluded). This body was to meet in a different province once a month, a practice meant both to foster secrecy and to show that every province was equal. This wasn't true, naturally. The Palermitans have always counted for more than anyone else in the Cosa Nostra, and the Greco family has always had more influence than any other. For a long time the Grecos wielded the real power inside the Cosa Nostra, regardless of who was formally at the head of the Region.

The regional commission—the body that coordinated the families of the Sicilian Cosa Nostra—was something quite distinct from the Palermo provincial commission. There has been much confusion between the two because unlike all the others, the Palermo province has never—apart from Badalamenti's brief attempt—had a provincial representative invested with enough power to stand up to individual families. There has been a provincial commission, with a secretary and elections among the province's eighteen district bosses. This secretary was a coordinator, a man like the others—not a boss who could command the district bosses or give orders to the men in the families.

Michele Greco, for example, who was for a long time the Palermo secretary, used to say whenever a decision of some importance had to be made at the regional commission: "Stop. I can't say yes or no. First I have to talk to the district bosses."

A district was a territory made up of three neighboring families. There were thus fifty-four Palermo families—more or less, given

*The mafia equivalent of the governmental region of Sicily (translator's note).

the decade—with nearly two thousand men of honor. What a difference from Catania, which didn't even have a district, since it had only two families! In Palermo the district boss had to be a family representative, while elsewhere, for example, in Agrigento and Caltanissetta, the tendency was to keep the two positions separate. That is how it was in Catania too. My brother was provincial representative, but not the family representative. The positions were kept distinct to avoid an excessive concentration of power.

Totò Riina tried to reduce the number of districts that had come to be represented by the Palermo commission. He would say that eighteen was too many, and that with a smaller number decisions would be made more quickly. Thus, for a while, some Palermo districts were incorporated into others to reduce the commission membership to between eight and ten.

The first meeting of the Region took place at the beginning of 1975, in February, and was held at Paolino Cancelliere's country house in Enna. The body was formally created and a secretary was elected. It should be noted that from the very beginning we called him secretary—not "boss" or "president" nor even "representative"—because the secretary of the regional commission counted for less than a member of the regional committee in the same way that a provincial representative or district boss counted for less than an individual family boss. When he became secretary, Michele Greco in fact called himself the representatives' "waiter," the person who would hear them all out and then set a time, day, and agenda for the meeting.

My brother was the first secretary of the regional commission. It was a well-deserved recognition of his work on behalf of peace and unity in the Cosa Nostra. But the vote was not unanimous. There was a surprise. When his turn came, Cola Buccellato, the Trapani province representative from Castelmare del Golfo, jumped up and said: "I vote for Binuzzo Provenzano from Corleone."

Stefano Bontade retorted: "Uncle Cola, you can't do that. Provenzano has nothing to do with this."

"Why?"

"You're asking me? Bino Provenzano isn't here. He's not a pro-vincial representative. Why vote for him if it's impossible?"

"I'm voting for him anyway."

It was strange. Buccellato wasn't a stupid man. He knew very well that it made no sense to vote for someone who wasn't a can-didate and who couldn't be elected. It was talked about after the meeting. Bontade was confused, but my brother said to him, "Ste-fano, don't you realize that he did it on purpose? That he came here to provoke, to give warning?"

The meeting nevertheless proceeded in an atmosphere of sol-emnity. It was decided that later meetings were to be rotated among the provinces, and an absolute ban was proclaimed, under pain of death for those responsible, against carrying out kidnappings in Sicily. Pippo strongly insisted that such actions made their per-petrators unpopular among the locals, and that the hubbub caused by kidnappings increased police pressure on the mafia and greatly harmed the families in whose territories they were carried out.

It was a simple and straightforward speech that no one could contradict, and in fact no one really raised objections. But it was a speech directed against the practices of the Corleonesi, against their privileges. Bontade and Badalamenti's anger at Totò Riina as a consequence of the Cassina kidnapping three years before still hadn't been smoothed over. Notwithstanding that all three were part of the temporary "regency" of the Palermo Cosa Nostra, Riina had organized the kidnapping without consulting them and in fact profited from the fact that they were in jail. Bontade's prestige had been damaged even before that, in 1971, because of the Vassallo kidnapping, and a certain amount of bad feeling remained from that episode.

But no one protested. The proposal was approved unanimously and everyone present declared themselves resolved to have it re-spected whatever the cost.

The consequence of this decision was the kidnapping of Luigi Corleo, the father-in-law of Nino Salvo, which happened a few months later, in July 1975. It was an extremely serious event that had a powerful effect on the Cosa Nostra. Nino Salvo was a man of honor, a *decina* boss in Salemi and in his turn the son of a man of honor. He, his brother Alberto, and his cousin Ignazio—who was a man of honor too, the Salemi vice-representative—had a contract for collecting taxes all over Sicily. The Salvos were extremely rich. Their family was as small, so to speak, as the Principality of Monaco. But they drew on the great power of money. With their funds they could buy off politicians. They bought everything. They could make or break anyone in Sicilian politics.

The Salvos were closely linked to Badalamenti and Bontade. To the Salvos, Badalamenti acted like he was the king of Italy. And now both Badalamenti and Bontade looked like shit to Nino because they had failed utterly to get his father-in-law's body back. The kidnapping had been carried out by the Corleonesi, who had asked for twenty million lire in ransom, which would be something like eighty million today. I don't think the Salvos ever paid anything. The kidnapping, however, hadn't been done for money. It was carried out to make the Salvos understand that the balance had tilted to the other side, to show them where—above and beyond all rules, understandings, discussions, and commissions—the power really was.

After the Enna meeting Pippo returned to Catania and told his friend Nitto Santapaola about his nomination as secretary in the Region. Nitto's expression changed, and instead of congratulating him he said: "You've made a mistake, Pippo. You were rash and trusted them too much. You shouldn't have accepted without talking to me first."

My brother was irritated. He wasn't expecting this from a close friend, and in any case it seemed to display a lack of respect on Nitto's part. Pippo brusquely replied that he didn't see a single reason why he should have talked to him beforehand. Nitto realized his faux pas and changed his tune, trying to retract what he had only just finished saying.

Now, when I reflect on what happened later, I have to think that Nitto Santapaola's statement did not constitute a threat or a show of arrogance. Nitto was still my brother's sincere friend, and he was afraid that Pippo would be destroyed by the Corleonesi's power games. Just a few months later, Nitto Santapaola's friendship would turn, very slowly, into its opposite.

Another threatening sign of the changing times occurred a few months after the Corleo kidnapping. In October 1975, on the twenty-fourth, the date of my son's baptism, two representatives of the Greco clan, Nicola and Giovannello Greco, showed up in Catania. They had come to inform my brother of an important development under way in Palermo. As often happens in the Cosa Nostra, such visits are also an excuse for social, convivial meetings between friends who celebrate anniversaries, go on excursions, and have fun together.

For this day Pippo organized a hunting party. It was Sunday, and after the hunt everyone came to my house for dinner. The baptism was to take place in the evening, and in the afternoon there was time to talk, even if those who had taken part in the hunt were a bit tired and sleepy. We sat down around the table. I had invited Nitto Santapaola too.

Many things were discussed, but Nicola Greco found a way to tell Pippo, and only him, that his brother Totò Greco "the Engineer"—a representative of the first rank in the Palermo Cosa Nostra—wanted to let him know that Gaetano Badalamenti had served his time as secretary of the provincial commission and that his successor would probably be Michele Greco. Badalamenti was being talked about because he had gradually begun to lose votes in the commission meetings. By now he was in the minority since many of the eighteen district bosses were regularly voting against him. His prestige had fallen so low that on one occasion Bino Provenzano allowed himself to say to him in public: "Uncle Tano, what you're saying doesn't make sense. Things aren't as you say. You must have bumped your head against something." Very serious words. Hence the idea of naming Michele Greco to his post.

Pippo immediately realized what it was all about. It was the first big official push against the Badalamenti-Bontade-Inzerillo group in Palermo, and indirectly against their allies on the rest of the island. He brushed over the deception and answered that as secretary of the Region he couldn't interfere in the internal decisions of the provincial bodies, but that he was not well disposed, in any event, to the nomination of a person as indecisive and uncharismatic as Michele Greco to such an important position.

"Yes. What you're saying is true," said Nicola Greco. "But behind Michele Greco we'll put Antonio Mineo, the boss of the Bagheria family, who's a man of great experience. He'll give Michele Greco the right advice."

Mineo was also a district boss, and he was quite influential. He was in a position to carry two or three other district bosses along with him, which would mean that the anti-Badalamenti front was large and consolidated, and that it had prepared everything carefully, preventing the objection of opposing fronts. Thus, at the end of 1975, Michele Greco was elected secretary of the Palermo provincial commission, one of the key posts in the Sicilian Cosa Nostra.

The period from the establishment of the Region to August 1977, when the *carabiniere* colonel Russo was killed, was one of apparent calm that fooled many people. On a few occasions the Corleonesi gave the impression of wanting to respect the rules set down by the Region, or at least the more important ones. After the Corleo kidnapping they were trying to recoup a bit of credibility by punishing a few infractions committed by minor characters.

One day in 1976 I was on the Favarella property with Pippo. We were sitting down and talking with Michele Greco when Rosario Riccobono and Vittorio Mangano—one of Pippo Calò's men of honor, whom I had already met in Milan—arrived. They had come to inform Greco about the carrying out of an order: they had just eliminated those responsible for the kidnapping of a woman, and they had freed the hostage as well. The victims had transgressed the extremely serious (for non-Corleonesi) ban against abductions on Sicilian territory, and they had been punished as an example. Riccobono said that they had learned where the woman was being held prisoner from the confession of one of the kidnapping's alleged perpetrators, whom they had captured and "interrogated" the night before. Then, having removed the dead men's ID cards and any papers that might identify them, they had put the bodies inside garbage bags and telephoned the police to come and pick them up.

The quiet inside the Cosa Nostra was in reality the calm before the storm, the silence that momentarily reigns before a battle. The Corleonesi were inexorably weaving their plan, creating a network of people they trusted within the various families. Traitors—power-hungry people who wanted to be the new family bosses, district bosses, provincial representatives—informed them of their adversaries' movements. The Region meetings took place regularly, at the agreed sites, only for the first few months. One of these, the one arranged for Catania province, was held in my house. Another was held in Agrigento, at the Falconaro property of Antonio Ferro. The one for Caltanissetta was held in the villa Di Cristina had just finished building at Riesi. The one for Trapani took place in an open field outside Castellamare del Golfo. The Palermo meeting took place in Ciaculli, near Michele Greco's Favarella estate.

After this first cycle, the regional commission's monthly meetings almost always took place at the Favarella property, around a large table in a house entirely surrounded by huge orchards. The power of the Grecos, allies of the Corleonesi, had been further confirmed.

Before continuing, I'll try for a bit to sum up the Cosa Nostra's situation in the middle of the seventies. We've already seen that in the past there hadn't been any continuing relationships with America, and until then no new ones had been established. There were always links of personal friendship and family, but the Cosa Nostra as such had no contact with the United States. Even relations with Tunisia had been broken off after the war and were never reestablished. There were no more families in Tunisia.

The only Cosa Nostra family existing outside Sicily was in Naples, and it was ancient. During my visit to Naples in 1974 a very old man of honor, originally from Palermo and now living in an apartment building in the Santa Lucia quarter, narrated to me the history of this family, which dated back to the thirties. The principal figures in the Naples family were the Zaza, Nuvoletta, and Mazzarella brothers. There were some more people, such as Nunzio

Barbarossa, the Sciorio brothers, and others. The entire Naples family was dependent on Michele Greco, but the Nuvoletta brothers constituted a *decina* of their own inside it, with even stronger and closer links to Michele Greco, who could command them without the mediation of the family's own leadership.

Relations between the Sicilian motherland and the Neapolitan colony have, in fact, never been idyllic. The Cosa Nostra claimed to rule Naples through its local branch, but in reality Naples was too big a mouthful for anyone. I once asked Giovanni Mongiovì what was going on in Naples. This was at the beginning of the eighties, murders were snowballing, and there was beginning to be talk of camorra. Mongiovì replied that the regional commission had met for two straight days at the Favarella property to discuss the Neapolitan question and look for a way to establish some order there. To keep the contents of the discussion from leaking out, the participants were all forbidden to leave the property before the final decision was made. Immediately afterward Nitto Santapaola and Salvatore Ferrera were sent to Naples to communicate the results of the meeting, but Ciro Mazzarella refused to recognize the validity of the decision.

In addition there existed two *decinas,* one in Torino and one in Rome. The one in Torino had been formed by Giuseppe Di Cristina, who toward the end of the sixties found himself obliged to stay in the area. The *decina* was composed of Riesi natives who had been made men of honor—who had had "their eyes opened," as we say in Cosa Nostra slang—by an old mafioso from Caltanissetta who was living there. But it was a question of illegal, unauthorized initiations, and these people didn't know whom to associate themselves with or to which Sicilian family they belonged. They were capable enough, but they had been abandoned. They were struggling by, working as laborers. Di Cristina thought he would straighten out the situation by forming the *decina* and bringing it into his family.

In Rome there was Stefano Bontade's *decina,* the one commanded by Uncle Angelino. I don't know whether or not Pippo Calò created another one later, in the seventies. Calò was a fugitive for a long time in Rome, living under a false name. He had people call him Mario, and he would often to go Palermo, where he had been made a district boss.

In Milan there was Pippo Bono. He was a representative in the family from Bolognetta, a small village outside Palermo. He moved to Milan and brought with him some men from his family, but he remained the Bolognetta representative. Bono went this way and that, never taking sides with anyone, neither with Badalamenti nor with Greco. He kept his iron in both fires. Bono was one of the first to become heavily involved in drugs. He was a friend of Joe Adonis, the American mafioso. Others had been involved in drugs before him, but he was the first to do things in a grand style. It's for this reason, probably, that he never decisively joined a given camp and always ran off in times of crisis. It's for this reason too that he didn't really welcome Liggio's arrival in Milan at the beginning of the seventies. Liggio wanted to get into drugs himself, and sold small quantities along with a mafioso from the Ramacca family who was living in Milan, but then he started to specialize in kidnapping.

In 1975, when Pippo was still secretary of the Region, I went with him to Milan, where we met the Bono brothers. Alfredo Bono was having problems with the Milanese underworld and had even been roughed up during a robbery in a gambling house. My brother advised Bono to leave the Bolognetta family and to form a true Cosa Nostra family of his own in Milan. The Bonos would have been able to defend themselves better, and the numerous men of honor running around Milan in those years could have helped him work more effectively in a very promising market. Bono didn't accept the advice, but our relations with him didn't sour because of it: when we left Milan he gave each of us a large deerskin coat made by a furrier's in which he had interests. The coats were a bit much for the climate in Catania, but Pippo and I would show them off, putting them on whenever we went around the city.

These were our relations abroad, outside of Sicily. We even had a "passport office" for whoever wanted to leave the country without problems. I'm joking, naturally. What the newspapers refer to in a certain way, with those pompous words that make people imagine who-knows-what, is, inside the Cosa Nostra, much more simple and straightforward. The passport office was nothing more than Aurelio Bonomo, the secretary of the parliamentary deputy Lupis. Bonomo could produce a passport instantly for any of us who needed one. He had ties to an employee responsible for issuing them in an Italian consulate in Germany. All Bonomo had to do was to send someone's photograph and vital statistics, and the employee would immediately produce the passport and send it back to Catania. The police wouldn't know anything because the employee would omit to tell the Catania police department about issuing the passport.

It was thanks to our passport office that Nitto Santapaola could take a nice trip to the United States with his wife around the end of 1980. I know this for a fact, because upon his return Nitto told us that he had had a lot of fun, and because his wife talked about it with the other women, singing the praises of the places she had been.

14

There are no Cosa Nostra families or men of honor in Calabria. One day in 1972 or 1973 Paul Violi, the well-known Canadian mafioso and a native of Calabria, arrived in Catania. He came to my office for half an hour, enough time for us to have a cup of coffee together and for him to ask me if I knew any men of honor in Calabria. Violi was a native of Sinopoli, a small town in the province of Reggio Calabria, and he explained to me that he was the boss of a *decina* in the New York family of Carlo Gambino but that he had been dispatched to Canada. He jokingly said that Uncle Carlo didn't want to hear anything, he just wanted dollars from his *decina* in Toronto. Violi could do as he pleased. Uncle Carlo didn't interfere; he delegated his power. But at the end of the year Violi had to bring him cash. They made money racketeering, which is why they planted bombs in dairies. Violi himself owned a dairy in Toronto.

Paul Violi didn't make a great impression on me. He was a braggart, a big, fat man who didn't seem to have much upstairs. In any case, he was going to Calabria because he thought there were men of honor there. Things are different, in fact, in America. American men of honor aren't just Sicilians, but even Calabrians and Neapolitans. It doesn't matter. At this point one could ask: if Violi was Calabrian and an important mafioso, how is it possible that he didn't have a direct channel, that he didn't personally know the *'ndranghetisti** of Calabria?

Let's return to the issue of secrecy, to the attributes of a man of honor. Even if Violi knew some *'ndranghetisti,* he would never have come to learn of any men of honor in Calabria, supposing there were any, because the *'ndranghetisti* wouldn't have known about them, and even if they had they wouldn't have been able to introduce him to them. And so, correctly, Violi came to Sicily to find a man of honor, a third person who would have been in a position to make the actual introduction. Only a man of honor could say if there were men of honor in Calabria, and consequently could introduce them.

We Sicilians, however, did not make Calabrians men of honor. It could happen that some Calabrians were affiliated on an individual basis, as in the case of the Neapolitans, for some particular occasion. But otherwise the rule held.

The Calabrians were in fact not looking to join the Cosa Nostra. They had their own organization, which was almost similar to ours, and they claimed to be more important than us. They said that their organization was superior to the Cosa Nostra. I don't know how their hierarchy was structured, but I do know that the *'ndrangheta* was widespread. It was in all their towns. In my brother's time the Calabrians would speak of Antonio Zoccali as the *'ndrangheta* boss.

When they knew they were talking to a man of honor they would start to use a special, colorful language to give themselves airs. They'd say: "Don Antonio Zoccali is the sunshine of our province." And Don Antonio Macri, the boss of the Calabrian Region, would be referred to in who knows how many exaggerated ways, and always in that florid manner of speaking.

And then the Calabrians would talk, talk, talk. They talked all the time. Not to others, of course, but among themselves. They would have endless arguments about their rules, especially in the presence of us men of honor. They felt uneasy because they knew that in reality they were inferior to the Cosa Nostra, and they

*Members of the Calabrian camorra (translator's note).

would try to confuse men of honor with all those quibbles and verbal snares.

They had endless rules. Whenever a man of honor spoke with one of them he'd become bewildered, he'd develop a headache. No one wanted to end up in the same jail cell as *'ndranghetisti*. It was the same tune from morning to night. They were tedious, wearisome, and obsessed. They would never stop talking, going on and on about the same things: "If someone acts like this, is he a *sbirro* or not?" And so forth. Or they'd start up with their nursery rhymes like kids in elementary school. The subject? The *'ndrangheta,* with its rules and customs.

They thought themselves important, the *'ndranghetisti,* but instead they would commit endless stupidities. Imagine—they'd let prison guards join them. Many guards were, in fact, part of the *'ndrangheta,* something the mafia could never tolerate. At one point it was even said that no one who wore a beret could ever be made a man of honor, not even local policemen. And judges were excluded too, because judges hand down sentences. But the *'ndranghetisti* would admit them. They admitted a huge amount of people and so they were legion, but they weren't organized as well as the Cosa Nostra. We would choose carefully, and our people were more reliable.

I know only one case in which a man in uniform was fully admitted into the Cosa Nostra: the military doctor Colonel Vito Cascio Ferro, a man of honor from Agrigento whom I met at the house of one of Stefano Bontade's cousins. He was the namesake of one of the century's most famous mafiosi.

It could be that there existed a more restricted circle, abler and more select *'ndranghetisti* capable of more secrecy, and it could even be that prison guards were admitted because they could relay messages out of prison more easily. We, however, avoided extending our recruitment to include such people.

And then there's the fact that the Calabrians—and the Neapolitans too—permitted prostitution. In these days a good number of them would strut around inside brothels, while the Sicilians never would. We've always excluded prostitution from the Cosa Nostra's business interests, and we've always despised those who make money off it. In the thirties, when the prefect Mori was even sending pimps to the Island, the men of honor who found themselves there would organize expeditions to go rough up these *ricottari*,* as they were called then.

For this reason we've always considered the Calabrians inferior, garbage. Not to mention the Neapolitans, who we've never trusted much.

*"Weaklings," from the name of the soft cheese (translator's note).

15

To understand the situation in the Catania family, we must start with the fact that we had thirty-five men of honor in a city of five hundred thousand. There wasn't the density in Catania that there was in Palermo. Our activities had always been freer because there was never a need to impose particular restrictions. The principle was that "everyone is his own master." Whoever wanted to commit a robbery, for instance, would do it, and that was that (after having asked for the authorization of one's *decina* boss or representative, and in some cases without asking at all: it was assumed that everyone knew whom to steal from). The only thing the bosses cared about was that the individual or business in question wasn't under the protection of some man of honor.

In Palermo it was different. Not only did authorization always have to be asked, but a percentage had to be paid to one's family if the action occurred on its territory, or to another family if it occurred on its territory.

Otherwise, in both Catania and Palermo responsibility fell on whoever carried something out. If someone was arrested for a robbery, that was his business. The same principle applied if one was killed during the action. As a rule the family would help someone get out of jail, or, in case of death, help his wife and children out a bit—but it wasn't obliged to do so. In smuggling enterprises, though, there was an obligation to help an associate who ran into a problem with the law or with competitors.

143

Some soldiers, on the other hand, were interested in securing the support of the *decina* bosses and representatives in their illegal enterprises, and in exchange they would offer them a share. They'd go to their boss and say, "Listen, I'm going to do this and that. Do you want a share? Let's become partners and split the profits." If problems arose, if someone ended up in a jam, the bosses would thus have an incentive to resolve the matter.

It was different in cases where the family ordered a robbery or a murder. If the perpetrator was arrested, the representative had to do everything possible to help him. He was obligated to pay for lawyers, to approach judges, to pay prison fees, to give an allowance to the arrested man's family, etc.

Any talk about the mafia as it once was—making sure that there were no burglaries or robberies, maintaining order, having a good relationship with the local population—is an old story. If a kid was committing robberies in a neighborhood and causing too much trouble, and he continued to do so after having been warned, then the mafia boss could say: "Let's eliminate this fool, since he won't see reason." But if at some point a promising kid appeared, with his wits about him, who could shoot well, who respected the men of honor, in that case he would be approached and told, "Look, if you really must steal, we'll tell you where and from whom you can do it." If the guy responded, if he realized it was better to get along with us than to act on his own, he would be brought into the family.

It's true that the old-time mafia didn't want abuses committed against the poor. But that was because there was no point to it. Why would you want to steal from someone who has nothing? It was stupid to steal from the poor. There was little to gain and you became unpopular. If someone was behaving badly because he was a friend of the carabinieri or was opposed to the mafia, a way to hurt him would be found. But one wouldn't hit decent people, that is, people who respected and protected men of honor; one wouldn't indiscriminately rob or steal from those who didn't deserve it. One didn't go after the little people. For as long as I was in Catania, I'm sure no mafioso would have taken 500,000 lire from a little shop. We focused on the big businesses, which we'd try to exploit.

They, on the other hand, would benefit from going along with us, and everything would work smoothly.

Then the big change happened. Vicious kids appeared—anonymous individuals who organized themselves into groups and telephoned storekeepers asking for a cut. This is why it's important to differentiate between the mafia and common criminals. In Catania the mafia never undertook extortion, at least not as long as I was there. Nor would the soldiers in our family do it. We would live off smuggling, fencing, robbery, some burglary, and legal activities, but not small-time extortion—it wasn't considered honorable. It had come to be equated with usury. I don't know if the mafia in Catania has gone into loan-sharking today, but in my time it wouldn't do it. It was a question of principle, like prostitution. Others organized prostitution—people in the underworld, the common criminals.

In Palermo, insofar as extortion goes, a different system was in effect. Everyone paid a cut, even small shopkeepers. The mafioso population was large and had to survive. Every district, every neighborhood, every street in Palermo was governed by a particular family. Every family had various *decina* bosses, and every *decina* boss had a certain number of men of honor. So the cafés and shops on a certain street would fall under the jurisdiction of a given man of honor, who would collect a cut. They were worse than tax collectors. In return they would furnish protection against bands of common criminals, but it was security against dangers more imaginary than real. Underworld gangs existed, as would be expected, even in Palermo, but they rarely tried extorting because they would be killed before getting started, or soon afterward.

Soldiers in my family didn't receive a salary, nor did those in the Palermo families. Everyone had to make a living on his own. Certainly there was solidarity within the family. If someone had money, he was in a sense bound to lend it to another family member who needed it to get something going. There was no risk of it not being returned. It was considered disgraceful not to repay a loan or to abuse the trust of other men of honor. I can't remember a single incident, apart from the case of soldiers killed in the course of action, of a debt not being repaid.

The soldiers in a family all knew one another. Woe if they didn't! Thus there were all the differences there are in normal life: some would be friends with each other and their families, exchanging visits, inviting each other over for dinner; others would greet each other and no more; others didn't get along and would avoid each other to keep from fighting and thus threatening the unity of the whole. But all the soldiers shared a certain sense of distinction, of superiority with respect to ordinary people, and they would end up slowly distancing themselves from old acquaintances, from childhood friendships, to start frequenting people like themselves, people with whom they could talk, discuss mutual problems, speak the same language. Sooner or later the world of the Cosa Nostra became all-important to the mafioso. Normal friendships lost importance and became empty, because after a while the soldier would start acting coolly toward any friend who wasn't a mafioso, growing bored with his company until the fact became pretty much obvious.

The family in Catania operated in a way very different from what came to be described in the newspapers. Those rigid and precise roles—such as the killer, the weapons supplier, the accountant—never existed at all. For a certain length of time we had a treasurer, but then we fired him because he wasn't honest; he took money from the cash box. When I joined the Cosa Nostra the treasurer of the Catania family was the uncle of a very well-known tailor. Illicit activities weren't producing a steady return at the time, and the communal cash box was being replenished by personal contributions. Every man of honor put in so much per month, but the funds were never enough. There was a *decina* boss, Giovannino *"u scemu,"** who was regularly arrested for pickpocketing, and the costs of his peculiar problem were enough to drain our reserves. The moment he was arrested, Giovannino would declare himself broke and ask for money for himself, his children, and the lawyers. He had two families—his regular one and another with his mistress and her children. It was fortunate that he didn't claim

---

*"The Fool" in dialect (translator's note).

money for his associate as well, a police corporal in charge of the cells in the central police station.

The same goes for weapons. There has never been a "mafia armory." The family would take a small percentage from the sale of one lot of smuggled cigarettes, buy a few weapons, and hide them with someone who had property in the countryside. Every now and then the *decina* boss would go to the property owner, ask him for a pistol, and that night a murder would take place. Weapons have never presented a problem; they're easy to get. Apart from the fact that every man of honor had his personal weapons, if the need arose for a pistol, all one had to do was bribe a night watchman. He would be told to sell his pistol for a million or a million and a half lire, and then to report the theft or loss after we had filed off the serial number. Armories were robbed for rifles, while explosives were obtained from small-scale contractors who were friendly with the family. Kalashnikov machine guns came later, after my brother's death. Alfio Ferlito introduced them along with hashish.

For me and Pippo the problem of getting weapons was less difficult than for anyone else: the brother of our foreman, the chief laborer at our construction firm, was exceptionally good at making weapons, or modifying them, or creating them out of the most unexpected objects.

There have never been paid young killers, kids who murder people for 200,000 lire. The mafia has never done anything of the kind, and I don't think it would do so today, because it doesn't need to. No mafia boss would approach a young kid he didn't know, who might "sing" if caught by the police. If a murder has to be committed, a normal mafia boss with a head on his shoulders uses one of his men of honor, someone who can be trusted. I've never seen or heard of a representative saying to some kid, "Go kill so-and-so and I'll give you a million." It can happen that, after having pulled off a robbery of ten million lire, a kid of fifteen or twenty will ask another youngster to go knock someone off for two million. But foolishness is foolishness and has nothing to do with the mafia.

The mafia isn't stupid. It knows how to add things up for itself and has proved it. Mafiosi aren't irresponsible people. Perhaps they have been on some occasions, when they've committed massacres, done brutal things, dirty things. But they've never done childish things. If the mafia acted that way, we'd have to conclude that it doesn't think. And if the mafia doesn't think, why is it that the state hasn't managed to defeat these brainless people?

The mafia families can allow themselves the luxury of choosing. They have no problems in terms of people wanting to come in. The basis of everything is the neighborhood in which the men of honor live. In the Palermo mafia the neighborhood is even more important than in Catania. No sooner do we Catanians make a bit of money than we move from the outskirts into the city center. No one wants to live in a place like San Cristoforo. We Calderones, the Santapaolas, Turi Palermo, and so many others were born in the city's worst areas, and we all moved into the center. The Palermo mafiosi don't go to live in the center of Palermo; they don't move from their own neighborhoods. They're born, they live, and they die in the same place. The neighborhood is their life, their families have lived there for generations, and everyone is related. There are four or five principal names. At most, one builds oneself a nicer, more magnificent house. Stefano Bontade knocked down his father's house in Santa Maria del Gesù and built a palazzo over it; his brother Giovanni and Salvatore Inzerillo did the same thing in Bellolampo. They never moved a foot away from their kingdoms, where they were absolute rulers for decades.

When the young men in a neighborhood see the respect, the deference, the solicitude with which a man of honor is treated, they fall in love with the mafia. They see Uncle X coming into a café and everyone running up to greet him, to pay him homage, and competing to serve him, or else they run into the place just to look at him, to admire him—like, one might say, young rock fans to Madonna. So they begin to think of the mafia as something great, something that allows one to outdo others, to rise up above the mass. These young men will do anything to join the family. And when they realize that even the newspapers are talking about this man, the one they've seen in the street, in a café, in a shop, their esteem for him soars up to the stars.

Some of them commit a robbery merely to stand out in the eyes of their zone's mafia boss, who keeps an eye on promising youths, beginning with the ones in his own family but extending beyond it too. Around every man of honor of a certain rank is always a circle of twenty or thirty kids—nobodies who want to become something. These youths are at his disposal, are always there to do small favors for him, to ask him if he needs anything. The influence of a mafia family is very great. It can have fifty active men of honor around whom gravitate, first of all, their own blood families (sons, nephews, brothers, etc.), and then this ring of youths ready for anything, who aren't asking for anything other than to be put to the test in order to be admitted into the Cosa Nostra.

For his part the man of honor doesn't stand there twiddling his thumbs, simply taking without giving anything. We shouldn't forget that the mafioso is also a sort of authority, a person to whom everyone turns for favors, to settle problems. The mafioso seeks power, assumes it, and is proud of it. But a large part of his power is given to him by others.

When we Calderones were at our zenith, every day there was a procession into my office. It was a constant coming and going of people asking for the most varied things. At a certain point these people became so numerous that to receive them we had to rent an apartment next door to my office. My brother would sit inside, with the doors firmly shut so that nothing could be seen from the outside, listening to requests. There were people looking for work, people who had taken a competitive exam and wanted to win it, people who were offering the Costanzos a contract, people who were dying of hunger and couldn't buy bread for their families. In the latter case my brother would ask me for fifty thousand lire to give to those poor people, and I would jokingly reply that we should hang a sign outside that said WELFARE OFFICE. They would come from all over Catania, even all over the province, and Pippo wouldn't say no to anyone; he would take charge of everybody's problems.

And we ended up not thinking as much as we should have about our own affairs, our own problems. It would have been so easy to grow rich at that point! It would have been enough to ask for a loan of 100 million lire from Carmelo Costanzo, buy some land, and sell it the next year for 150 million. But we never did it because we never had enough time to concentrate on getting rich. People didn't leave us enough time to think about ourselves, to tend to our own interests.

I would get up every morning around seven, have my coffee, and say good-bye to my wife before she left for work at the university. Then I'd wait for my brother, and together we'd go to our offices on the ground floor of my house. We always were inseparable. In front of the office door there would already be people waiting for us: some wanting work from the Costanzos, others looking for help in dealing with city hall or with the hospital. Still others would have a problem with the wharfside criminals in their neighborhood and come to ask for Pippo's intercession. He would make a mental note—we never wrote anything down for fear of a possible police search—and try to settle things himself, or by telephoning people of his acquaintance who would know, who would be able to intervene.

Others would come to tell us about a certain brawl that happened the night before, or about a gunfight in which they were somehow involved. Others would have problems with a debtor who wasn't paying, with a policeman who was harassing them, with a group of hostile people who were threatening them. Pippo would set up an appointment for a few days later to hear out the other side, and finally would bring everyone together to work out a solution. These were common people, with common, everyday problems, who saw in Pippo an authority, someone in a position to help. They weren't men of honor, of course. Men of honor didn't fight over little things, and when they had a problem they would resolve it inside the Cosa Nostra, according to Cosa Nostra rules. On a few occasions, however, even they would ask for favors and recommendations. Rosario Riccobono, for example, recommended to my brother a Palermo man of honor who wanted to claim the catering service at the Catania airport. Pippo was meant to "dissuade" competitors from bidding for it. This fact created a certain amount of discord between him and Nitto Santapaola's brother Nino, who worked in that area and would have liked to have claimed the commission for himself.

My brother even reached the point of making recommendations at the university, for exams. A young man nicknamed "Puntina,"* from the Di Mauro family, a Catania underworld group, was enrolled at the University of Palermo Law School because it was said to be easier than the University of Catania. His father held Pippo in great esteem and more than once asked him to intercede for his son in the case of the more difficult exams. Pippo would pass the request on to the Palermo men of honor, who would want to know the name of the professor and where he lived. The representative who "governed" that territory would then go to the professor and ask him to look at this Catanian student with a benevolent eye. When the young Puntina graduated, his father said that, given the number of recommendations Pippo had made, the degree should really have been given to him.

A professor at the University of Palermo School of Engineering was very closely tied to the Costanzos. Two of the Costanzo kids, in fact, graduated under the supervision of this instructor, who also knew a great number of engineers engaged in building projects and who was, in practice, the Costanzos' *longa manus* in Palermo as far as the university went. He was also the arbitrator of disputes between them and the contract commissions, and the Costanzos would often call him in as a consultant or planner for their projects. A few times the professor called Catania and asked for something, a car or whatever. The Costanzos would blanch at these requests, but then would immediately run off to fulfill them.

Pippo was very fond of his role and was passionately interested in other people's problems, even the most bizarre. He liked to reestablish harmony. Every day he would sit down in that office, listening, and he never lost his patience or grew bored. One of the Costanzo brothers once asked him to step in on behalf of his son, who had fallen in love with a girl about whom there was a fair bit

*"Thumbtack" (translator's note).

of talk. They had gathered some information on her, and it turned out that she was a frivolous type who liked to have fun, and thus probably wasn't a virgin. Pippo was asked to distract the young Costanzo by introducing him to new people so that he would get the girl off his mind. Pippo intervened, but without success; the boy was obstinate and the story ended with their marriage.

The hardest disputes to resolve were the ones that arose in the city's common criminal underworld. One time the Laudanis, another underworld group, had a fight with a young man they believed belonged to a rival clan, the Carcagnusis, who in turn were waiting for nothing more than a chance to open hostilities. Even though the young man had nothing to do with the Carcagnusis, after a few hours they were on their way to open fire on the Laudanis. Pippo found out the real roots of the matter and drew upon all his authority to make the parties realize that it was a misunderstanding, and that it was neither right nor plausible to start a war without a real reason. He arranged a peace summit and saved the life of the unfortunate young man—who, besides, had five or six brothers and a group of friends ready for vendetta and war.

Today there are all these killings because there no longer are people like Pippo to jump into conflicts, slow the antagonists down, and take action before there are any deaths. The reputation we mafiosi had was of being above all parties, above all these peripheral underworld groups, who would trust us and accept our intervention in their controversies. When Nino Santapaola started indiscriminately killing people in these groups, we lost our prestige and descended to their level.

Pippo never took a lira for his activities. From this point of view he was like a mafioso of fifty years ago. When someone came to ask a favor, he couldn't mention money in his presence. Pippo would have thrown him out. If someone came to ask for our protection and at a certain point proposed that we become partners, we would do so, but we would never even dream of claiming compensation for the favors we'd done.

At Christmas, true, all sorts of presents would show up at our house, but no more than what Pippo himself gave away. A week or two before the holidays Pippo would shut himself up in the apartment next door to our office and bottle and label the wine he had produced on his property at Monterosso Etneo. He was very proud of his wine. He would age it in oak casks for seven or eight years, then bottle it and give it away as presents, along with the best mandarins and artichokes in oil. When his gifts were ready he would have a pair of boys run around the city delivering them to this lawyer, that doctor, this official, that professor. There would be scores of these gifts, which cost millions, and at the same time Pippo would receive as many gifts for all the favors he had done.

And then there was life inside the Cosa Nostra. The inexhaustible, interminable talks about the Cosa Nostra; the discussions never ended. My brother was a real man of honor. He could have become richer than Gino Costanzo if he'd wanted to. But he liked the Cosa Nostra more than anything. So much time was spent talking about events in the "families," getting information, judging, thinking, establishing who was wrong and who was right!

■

The recruitment of young men is essential to a family's power. Every boss wants a big family with many young and active soldiers. Even old soldiers are important because they have relationships with the older figures in the area, they know many influential people inside and outside the mafia, and they're experienced in the affairs of the Cosa Nostra. But the principal staff at the soldier level is made up of the young. It's they who produce, who represent the muscle upon which a given family's power is based. For this reason, careful attention has to be paid to not overloading, to not letting too many into the family at a time, to not making a mistake by bringing in unfaithful, untrustworthy people out of a love of power and greatness.

Young men of honor are valuable because they're stronger and more alert than old ones; but they're restless, they tend not to respect discipline and hierarchy, and they must be governed with a firm hand. Obeying orders is everything in a family. The *decina* boss is vitally important for this reason, because the soldiers and the most dangerous actions depend on him. The *decina* boss must know men. He must understand how to use the men at his disposal:

if so-and-so isn't capable of committing a murder, then he'll steal a car, a gun, or he'll be sent to shoot someone in the legs or to sell stolen goods or contraband. One tries to use every man's qualities to the best advantage. Being a *decina* boss is a delicate job. He must know how to command, but he must also be close to his soldiers because they answer only to him, they talk directly only to him. When a murder is committed, for example, there's no obligation to tell every member of the family that it was this soldier or that who pulled the trigger. Not every killing is advertised inside the family. One intuits that a given murder has been carried out by someone in the family, but only the *decina* boss knows the killer's identity and passes it along to the representative. When a soldier is ordered to kill someone, the *decina* boss's involvement is total. He always stakes out the area, and he's very nervous and emotional, as though he himself is committing the murder. And he doesn't stop worrying until he sees the soldier return, because he is aware that he has exposed him to mortal danger. And if the soldier is arrested or wounded during an action, the *decina* boss feels the responsibility; he's tortured by the thought that he might have made a mistake in choosing the man, the time, the circumstances.

The bond between soldier and *decina* boss comes before everything. It comes before important obligations like telling the truth to other members of the Cosa Nostra. If a man of honor asks me about something my *decina* boss has told me to keep quiet about, I must answer that I know nothing. If the *decina* boss says to me, "Go do this murder and don't talk about it to anyone for any reason," I have to obey. I can't talk about the murder, even to the family's representative. I follow orders. I go kill and then I return. Whether the *decina* boss has ordered me to do it after talking with the representative or not is his business, not mine. And if the family boss calls me to a meeting and asks me in front of the *decina* boss whether I committed the murder, I answer, "I take his orders. Ask him about it."

The *decina* boss's great power arises from the fact that the orders he gives represent the will of the family. And the family is above and beyond anything else. On the night of my initiation into the Cosa Nostra it was stated to me very clearly that when the family requires it, one must go, no questions asked. One must drop whatever one is doing and run to answer the summons. Once they've decided something, I'm no longer my own master. They can order me to kill an acquaintance, a relative, someone dear to me, and I have no choice: I have to do it. If they've decided to kill my brother, they will almost certainly ask someone else to do it, but I have to accept the decision. One bows down or it's death. There is no middle path. I was told this again and again the night I joined the Cosa Nostra.

It can happen that the family—through the *decina* boss—communicates to a soldier that he must kill a friend of his. If the soldier cannot bring himself to carry out the murder, the family will appoint someone else, will assign him a partner whose task is to do the shooting, strangling, stabbing, etc. But first he must collaborate, help the killer get near the victim without the victim suspecting, precisely because they're friends, because the trust inherent in ties of friendship is being exploited.

Relations and friendship are worth nothing compared to fidelity to the Cosa Nostra. If the interests of the family are at stake, all those sentiments vanish; they drop to a second level. They're used, in fact, to strike more effectively, to achieve the goal more easily. No one feels particularly troubled by it, and under such circumstances no one speaks of "betrayal."

In this respect, the killing of an old Palermo district boss, who was called Matranga, I think, an event that took place a little while after the elimination of Michele Cavataio, is a story that has stuck in my memory. One day Stefano Bontade and some other Palermitans arrived at Catania to confer with my brother, me, Salvatore Ferrera, and Calogero Conti. The purpose of the visit was the problem of hitting Matranga, who lived in Milan, where he kept himself extremely secluded for fear of being killed. Matranga very much trusted his brother-in-law, who had a stand at the fruit market in Milan. The latter was in turn good friends with Salvatore Ferrera, who was to approach him and convince him to put Matranga at ease about his safety. So Ferrera and Conti flew to Milan, contacted Matranga's brother-in-law, and through him reassured the old mafioso: they all wished him well in Palermo, the hatchet had been buried, and a future of peace and harmony among the families was beginning. The victim believed these friendly words, which were expressed to him by his trusted brother-in-law; he gradually lowered his guard, and he started going out of his house. And then it was very easy to kill him.

Episodes like this aren't rare, but they aren't very frequent either, because the rules of the Cosa Nostra aren't always carried to the extreme. Sure, in times of war one is more severe and thorough, but in normal times one can even opt to let things lie. My family, for instance, left Nick Gentile alive, the American *decina* boss from Lucky Luciano's time who was hiding out in a village in the province of Agrigento after he fled the United States for having collaborated with the police. Gentile had even written a book about his life and granted an interview to *Espresso*. Everyone criticized him. He had tried to approach Pippo and my uncle, who didn't pay any attention to him. On a few occasions we had been asked by Palermo to get rid of him as a courtesy to our American cousins, and my brother had even given the order to kill him, but no one did. He was allowed to waste away, the poor man. At the end of his life he was reduced so low as to survive thanks only to the charity of his neighbors, who would occasionally give him a plate of pasta.

In other cases, family members appointed to pull off a murder and who have no intention of doing so take refuge in stratagems, faking unforeseen complications, even warning the victim. There are also cases in which the order to kill is countermanded against Cosa Nostra rules, or is contested and put before another authority in the same family, district, or province. Long discussions are then opened, which never bodes well for the future of the family itself. The faction that caves in always accepts the final decision with great reluctance, or pretends to accept it and then waits for an opportune moment to get its own back.

■

Soldiers are used for all sorts of dangerous actions, but some murders are carried out by the family representative in person. If a particularly strong and smart man has to be killed, or a man of a certain importance, then it's likely that the boss himself will come into the picture. I remember the case of the murder of Stefano Giaconia, a brave man of honor from the family of Palermo center—the family of the La Barbera brothers, which was dissolved by the Palermo commission. I've already talked about him: Giaconia had shown up, wrapped in explosives, with Angelo La Barbera at the meeting of the provincial commission during the time of the first mafia war.

Stefano Giaconia would certainly have become boss of the family of Palermo center the moment it was reconstituted had he not committed the grave sin, in Stefano Bontade's eyes, of becoming partners with Totò Riina. One day in the second half of the seventies, Pippo and I went with some other people to an appointment at a motel at the very beginning of the Catania-Palermo highway. Michele Greco and another man of honor from Palermo arrived to talk to us about the problem of a share the Costanzo firm had to pay because a section of the ring road it was building around Palermo passed through the Ciaculli territory. Bontade arrived an hour later in his Porsche Carrera. He was very annoyed and apologized to everyone present: "Excuse my lateness, but I had to fix a flat tire and strangle Stefano Giaconia."

Michele Greco approved: "Don't worry about it, Stefano. We were waiting for you. In any case, you did very well getting Giaconia out of our hair."

"That idiot kept bothering me right to the end. After I killed him I burned his clothes, and while they were on fire there was an explosion. It was a little twenty-two-caliber pistol Giaconia had been carrying."

"What a man of honor! Shoots even after he's dead!" was the sarcastic remark of someone there.

I think I've already mentioned that in a number of mafia families today the habit is spreading of direct contact, without the mediation of a *decina* boss, between the representative and a few individual men of honor he can rely on absolutely, and whom he can use for secret actions that no one else in the family knows about. This habit is based on the fact that there exist a few very peculiar, unstable, senseless individuals who lack a point of reference to the world—men without a flag, so to speak, lacking a father, to whom it makes no difference if they lose their own life or take those of others, who run around asking to be killed. For the shrewd mafia boss, the trick is to bind them to himself personally and use them for the most dangerous tasks, and above all for murders. In the right hands, these men can be a formidable weapon. They end up venerating the boss, thinking of nothing but him and his orders, as though he were their lost father.

The story of Damiano Caruso and Giuseppe Di Cristina illustrates this. Caruso was a madman, a maniac capable of nothing but causing trouble wherever he found himself. But he had boundless courage and was as ferocious as an animal. He had no idea of what he was doing. Damiano Caruso's world began and ended with one person: Giuseppe Di Cristina, who protected him, encouraged him, and called him "my pupil." To keep him from being killed (Caruso had already fallen into a good deal of trouble) and to tie him to himself unequivocally, Di Cristina made him, at a certain point, a man of honor in the Riesi family. It was an act of force, a completely illegal initiation, because it was done on the sly and without asking the permission of the family from Villabate, Caruso's birthplace.

But the rules of the mafia are a little like the laws of the state: they apply to nearly everyone. There were a lot of protests, but then things calmed down and Di Cristina even brought Caruso to Palermo, where he put him to work as his personal slave. He had him do a whole number of things—which Caruso did, but in his own way. Di Cristina commissioned him to kill the parliamentary deputy Nicosia, that fascist from the Social Movement. Caruso's orders had been handed to him as a consequence of the "destruction" strategy Badalamenti had imposed at the beginning of the seventies, and Caruso tried his best to fulfill them. He was such an animal that he showed up at the execution spot with an ax. Not with a knife; he wanted to kill Nicosia with an ax. But he was clumsy, a maladroit; when he swung at him with the ax he missed and hit his own leg instead. Because his own leg was split open, he didn't manage to finish Nicosia off. Although Caruso managed to hit him a few times with the ax, Nicosia survived.

Caruso was also commissioned with the murder of Ciuni, a hotel keeper who had had a falling out with Di Cristina. Caruso went looking for him one night at his hotel and stabbed him. But he didn't manage to kill him. He wounded him seriously, and Ciuni was taken to the city hospital. Totò Di Cristina had just read *The Godfather,* and the idea struck Giuseppe of doing what they did in the book. He sent Caruso to the hospital, but this time with reinforcements, who disguised themselves as doctors, with white coats and everything, and killed Ciuni in his bed. The event caused an uproar because a murder inside a hospital had never been heard of before.

I've already described Caruso's behavior, his great stupidity, during the *viale* Lazio action. I can add only that this hothead behaved himself badly in America too, where he had been sent after the massacre to rest and recover from his wounds. It was Pippo Bono who helped him get out of the country, and it was he who went with him to Carlo Gambino, the boss of bosses in America, the number one. As soon as he found himself in Gambino's presence, Caruso started boasting. He described the whole *viale* Lazio action down to the smallest detail, bragging about his deeds, exaggerating his own role and, of course, that of Giuseppe Di Cristina. He thought he was doing well. He felt himself a hero because in those days everyone, even in the United States, was talking about the *viale* Lazio.

But he didn't notice that the more he went on, the more Carlo Gambino was getting annoyed. Pippo Bono was on tenterhooks and feeling deeply embarrassed because he realized what a gross mistake Caruso was making. In the first place, he had started talking about something no one had asked him about. In the second place, Gambino and the others were perfectly well informed about it all, and they had willingly agreed to harbor Caruso and have their most trusted doctors take care of him, but they didn't have the least desire to start talking about the event with the first person who showed up. And in the third place, who had given him permission to start pontificating like that in front of a person like Carlo Gambino of New York, a man who had half of America in his hands?

But that's the way Caruso was. He didn't weigh his words, he couldn't control himself. After the *viale* Lazio, Damiano Caruso ended up with a swollen head and a feeling of invulnerability, a feeling of superiority to anyone and everyone, except his boss. He had no respect for anyone and started doing all sorts of crazy things. He stole from the taper warehouse of Enzo Vasile, a man of honor from Palermo. He refused to return the loot from a robbery committed at a jewelry shop that belonged to another man of honor, and he replied arrogantly when Bernardo Provenzano asked him to explain his behavior.

On one occasion, which I witnessed, he even insulted Luciano Liggio. We were at my brother's house. We had just finished coffee and the conversation turned to how we could get the Rimis out of the Ragusa prison. We began talking about the position of the main wall and were using espresso cups and teaspoons to diagram the operation. Caruso immediately jumped into the middle of the discussion and began saying that this and that needed to be done. When Liggio contradicted him and objected to one placement, Caruso quickly replied: "Don't take this wrong, but I know more than you do about these things." Liggio looked at him like he wanted to kill him, but he said nothing. His look silenced us all.

It was by Liggio's hand, in fact, that years later, around 1973, Caruso's life came to an end. He was killed along with his mistress and her daughter. Liggio hated Caruso because he believed that he was responsible for the elimination of a young man he liked very much, the Nino Guarano of Vallelunga who was nicknamed Big Heart, the one who used to go off with him in his Fiat 500 to look for the investigator Mangano. Caruso had killed Guarano because he suspected that he was distancing himself from Caruso's beloved Di Cristina to join the Madonias, Liggio's allies at the time, and to remove an obstacle to Di Cristina's nomination as the Caltanissetta province representative. Liggio ran into Caruso in Milan, where he had fled after escaping from internal exile, and he had him killed by Nello Pernice at the first opportune moment. Then, because he knew Caruso had a woman he confided in, and knew that the woman had a daughter with whom Caruso was sleeping

Members of a *carabiniere* paramilitary unit surveilling one of Palermo's main thoroughfares FOTO ANSA

Carabinieri at a roadblock in Palermo FOTO ANSA

Guiseppe "Pippo" Calderone   FOTO ANSA

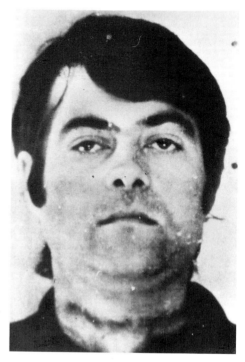

Benedetto "Nitto" Santapaola

FOTO ANSA

Salvatore Greco

FOTO ANSA

Salvatore Marchese

FOTO ANSA

Gaetano Badalamenti FOTO ANSA

Costanzo Brothers, Palermo, 1988

FOTO ANSA

Pasquale Constanzo   FOTO ANSA

Francesco Madonia   FOTO ANSA

Luciano Liggio   FOTO ANSA

Stefano Boritasle   FOTO ANSA

Guiseppe Di Cristina   FOTO ANSA

Palermo street scene   MIMMO FRASSINETI, AGF

Judge Giovanni Falcone   MIMMO CHIANURA, AGF

Salvatore Greco, 1991   PUBLIFOTO

Salvatore Greco, 1970 PUBLIFOTO

Angelo La Barbera

NICOLA SCAFIDI

Bernardo Provenzano

Michele Greco

Carabiniere roadblock in Agrigento   LUIGI BALDELLI

View of Corleone   ROBERTO KOCH

View of Corleone   GERBASI, AGENZIA CONTRASTO

View of Catania, 1980   ROBERTO KOCH, AGENZIA CONTRASTO

Tommaso Buscetta at the Maxi
trial, 1986–1987

FOTO ANSA

Giuseppe Madonia   FOTO ANSA

Pino Arlacchi and Paolo Borsellino at the reception for the just pub-
lished *Men of Dishonor*   FOTO SERGIO POZZI, LINEAPRESS

Judge Giovanni Falcone in his office in Palermo

Salvatore "Totò" Riina being charged at the Ucciardone Prison

Giuseppe Calò   MASSIMO SESTINI

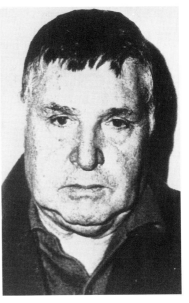

Salvatore "Totò" Riina
FOTO ITALPRESS

Antonino Calderone   FOTO ANSA

as well, he sent for both by telling them Caruso had been wounded and needed clothes and bandages. The women came immediately. Liggio killed the mother and fucked the daughter, who was maybe fifteen or sixteen, then killed her too. A cousin of Caruso's who had come from Palermo to look for him disappeared soon after. They all disappeared.

16

Caruso's two women died because of Luciano Liggio's perversity, but also because they knew things, and when women know things there's always a risk they'll talk. The men of the Cosa Nostra are very careful about what they tell their wives. For starters, women think in a certain way—all women, even those who have married mafiosi or who come from mafia families. When a woman's deepest feelings are affected, she no longer reasons. *Omertà,* the mafia code of silence, no longer applies; there's no more Cosa Nostra, no arguments or rules that can hold her back. Women become crazy if their sons are touched, because there's no greater love than that of a mother for her son. The bond between mother and son is the strongest of all, stronger than the one to husband, father, or brother.

The pain of losing her son is unbearable for a mother. If her husband is killed she can resign herself to it (which isn't to say she doesn't suffer), but if her son is killed she loses her mind, she doesn't recognize rules anymore, and the pain makes her do and say the unthinkable. Did you see, on television, that woman testifying at the maxi-trial? They had murdered her son, and her pain came through with every word. It wasn't cinema or the stage. It was real life. It was his blood that was speaking through her mouth.

If they know something, women will talk. Sooner or later they'll talk. The Sicilian man of honor knows that, and tries to keep his wife, sister, and mother at a distance from the Cosa Nostra. He does it to protect them, to save them, because if a woman knows something, it may end with him having to kill her, or having to get someone else to kill her. Confiding mafia matters to a woman means betraying one's oath to the Cosa Nostra, and it also means betraying other men of honor. If I tell a woman, "This person has committed such and such a murder," the man in question will take me to task for it: "You've put me in the hands of that woman. At any time she can accuse me and have me packed off to jail. How could you discuss my business with her? What right do you have to tell her about me and my actions? How could you trust her, even if she is your wife or sister, when you know that women will talk?"

In practice, however, it's not easy to keep women in the dark about one's activities. Every Cosa Nostra family sets down rules and harsh punishments for whoever reveals mafia business to his wife, although I don't know how realistic it is to expect them to be enforced, especially because it's not always easy to find proof of an infraction before it's too late.

In my uncle's time, after the war, there was a man of honor who was a wonder with guns. When he was in the service he had been selected by the German command, after a series of shooting contests among Italian soldiers, to join a special squad. He was made a noncom in the German forces, and he'd kept his uniform. This man of honor was responsible for many murders in Sicily, some of them on my uncle's orders. Word then began to spread about his skill and everyone sought him out. From the moment he stopped informing his own family about the work he was doing for other families, it was decided to punish him. He realized that he'd gone a bit too far and got scared. He started to confide in his wife, telling her whom he was seeing and where he was going on each appointment. But because his wife was a relative of Lillo Conti and would tell him everything her husband told her, the family found out about the second grave infraction the man had committed.

So it came down to killing either just him or both him and his wife. But the assignment was given to Lillo Conti, who was already fairly influential in the family and who had no intention of either killing or having someone else kill a relative of his. So it was decided to confront the man of honor with only the sin of having told his wife about his activities, and to reproach him by throwing him out of the family for a time. And that was that.

I was saying that it's hard to hide one's life as a mafioso from one's wife. Apart from the fact that many mafia wives—almost all the ones I've known, in fact—come from mafioso families, have breathed mafia air since they were born, and thus know very well how a mafioso thinks and behaves, I don't need to explain that the wife herself ends up intuiting everything, and whatever she can't figure out on her own she is told by her friends or her sisters and sisters-in-law, who themselves are often married to men of honor.

Nitto Santapaola didn't marry a mafia woman. His wife came from a very humble family; before she was married she worked as an underwear maker, making bras. Later on she fitted very well into the mafia. She was a through-and-through mafiosa! Nitto's sister was even more of a mafiosa than his wife, and he would even take her along on robberies. They'd stake out places together by pretending they were a pair of lovers in a car. Nitto told every possible secret to his women, and then later he led me to understand that I was the one who said too much to my wife! But then, Palermitan women are special. They pretend to be ignorant, but they know more than their husbands.

Women are treated well in the mafia. Being the wife of a mafioso entails many privileges, great and small, and is even, in a certain sense, an honor. In some apparently innocuous circumstances one can even have someone's life in one's hands, as in the case of the foolish owner of a driving school in the Monserrato area of Catania who had given lessons to Nitto Santapaola's wife. After she passed her driver's test, the instructor thought he might bring the license to her house, where he had the bright idea of saying to her, "Haven't I earned a kiss?" The woman was worried because the stupid fellow didn't know with whom he was dealing, and he didn't realize what he was really going to "earn" once Nitto got wind of the episode. She felt compassion for the poor, deluded man and chose not to tell her husband. But she did mention the episode to my cousin Salvatore Marchese, who decided to teach the instructor a lesson anyway. Along with Salvatore "Tobacco" Guarneri, he went to the driving school to pay the man a visit. But they made a mistake and instead shot the legs of the man's brother, who's probably still asking himself what happened.

Women are attracted to the mafia. Until they're seared by pain, by the terrible things that can happen in the Cosa Nostra, they live very well inside it. They like mafia types. I'll never forget the time we went up to Enna to meet a famous fugitive who had been in hiding for thirty years. This happened a very long time ago. We were a party of men of honor, very young and self-confident. We were going to sleep out in the countryside, but first we went to have dinner at a certain mafioso's farm. We ate outside, around a big table under the trees, and there was a woman coming in and out of the house bearing dishes of food. She was the owner's wife. When she saw us she exclaimed: "Aaah! So many beautiful mafiosi I have here today! What a great pleasure to see all these beautiful young men in the mafia! Come here so I can give you all a kiss!" The husband's face turned red, but it wasn't too embarrassing because she was an older woman, some sixty years of age, who was speaking sincerely and spontaneously.

My poor wife, on the other hand, came to understand more gradually what it means to be attached to a mafioso. When we were first getting involved she was employed at the University of Catania, and every now and then I would go to University Square to have coffee. Since she knew roughly what my hours were, she would appear at her office window and we would stand there looking and smiling at each other for a while. One time, a few friends who were staying at a hotel in the city center and who looked me up whenever they came to Catania came into the café on the square. They were mafiosi from the Alfano family who had a contract for cleaning cars on the railroad line. When they came into the café I was still standing with my nose in the air exchanging signs of affection with my fiancée. I kissed them, and soon after I waved good-bye to my girlfriend, who was standing at the window and saw everything. Sometime later she asked me, perplexed, "Hey, what is this, you kiss men?"

"Sure. That's obvious, my dear. Men kiss each other nowadays," I replied, embarrassed, because it wasn't in fact true, and she had seen me greet other men without exchanging kisses. But what could I do? Could I tell her straight out that I was a mafioso?

Later she realized it on her own, unbeknownst to me. Sometime after we were officially engaged, we went out for a picnic with a group of families. Pippo and I had thought we'd bring along Luciano Liggio too. We had a great meal, and while I was stretching out on the grass she came up to me and asked, point-blank, "Listen, Nino, who's this gentleman everyone's treating so respectfully and calling 'the professor'?"

"He's a friend, *u professore*. A very good man. He's been a friend of Pippo's and mine for a long time."

"What are you saying to me? I've seen his photo in the newspaper. That's Luciano Liggio," my future wife said to me triumphantly.

"Are you crazy?"

"Why are you telling me stories? I know it's him, and I've talked about it with your sister. Your sister-in-law knows too. But while your sister-in-law doesn't tell your brother, I'm telling you. To let you know I'm not as naïve as you think. No one said anything to us; your sister-in-law and I figured it out on our own."

I mentioned to my brother that our women were onto Liggio, and I admitted what had to be admitted to my fiancée, but asked her not to say a word to anyone. When she said yes, when we got married, she knew what she was getting into.

—

There's never been a rule against killing women in the Cosa Nostra. A woman who talks, who raises accusations against men of honor, can be killed, and many such cases have occurred in the past and still occur today. It's true, on the other hand, that the Cosa Nostra doesn't kill innocent women whose only sin is being the wife or daughter of an enemy. There have been many cases in which men of honor spared the life of women even though they testified against them in court and caused more than negligible damage. Let's take the case of the Battaglia widow, Serafina Battaglia, and the Rimis from Alcamo who went to the penitentiary because of her. The Rimis hadn't wanted to kill her. They could very well have killed both mother and son, and they could have saved themselves all sorts of trouble. But they didn't do it.

The Battaglia widow was a shrew, an instigator, a nurturer of vendettas. After her husband's murder she would say to her son every morning: "Get up! Get up, they've killed your father! Get up and kill them!" But the son didn't want to get up. He was married, a man of peace. And moreover, the dead man wasn't even really his father. Nevertheless, he had left him a fortune because he had been very rich. But his mother would prod him and not stop haranguing him until he hired an assassin to murder the Rimis. They heard about it and eliminated both principal and perpetrator, but not her. The moment her son was murdered, the Battaglia widow turned from shrew into informer—a *sbirra*—and she told everything to the authorities.

Now it's us men who talk, while it used to be the women who did.

Even the mother of Salvatore Lanzafame, in Catania, went to the police to inform on the Cosa Nostra after they'd killed her son. Lanzafame was my godson. It was I who baptized him a man of honor. I was always very fond of him and followed his entire career as a soldier. He needed a lot of affection because he was born illegitimate, from his mother's affair with a married man. He had also undergone a great trauma that left him reserved, introverted. He never spoke much and opened up only to his mother, and sometimes to me. Mother and son were very close. He would tell her everything. I think he even spoke to her about murders he committed for the family.

He grew up a loner, Lanzafame, and began stealing when he was small. He formed a gang of five or six boys like him, also sad and unhappy. They lived off thefts and robberies, and they were ferociously serious about their work. They weren't like those who pilfer here and there and might be arrested from one day to the next. These boys planned their jobs carefully, and always aimed high, for bigger things. They would strike every year or two after having prepared for months and months. They would make a good amount of money, then retire to live calm, quiet lives for a while. So Salvatore Lanzafame led a more or less normal existence. He went to school regularly and got himself a surveyor's degree. He was nicknamed "the student."

Salvatore's gang included an adult, Uncle Angelo—a fine, distinguished person some forty or forty-five years old—who would reconnoiter the site of the boys' next job. They would send him, for instance, to a city in the North where there was a large pawnbroker's business. Uncle Angelo would go with his wife, rent a house in the same neighborhood as the pawnshop, and live there for two or three months while studying the hours, movements, and habits of the staff and the agency's security system. The house didn't attract attention, even if from time to time strangers showed up and spent the night there.

Uncle Angelo would go to the pawnshop with something to pledge, or he'd attend the auctions of unredeemed items, and he would study and take note of everything. When the right moment came, the boys would take over and hold up everyone who happened to be in the agency at the time, or they would break in on a Saturday or Sunday and empty it of the most valuable objects. The job done, they would hide out in Uncle Angelo's house for a few days, then go down to Naples, where they would sell the loot to a middleman, a fence. They would take their money and return to Catania, happy and content, to live a bit of the good life in the best places. But they weren't the types who within a couple of weeks spent the results of months of work. They were careful, cautious kids who saved a good part of the proceeds. There were many windfalls of ten million lire for Lanzafame's mother!

Every so often the possibility of a good job in Catania itself arose, and it was on one of these occasions that Lanzafame made the mistake of robbing an illegal gambling den run by Giuseppe Ferrera. Lanzafame wasn't aware of that fact, and when Ferrera raised a stink, Lanzafame slapped his face. This cost him a death sentence. When the poor fellow realized what he'd done, he dropped out of sight for a time and then did all he could to make amends, to reconcile himself with us in the family. He had, for good reasons, a terrible fear of being killed.

He tried to get close to Pippo and me, gave us many presents, and put himself at our disposal. And when the war broke out between us and the underworld people, whom he knew very well, Lanzafame and his men moved even closer to the family and did much on our behalf. And so we decided to pardon him, and we brought him into the Cosa Nostra. His mother was ecstatic because she saw that her son was finally in safe hands, and because she thought that the business of the death sentence was definitely over. The woman couldn't do enough for my brother, and she couldn't stop thanking and kissing him: "Uncle Pippo, Uncle Pippo, thanks to you my son is saved at last!"

Lanzafame was wounded in the head during the attack that cost my brother his life, since the two were together at the time. But Lanzafame survived, and later, when conflict erupted between the Ferlitos and the Santapaolas, he joined the former.

Salvatore Lanzafame's time came the day his faction found out where Nitto was hiding and arranged an expedition to kill him. Alfio Ferlito, Lanzafame, and others armed themselves to the teeth with hand grenades, machine guns, shotguns, and pistols, and stormed the country house in which Nitto supposedly was staying. But he wasn't there. His brother Nino and his nephew were, however, and they immediately returned fire. Lanzafame got out of the car and took cover behind a boulder, but Nitto's nephew hit him square in the chest with a shotgun.

Lanzafame's mother didn't accept the idea (which was only too true!) that her son had died during an attempt to kill someone, but was convinced that he had been assassinated as a result of the old story of the robbery at Ferrera's gambling den. And so one day my lawyer came back from court and said to me, "Rumor has it that Lanzafame's mother has started to collaborate."

Nitto commissioned Turi Palermo to kill the woman, but Turi refused and did nothing. Some others in the family were also against eliminating her, and thus nothing happened. No one touched her. A trial took place, which resulted in a deadlock.

The tendency to spare the lives of women doesn't apply anymore. In Catania as elsewhere, if it comes to be known that a woman has talked, she's killed without a second thought.

17

I had a lawyer I trusted, as did the other family members. It often happened that the same lawyer represented a number of men of honor, but each of us had his preferences. The obligation to hire a very good, expensive lawyer arose only when soldiers were arrested because they had followed the representative's orders. The soldier's day-to-day lawyer then took a backseat and his defense was assumed by a famous lawyer paid for by the family. For a prosperous family, the expenses of a celebrated professional weren't a problem. But until the middle seventies we weren't prospering. In those days, lawyers' fees were a burden and we had to limit our soldiers' "missions."

And then there are men of honor who are lawyers, but not like in *The Godfather,* in which they gave advice about everything to the family representative. The mafia doesn't need the advice of lawyers to carry out its operations. If someone has to be consulted before deciding something, the representative has his *consigliere,* the family *consigliere,* who isn't a lawyer. If the family boss has a problem with the law—a trial, for instance—then he asks for a lawyer's input. But what do they know about making war, smuggling, how to make the family "work," how to conduct business, how to kill? For these things there are *consiglieri.* A family is directed by the individual talent of its men of honor.

But lawyers are useful for something else as well: they can enter a prison as they please and talk to their jailed client for as long as they want. For this they are vital. Talks with a jailed person's relatives last for half an hour and must be authorized by a judge. The lawyer can go to his client whenever he wants to. One of Stefano Bontade's lawyers, a young attorney, was a man of honor, and he'd go to see him in prison every day. They would sit there talking calm and undisturbed, for one hour, or two, or three.

The lawyer sits in during interrogations, and if he's a house lawyer he watches, pays attention to what the accused tells the judge. The family's benefits from having a man of honor as a lawyer are enormous. If he's a man of honor and a trusted person, he can carry messages out of prison. Through him Michele Greco can tell Totò Riina if war should be made or not, if this murder should be carried out or not. Certainly, it's hard to avoid being overheard when one is talking to someone in prison. One never talks openly during these encounters, not even with family members. I remember that during talks with my wife in Marseilles we could even hear the sound of the recorder. We would talk little, therefore, and instead use gestures and movements of the head and eyes. Only when I decided to repent did I allow myself to be heard by the recorder. The lawyers also know that one is spied on during talks, so we rely on nicknames—on names in code known only to the recipients of the messages.

I found my trusted lawyer only after a terrible experience with his predecessor, whose life I had even spared. The lawyer was Tommaso Bonfiglio from Catania, whom Liggio's great friend Nello Pernice wanted to kill because he believed he had behaved badly toward him. Pernice asked my permission for the murder both because I had an official role inside the family and because he knew that Bonfiglio was my lawyer.

I didn't have any sympathy for Bonfiglio; he had treated me badly too. He had defended me too off-handedly when I was in court on charges brought against me by the Catania Police Department in 1974.

The accusation was that my wealth had been acquired illegally. It wasn't true, because I was able to show that my modest estate came from legal earnings (the gas station and the heating-oil distributorship). Bonfiglio claimed that it was unnecessary for me to produce any documentation. On the day set for the hearing I ran into another lawyer by chance and showed him the documents. He told me that I was right and that I should speak about it with the minister of Public Courts, Mr. Sebastiano Campisi.

The minister realized that my accounts were in order, and he declared that he would withdraw the accusation when my case was called. The court was presided by Judge D'Urso, the same one who was later abducted by the Red Brigades. The minister's request was granted and I was acquitted. Notwithstanding this, I didn't authorize the elimination of the lawyer Bonfiglio. His negligence wasn't enough to justify the death penalty.

Sometime afterward, the lawyer who intervened on my behalf with Mr. Campisi called me on the phone. He told me that Judge Campisi had a problem: his wife had a small piece of property that was going to be cut through by the Catania-Enna highway, then under construction by the Costanzo firm. He was evidently aware of the close relationship that existed between us Calderones and the Costanzos. Wouldn't it be possible to move the roadbed a little to avoid cutting into the property? An inspection of the site, near Catenanuova, was carried out in the presence of Campisi himself, his friend the lawyer, and my brother, who was representing the interests of the firm. The road was shifted, and the Costanzo firm even rearranged the layout of Mrs. Campisi's property.

In the course of the inspection, Campisi revealed that during my trial the lawyer Bonfiglio had suggested that the prosecution ask for a sentence of four years in internal exile, against the eventuality that I would be given two, and thus Bonfiglio could have made it look like the reduction of the term was due to his efforts.

We became friends with the judge, and when my brother was recovering in the hospital Campisi suddenly showed up. "But, Your Honor . . . you, here?" Pippo exclaimed, surprised and flattered. He was alluding to the uproar that could possibly ensue from the judge's visit to a noted mafioso. "Hey, don't worry about it," Campisi cut him off quickly, "everyone knows we're friends."

Years later, around 1980, I saw Judge Campisi again on a number of occasions. An agricultural-products broker, Pietro Castelli, asked me to go to Adrano, a town in Catania province where Campisi had property, to meet the judge. Campisi had in the meantime been transferred to Cuneo, but every summer he came to Adrano to oversee the pistachio harvest. Castelli informed me that Campisi had just done a great favor for Tommaso Buscetta, who was detained in the Cuneo jail. He had obtained parole for him through a friend of his who was a judge or official in the Ministry of Justice, and Buscetta had disappeared immediately afterward. To put himself in a good light, Buscetta had told Campisi that he was a friend of the Calderones.

I saw Campisi, who confirmed that he had intervened on Buscetta's behalf, though he didn't seem troubled by the latter's disappearance. So I thought I might try to ingratiate myself with the Corleonesi and I asked him if he could get something done for a poor jailbird (I was referring to Liggio, but not by name). Campisi answered that it was a bit difficult, but that some permission or authorization might, however, be possible. I let Nitto Santapaola know so that he in turn would pass it on to the Corleonesi, but there was no response.

I often went to see Campisi after that, each time bringing him presents like fish or black-market cigarettes (Marlboros for him and Muratti Ambassadors for his family). He told me that he had many children and that somehow or other he had settled them all into jobs up there in Cuneo.

On the occasion of another trip of his to Catania, Campisi asked me if it would be possible to get the mafia to catch some terrorists who, it was said, were hiding out in Sicily. I quickly replied that we were opposed to police actions and had never arrested anyone. I informed Nitto Santapaola, in his capacity as representative of the Catania family, about this strange request. Nitto approved of my reply.

In the course of my mafia career I met a number of judges, politicians, and carabinieri, though I never got a clear picture of the world of our adversaries. It seemed similar to the Cosa Nostra in one respect: there were honest ones and dishonest ones, those who believed in their work and those who took advantage of it, and sometimes it's hard to tell them apart at first sight. In any case, until 1983, the date of my escape to France, the Catania family didn't need to think much about them. We were well protected and well informed. We would safeguard the large enterprises against demands from the local common criminals and from the mafia families outside Catania, and they would protect us from troubles with the forces of law and order.

The Costanzo firm had many judges in its pocket. It would cultivate them for reasons of its own, because it had an endless series of legal problems. A large firm has headaches to contend with almost daily: breaches of regulations, workplace accidents, conflicts with other firms, etc. And given that it was in the possession of such contacts, it would also use them to help us with trials, legal charges, and so on. At the procurator general's, the Costanzos had Di Natale. At the Palace of Justice they had a powerful judge, someone who gave orders to trial judges and lived in Adrano. He was referred to by the pseudonym "Napoleon." The Costanzos did an extraordinary amount of work, gratis, on his land in Adrano.

The Costanzos had also built that big apartment building on the piazza Santa Maria del Gesù, the best in Catania at the time, where a number of judges lived. And what kind of rent did they pay? Every month the manager gave the tenant judges a receipt in full for the rent, with the word "Paid" stamped on it, but the money had been paid by Gino Costanzo. So the judges were in a position to prove at any moment that they were paying.

But we also had our own independent sources of information. At the Court of Law our man was Agatino Ferlito, who knew a number of judges and also had acquaintances at the Court of Assizes. The procurator general's office was a sieve, and arrest warrants in Catania were a joke. I knew a carabinieri commander who belonged to the section responsible for arrests. We were friends, or pretended to be. It's hard to tell. One night I invited the commander to dinner at my house, and he arrived in the company of two other carabinieri. One of them was nicknamed "Skinny" because he was so fat. The other one had a face I re-

175

membered well: he was one of the men who had arrested me a couple of years earlier.

The task of the arrest section is to make sure of the whereabouts of people about to be arrested in order to find them at home on the night the operation—the blitz—is launched. One day I found the commander waiting for me outside my house. I invited him to come in, but he replied that there was no need to. We sat in my wife's car, which was parked by the front door, and he let me see the list of arrest warrants to be executed during an upcoming operation against drug traffickers. There were some twenty names, all of them people outside our family, with the exception of my cousin Salvatore Marchese. Then I gave the commander a gift of 500,000 lire, which he accepted after a few weak protests because, he said, he wasn't doing it for money. The commander told me that he'd already shown the list to Nitto Santapaola, who had replied that the only person who concerned him was Marchese and that the others were trash. I confirmed to the commander that for me too the only name on the list that meant anything was that of my cousin, but he answered that by now there was nothing that could be done about it. He couldn't strike the name because the list was in the hands of the judges.

I knew what to do under the circumstances. I went to Pasquale Costanzo, who among other things was the uncle of my accused cousin, who had married a niece of his. Costanzo assured me that he would intervene through a director of the Justice Department, the prosecutor Di Natale. And he did. Di Natale took charge of the trial, which was in the hands of one of his deputies. My cousin's name was struck from the list of the accused, and because its position was linked to another, that name had to be struck too.

Afterward my cousin and I were called to Carmelo Costanzo's office. We had to sit through a long reproach at the conclusion of which the *cavaliere del lavoro** mentioned that the whole business had cost him thirty million lire, the sum he had to give Di Natale, who was very fond of cards. Maybe it was true, or maybe Costanzo

---

*"Knight of Labor"—an Italian civil title bestowed on prominent businessmen, industrialists, and large-scale farmers (translator's note).

was taking us for a ride. That was his habit: whenever he did someone a favor, he acted as though he had moved mountains even if he hadn't lifted a finger.

In any event, the business was over for us. We didn't think more of it until one night when I saw Domenico Compagnino—a ballistics expert at the Department of Justice who knew everyone and addressed everyone with the familiar *"tu,"* even Captain Guarrata and Colonel Licata, who commanded the Catania carabinieri— arrive at the Costanzo firm. I was in the waiting room, biding time until I could be seen by one of Costanzo's nephews, with whom I had to discuss a work question. As soon as he saw me, Compagnino came up to me and told me that he was very worried. The Catania carabinieri were preparing a massive antidrug operation, and he had noticed that on the list of people to be arrested were my cousin Salvatore Marchese and Giuseppe Ferrera, a Cavadduzzi man (and thus a close relative of Nitto Santapaolo) who was a provincial representative at the time. I was dumbfounded. "But how?" I wondered. "Carmelo Costanzo went on and on about having had the names struck from the list, and none of it's true! Or else he's been taken in by Di Natale."

I asked Costanzo's secretary to let me see the *cavaliere* immediately, even though he was busy with someone else. I went in and found Nitto Santapaola sitting down in front of him. I explained the problem to both of them. Nitto pretended not to know anything and acted upset at the prospect of his cousin Ferrera being arrested on drug charges: "What a disgrace! It's a shameful accusation! The mafia isn't involved in drugs! It would be better if he'd been accused of murder. We don't deal drugs!"

Incredible gall. He was playing this scene to impress (or fool?) the *cavaliere*. Nitto left soon after. I subsequently found out that Costanzo had sent his secretary to the prosecutor Di Natale for an explanation of Salvatore Marchese's arrest warrant and to remind him again that Marchese wasn't just anybody, but the nephew of the Costanzos. On his way into the prosecutor's office, the secretary had run into the carabinieri captain Guarrata. They greeted each other because they were friends, notwithstanding the secretary's attempts to corrupt Guarrata and put him on the *cavalieri*'s payroll.

Guarrata figured out the reason for the secretary's visit to Di Natale and was very concerned: it was he who had carried out the investigations and had charged Marchese and Ferrera, precisely to strike at the Costanzos.

The meeting with Di Natale cleared up the misunderstanding. There had been no evil intent on the prosecutor's part and there was no arrest warrant for Marchese and Ferrera. There had simply been two versions of the arrest warrants—the original and the one drawn up after the Costanzos' intervention. The ballistics expert had seen the old version, on which the names of Ferrera and Marchese still appeared. But Giuseppe Ferrera's name hadn't been struck due to pressure from the Costanzos. There was no need, and Di Natale had nothing to do with it. There was yet another channel—an "occult" channel, one could say—between us and the Catania magistrature. I'm asking you to believe me, at this point, and not to laugh. Or laugh anyway, but believe what I'm about to relate.

The deputy prosecutor who handled arrest warrants was called Foti; he was separated from his wife and had a mistress. This woman's sister, who lived with a cousin of Giuseppe Ferrera, was a fortune-teller. Like many judges, Foti would bring work home with him. His mistress would look at the documents and pass the names of those about to be arrested on to her sister. And thus from the fortune-teller's crystal ball came quite precise predictions about the movements of the Catania police and magistrature, and about the immediate fate of a number of mafiosi. Word spread and the woman's clientele grew. It's not every day that you find a witch who can say to a woman, "Your husband's about to be arrested." Even my wife went to her at one point to find out about my juridical future!

When the witch came across Giuseppe Ferrera's name among those passed along by her sister, she immediately told her man that his cousin was on the list of suspects to be seized, and she asked her sister to arrange for the judge to strike him from it. And so not even Ferrera was incriminated for drug trafficking.

When the procurator of the Republic's office handed down arrest warrants for many fewer people than were named by the carabinieri, Captain Guarrata was furious and immediately resolved to raise a fuss. He wanted to present a formal statement to the procurator general, the direct superior of the procurator of the Republic, to protest the fact that the Costanzos were meddling with the city's judiciary offices. But his commander, Colonel Licata, ordered him not to do anything. There was then a very loud verbal conflict between the two in the carabinieri barracks.

This episode of the revised and corrected arrest warrants occurred in 1981 and is only one example. Things went the same way in the Catania courts both before and after. When an order to arrest me was finally handed down in 1982, I had been expecting it for three months!

Everything the judges did came to be known. And many times there was no need to rely on the Costanzos or the others because lesser sources would suffice. It was enough to know a minor employee—a clerk, a secretary, a doorman—to collect information about how an investigation was proceeding, if a given verdict had been reached, or how an inquest was developing. Just one example: there was a girl who worked as a secretary or clerk for Judge Grassi and who bought chicken and fresh eggs from a prominent character in the Catania underworld, Saro Zuccaro. This Zuccaro had reached the point of being able to ask the girl every now and then, while he was wrapping up a chicken leg or breast of turkey, "Has Judge Grassi signed those arrest warrants yet?" Everything was known. And when they did in fact hand the arrest warrants down, after the death of General Dalla Chiesa, they barely managed to arrest anyone because the suspects had all had ample warning.

—

We had inherited the friendship, the relationship with the Costanzos, from my uncle Luigi Saitta, who had been protecting them since the fifties. It was my uncle who introduced Totò Minore, the Trapani mafia boss, to Carmelo Costanzo: an indissoluble friendship that was born around 1956–1957 on the occasion of several large contracts the Costanzo firm was to undertake in Trapani province. Early on the Costanzos had been simple masons, master builders who became building contractors thanks to the help of one Giovanni Conti, who wasn't a man of honor but who had excellent contacts with politicians, and in particular with the parliamentary deputy Milazzo. Their start as builders came with Milazzo's rise to the governorship of Sicily. The Costanzos thus survived all the subsequent political upheavals and became increasingly more powerful. As a reward, much of Giovanni Conti's property was transferred, after his death, to the Costanzo brothers.

The other *cavalieri* in Catania also used our services on various occasions. From the start Gaetano Graci was under the protection of Francesco Madonia, who would step in only when serious problems arose in terms of Graci's building yards and other activities scattered all over Sicily. After Francesco Madonia's death, his son Giuseppe preferred not to follow the Gracis' interests too closely, so they then joined up with Nitto Santapaola and Rosario Romeo, a Catanian man of honor who I consider worse than Judas because I think he betrayed my brother.

On the other hand, the builder Finocchiaro relied on an important personality in the Cursoti gang, an element of the common criminal underworld in Catania that was separate from the Cosa Nostra.

The Rendo group always kept itself a bit removed from the underworld. Contacts with mafiosi were maintained by dependents of the Rendo firm rather than by its owners directly. One time around the start of the sixties, Rendo applied to my uncle at the direction of Nino Succi, Catania's Socialist vice-mayor whom I've talked about in reference to the license for the gas station. A bomb had gone off in the firm's offices and Succi had suggested that Rendo contact the Costanzo firm, which was protected by my uncle. An appointment was fixed at the Costanzo residence, and Rendo climbed out of the car shaking with fear. Costanzo puffed up with satisfaction because Rendo had never come to him before while he himself had had to go to Rendo so many times. The meeting with my uncle was reassuring. "Take it easy, don't worry yet. It's possible that nothing at all will happen to you," my uncle said to him with a sly air.

"But how can I pay you back? Tell me what I can do for you," Rendo replied.

"Do you smoke, by any chance?"

"Yes, certainly."

"Good. Smoke these cigarettes to my health," my uncle concluded, handing him a packet of Nationals. A grand gesture, truly mafioso. Then, naturally, Uncle Luigi told Costanzo to ask Rendo to come up with the cash. I don't know what the whole sum was, but Costanzo subsequently had the courage to maintain to my uncle that he himself had paid it. Our family had placed the bomb at Rendo's with the aim of getting a bit of money out of him and to bring him in, to take him in hand. But Rendo paid and wouldn't allow himself to be subordinated. With the cigarette gesture my uncle had meanwhile covered himself, because he didn't feel comfortable accepting money from a character like that.

We continued to cause much damage to Rendo, both to intimidate him and to do a favor to the Costanzos. But we didn't manage to subdue him because he also had the support of the police. He was closer than all the others to the police and magistrature. Rendo understood very well where the hostilities were emanating from, but he wouldn't give in. And Costanzo would puff right up whenever he heard about damages to his rival's construction sites. He would have done anything he could to grow larger than him. He always saw Rendo as a step in front of him, above him, as more intelligent and powerful than him. And he would try to get the better of him the only way he could: by frightening him. He would run to Pippo and say to him, "Ah, look how badly he took it! He did this and he did that . . . " And then bombs in Rendo's construction sites in Gela. "Look at how awful that guy is! He did this other thing . . . " Then bombs in his construction sites in Catania. Then bombs somewhere else.

In meetings with other large builders, Carmelo Costanzo made it clearly understood that there were going to be no games with him because he had the mafia behind him. Sometimes they would bow their heads, acquiesce, and Costanzo would behave like a lion. But often the others balked because they too were protected, and massive disputes would break out. Costanzo, Rendo, and Graci had created various consortia so that they could join forces and win contracts worth tens of billions, especially for waterworks and airports. Then their interests conflicted, they fell into violent arguments, and they decided to go their own ways. They split up the remaining work and drew each of their shares by lot. To Graci fell the Enna dam and a cash compensation. Rendo got another dam, which was to be built in (I think) Agrigento province, and Costanzo was assigned the airports on the smaller islands around Sicily. They ended up insulting one another with truly harsh words. We were shocked just listening to them. At a certain point the conflict reached such a level of vulgarity—the three could no longer sit down at a table together without insulting one another—that mediators had to be called in. Two of them were noted professionals, and the third was an important politician whose name I forget.

Catania's *cavalieri* were never victims of the mafia, or at least not as long as I was there. Sure, there were differences between a Rendo on one side and a Costanzo on the other. But essentially they all benefited, even from the mere reputation of being associated with us. Now they claim they don't know us.

Later, Gino Costanzo practically denied that he had attended my wedding and that of my brother. He couldn't remember! Meanwhile, his brother Carmelo admitted to having been escorted by us to the feast of the Madonna del Carmelo. He was very devout, and every year on the morning of the feast he would carry a taper to the Madonna. He had vowed to increase the size of the taper every year. One night when we were all together, Gino Costanzo said to his brother, "It's time to go, Carmelino. We must go to bed soon because tomorrow we get up early. We have to carry the taper to the Madonna del Carmelo." He said that and repeated it in front of us to let us know that they wanted an escort the next day. Carmelo Costanzo lived a bit outside of the city, in Cibali, near the stadium. He would leave from there, barefoot and in pilgrim's clothing, and walk, taper in hand, to *via* Etnea in the city center, where the fair was. His brother Gino would follow him in a car with shoes and normal clothes. And my brother said, "Tomorrow morning we'll come with you too." "No, no. There's no need. Don't trouble yourself," the Costanzos replied ceremoniously. The next morning we showed up in front of his door and accompanied him the whole way.

The episode became folklore. To have the mafia on one's side meant a lot to businessmen like the Costanzos. It meant they could work in peace and make money without the risk of seeing their construction vehicles harmed, without strikers stopping their projects halfway through, without the demands for payoffs that even the littlest mafioso feels a right to when anyone undertakes an investment in his territory.

This was the service that my uncle Luigi and my brother carried out for the Costanzos. When my brother's building partnership collapsed, he became the Costanzo firm's factotum. He would examine every worksite on the spot, and he'd fly to Rome. He would take care of everything. He put his friendships all over Sicily at the firm's disposal, and in return he received a salary of a million lire a month. It wasn't a mafioso's salary, but that didn't matter to him; he never thought much about money. He was a sentimentalist. Nor did he ever officially become part of the firm.

They would say, for example, "We have to do some work in Caltanissetta. In what part of the city should the site be?" And Pippo would go there, look for terrain to lease, and reach an agreement with the area mafia boss for protecting the construction site and the machinery. The local mafiosi would be paid for their services, and when Nitto took over the protection of the Costanzos after my brother's death, I handed him a little piece of paper on which the sums owing to the mafia bosses in various areas were indicated.

But there wasn't just the fact of protection. Pippo was welcomed everywhere because he provided work. When he went to a city or town, everyone would pay him their respects, seek him out, because he was not only a Cosa Nostra provincial representative but also the representative of the Costanzo firm, which provided bread for the men of honor's people. All this had helped his mafia career and made him known and liked by everyone. In the seventies Sicily was filled with mafiosi who had bought trucks and construction equipment and needed work to pay them off. When the Costanzo firm won a contract for twenty or thirty billion lire, the contract would turn into three or four years of assured work for the jobless. The firm's subcontracting—providing sand, gravel, carpentry, etc.—would be doled out through small local biddings in which jobbers who weren't men of honor could participate as well. The firm's policy was to ask for a bid from each applicant, then to favor the mafiosi by telling them what the other bids were. The mafiosi would propose a figure slightly lower than the lowest bid and so would win the contract. The firm could then justify its preference for the mafiosi over the other bidders and save itself a good bit of money too!

Pippo saved huge sums for the Costanzos. "We need this material," they'd say. Pippo would then find out about prices and the reliability of the suppliers, and after that compile a list of names to choose from. For gasoline and heating oil the Costanzos would turn to us, to the company I had started with Pippo, but without asking for special deals. We sold them considerable quantities of heating oil for the apartment buildings they owned.

And how much trouble Pippo took care of! In 1973 the Costanzos were suffering heavily because one of the firm's workers, a surveyor, was blackmailing them. They had built a viaduct over the Catania-Messina highway, and its columns were giving way and threatening to collapse. The surveyor had been fired and wanted to report the mess to the authorities. He'd written down everything. He knew that the firm used all sorts of shortcuts, had made a list of the defective columns, and he was threatening to expose everything to the contracting board if he wasn't given five hundred million lire. But he'd done it already, he'd turned in his statement, and samples from the columns had to be taken to verify his claims. The surveyor didn't show up on the day set for the inspection. But things had been muddled up to the Costanzos' advantage, and the tests were performed elsewhere, on other columns. The surveyor hadn't appeared because Pippo called him up and told him that if he didn't stop making trouble he'd break him in two.

Pippo had even had the Costanzos made *cavalieri* through his friend Lupis, the Social Democrat deputy, who was born in Ragusa. Carmelo Costanzo became a *cavaliere* in 1968. At the time Lupis was an undersecretary, and was closely tied to another undersecretary named Evangelisti. A figure of 80 million lire was set, which later became 110 million lire because some difficulties arose. It was Pippo who took care of everything. He went to Rome with the money and first met Lupis's private secretary, Felice Ciancio, a former baron, who sat in a room next to that of the parliamentary deputy. When Pippo came in carrying a bag stuffed with bank notes, Ciancio announced him to Lupis by saying, "Sir, Pippo's arrived with the mail." "Good. Put it down and have him come in." And thus Costanzo was named a *cavaliere*. Rendo too was made a *cavaliere* in the same year, but in agriculture, which made Costanzo extremely happy because it wasn't Rendo's field, and in any case it was less prestigious than being a *cavaliere* of industry.

It can't be said that Nitto Santapaola received the kind of treatment my brother enjoyed after he succeeded him as the Costanzos' right-hand man. When it came to money the *cavalieri* were pretty stingy, and they didn't think much of the benefits they obtained through the mafia. Nitto confided to me one day, "That Carmelo Costanzo is never pleased. Totò Riina won him a huge contract in Palermo for the construction of an apartment building. And you know how much Riina got out of it? A hundred million. A hundred million for business worth billions! What does he think? That we're idiots? Just imagine, after the first year I worked in Pippo's place Costanzo only gave me fifteen million! Nothing! I didn't even use it. I bought spumante and panettones for all the internees at Christmas, like Alfio Ferlito suggested."

And to think that Nitto even killed someone for the Costanzos around the end of the seventies! I'm not sure if they knew about it beforehand, but certainly they weren't displeased when they heard the news. The Costanzos had set up a construction site in Messina, and they had received a demand for extortion money. A group from the local underworld made up of ex-employees of the Costanzos had asked for money from the foreman and from a nephew of Nitto's who was a worker there. A number of Costanzo employees were close relatives of men of honor: the son and the brother of the smuggler Francesco Mangion, for example.

Gino Costanzo met with me and told me about the problem. I

asked him if he'd spoken to Nitto and he said that he had. One of the extortionists was killed sometime afterward in Messina, and Nino Santapaola and Salvatore Tuccio were tried and acquitted for the murder. Nitto subsequently told me that the killers had in fact been Tuccio and his brother, and that they had avoided being arrested red-handed by a hair. On the same occasion Nino Bua, the Catanian mafioso who was the firm's chief at the construction site and who according to Nitto was stealing money from the firm, was to have been killed too. But the murder didn't take place. In fact, Nitto and Bua later became close friends.

With respect to Bua, an episode comes to my mind concerning the *cavaliere* Graci that illustrates the kind of links that existed between the mafia and the major Catanian builders, how many advantages these links could produce, and how dangerous it could be to exploit them without respecting the mafia's unwritten rules. One day in 1980 or 1981 a friend of mine, Salvatore Santamaria, who owned a small machine shop that did metal work for the Costanzo firm, asked me to come with him on a visit to his friend, the very same Nino Bua, whom he hadn't seen for a while and who lived in a villa off the Syracuse road. I knew Bua too, and when I saw him I found him in a very worried and agitated state. He couldn't hold back, and he related an event to me that—as I said to him myself—he had no business to be telling me.

Bua was nervous because, having planned to set up an earth-moving business with two other partners, he had gone to ask Graci for some subcontracting jobs. To give the request more weight, he and his partners claimed that Filippo Di Stefano, the boss of one of the two mafia families in Favara, a town near Agrigento, was backing them. Since it had never been recognized, however, the family wasn't part of the Cosa Nostra. Sometime after his talk with Graci, one of Bua's partners, an internee let out on parole named Camilleri, was murdered. Bua was nervous because he was afraid of meeting the same end, and he couldn't figure out why Camilleri, who hadn't done anything wrong, had been killed. The only thing he'd done before his death was to have asked Graci for work.

Later on I mentioned Bua's fears to my cousin Marchese, who

shed some light on Bua's story. "Those fools" had asked for work from Graci without any authorization, because the Favara family was not part of the Cosa Nostra, and even if it had been, the request to Graci should have gone through the Catanian family in charge. Camilleri had thus been killed by "that lunatic Franco Romeo" in a car parked on a very busy street in Catania, and in the middle of the morning to boot, with a great risk of being seen by someone.

Requests for work and favors have always been a problem for the Catanian *cavalieri*. They reaped considerable advantages from their relationship with the Cosa Nostra, especially since many men of honor worked for them as subcontractors, drivers, truckers, jobbers, clerks, overseers, suppliers, etc., and were trustworthy, capable people who didn't cause trouble and did their jobs well.

But there was also a limit to the number of favors and contracts that could be handed out, and this is why Gino Costanzo never entered the Cosa Nostra officially. Pippo would tell me that Gino had the qualities to be a man of honor, and that for a certain amount of time he had been undecided about joining, at least as an associate, but in the end he stayed outside. Had he become a man of honor he would have been introduced as such to other men of honor, who would have felt free to turn to him directly for recommendations, orders, and various favors. He would have exposed his fortunes to the risk of entailment by the family, and thus he would have lost his peace of mind. It was more convenient to leave everything unpleasant to my brother, to Nitto, and to the others.

My impression, in any case, is that had they been faced with making a decision about Gino Costanzo joining the family, Pippo and the others would have been perplexed for other reasons as well. Gino simply had too many contacts with the police, the carabinieri, judges, taxmen. These contacts were very useful to the Cosa Nostra, but they are not suitable for a true man of honor.

The Cosa Nostra's protection was not just sought by the Costanzos and the other Catanian builders. Almost every Sicilian business of a certain size would resort to the mafiosi in order to work in peace and keep firms from the North out of their markets. Many northern firms had abandoned Sicily because it was too risky to work there. They would have no end of troubles with extortionists and hostility from local firms and bureaucrats who wanted their own share too. When a large northern firm competed for a contract in Sicily it would add a "mafia risk" of 10 percent to its costs—which would prevent it from underbidding the competition the way it usually did. Working in Sicily also meant greater transportation costs. This is why northern companies lost so many bids in Sicily.

For various reasons, many companies went away. I remember one company from Florence that had a huge dispute with the Costanzos. There was even a court accusation against Carmelo Costanzo, but in the end the company had to withdraw.

And so local firms flourished; they weren't subject to the mafia risk since they were already dealing with the mafia. Then, as I said, in the seventies, the Gracis, Rendos, and Costanzos started forming consortia to win the larger contracts and to be more competitive with the firms from the North. It was also much more convenient at the time for the *cavalieri* to work on projects in Sicily because it was very difficult for them to work in the North; the northern firms would raise all sorts of obstacles against them in retaliation for the treatment they endured when they showed up in Sicily.

For our family the advantages accrued from friendships with the *cavalieri* were, all told, marginal. Little things, crumbs. The Costanzos knew our weak points, our little passions, our vanities, and they would pay us accordingly. They were good at conferring rewards that cost them little or nothing but that in our eyes appeared significant.

They knew about our passion for hunting, for example. A good number of men of honor were hunters. Stefano Bontade was a great hunter. Michele Greco was a hunter and had a passion for guns. He was an excellent skeet shooter and also had a shooting range frequented by the best names in Palermo. My dear friend Angelo Padrenicola would organize hunting parties every year on the banks of Lake Pergusa—in the innermost part of Sicily, on the flanks of Mount Carangiaro—in which Stefano Bontade and Gaetano Badalamenti would participate. The best hunting reserve in

Sicily was called Ntrunata and was located in the province of Enna, near a property owned by Ciccio Mancuso, a Nicosia man of honor. I once went to Ntrunata with a fugitive sometime around the beginning of the seventies.

The Costanzos knew that we liked to be in the company of the important, the powerful, from both inside and outside the mafia. And so they would arrange meetings, dinners, and hunting parties to which they would invite the best names in the Cosa Nostra. Or else they would put up men of honor and members of "the forces of law and order" at the hotel they owned, La Perla Jonica, most times without making them pay, and treating them with the utmost respect. They would have them meet and get to know one another. At the wedding of Gino Costanzo's son, after my brother's death, the cream of the Sicilian mafia was present, along with a pair of carabinieri officials. Captain Guarrata almost ruined the party when he realized that Totò Minore and Nitto were there. Guarrata wanted to do something about it, but Gino told me that luckily his superior, Colonel Licata, was there too and quickly intervened to calm him down.

I remember one hunting party that took place at the opening of the hunting season, toward the end of the summer of 1979, at a marvelous preserve on the flanks of Mount Etna, between Bronte and Maletto, that belonged to the Costanzos. Michele Greco, Totò Minore, and Totò Riina, accompanied by his inseparable Giacomo Gambino, had come expressly from Palermo and Trapani. There were also Nitto and other prominent Catanian mafiosi, among them Natale Ferrera, who had brought a couple of crates of fish to broil. The only nonmafiosi present were Gino Costanzo and his secretary, De Luca. The hunt lasted the whole day. Toward evening Michele Greco went back to Palermo, while the rest of us went to have dinner in the offices of the Costanzo firm, which were on the Scia property. Then something unexpected happened that spoiled the whole project. Nitto, Totò Riina, and some others suddenly went off into the secretarial offices, then came out a half hour later saying that it wouldn't be possible to make dinner and that the group would have to split up.

Nitto used to boast about having free use of the Gracis' splendid hunting preserve in the countryside near Enna's Poggiorosso. He went there very often and invited whomever he pleased. It wasn't unusual for his guests to run into those of his hosts. One day he told me he had even run into a carabinieri general there. In fact, Nitto was a very close friend of Gaetano Graci's son-in-law. He would often talk about him, and one night around 1979 I went into the La Costa Azzura restaurant in Catania and found both of them having dinner with the parliamentary deputy Lo Turco, from the PSDI,* and a few others. They invited me to join them and I accepted.

The arrival of General Dalla Chiesa in Sicily made the *cavalieri* intensely nervous. In May 1982 I went to the Costanzo offices to collect a bill. There I ran into a preoccupied Gino Costanzo, who said to me that Dalla Chiesa's arrival was a disaster because the general was an extremely dangerous man. Their business would be heavily affected. Measures would surely be passed that would force them to close their construction sites and shut down their operations. "What are our Palermitans doing? Sleeping? Don't they realize the situation is serious?" he said excitedly. The extent of his exasperation was obvious from the fact that he said those things to me, who by that time counted for almost zero inside the Cosa Nostra. If he expressed himself in those terms to me, one can only imagine what he was saying to the bosses of the Catania families.

After the death of General Dalla Chiesa a warrant was handed down against Nitto Santapaola accusing him of having participated in the massacre. It had been discovered that the weapons fired on that occasion had been the same ones that killed Alfio Ferlito, Nitto's bitter enemy, a few months before. But Gino Costanzo told my cousin that there weren't any problems for Nitto: at the time of Dalla Chiesa's ambush he had been at La Perla Jonica with the carabinieri colonel Savino. The colonel was living there free of charge, while Santapaola had to pay a ninety-million-lire bill because, according to Gino, it was better to have proof of Nitto's stay. But Santapaola didn't show up before the judges to exhibit his alibi for the night of September 3. He said that it wasn't nec-

*The Italian Social Democratic party (translator's note).

essary and that he would have done it only had he been arrested. He didn't believe there was a need to expose a person like Colonel Savino, and he thought that in any case the trial was going to turn out well for him.

Relations between the Cosa Nostra and the *cavalieri* weren't always peaches and cream. There were moments of friction and danger that were extremely serious for some of the *cavalieri*. From our very close contact we came to know them well, and it wasn't possible to avoid, from time to time, a man of honor nourishing the idea of becoming rich like them, of substituting himself for them, or at least of getting a good deal of money out of them. "Why them and not me? Why should they have all that wealth when I'm basically more powerful than them, when I'm able to do things for them that they'd have difficulties doing for me? And after all, how did they make and keep making that money? Through us, who are satisfied with crumbs, scraps from their table. We have the right to make them give us what we're due." This is what some of us said to ourselves on more than one occasion.

Every mafioso knows perfectly well, when all is said and done, where his power comes from. People are scared of being physically hurt, and, more than that, no one wants to risk being killed. The mafioso, on the other hand, is not scared, is open to risks, and by consequence puts the lives of others at risk.

All this is to say, in short, that at a certain point the idea entered Giuseppe Di Cristina's head to kidnap Gaetano Graci. Di Cristina had spoken on the telephone to his dear friend Totò Greco Cicchiteddu, who had fled to Venezuela, where he was in deep trouble. Cicchiteddu didn't have a lira to his name, while until just a few months earlier he had been one of the most powerful men in Palermo. Di Cristina said that he was deeply saddened by the conversation, that the world was really unfair and something had to be done to rescue Totò from poverty. So he proposed kidnapping Graci to my brother. Pippo told me that he didn't believe Peppe Di Cristina's altruistic motives—Di Cristina hadn't become a convert to the love of one's neighbor, but just wanted to get rich and at the same time insult Francesco Madonia, Graci's protector and Di Cristina's enemy.

Pippo reminded Di Cristina of the absolute prohibition against kidnappings set down by the regional commission, of which Di Cristina himself was a member. Di Cristina replied that they wouldn't violate the ban. They would kidnap Graci outside Sicily, for instance in Rome, where Graci usually stayed at the Hotel Jolly. My brother declared himself absolutely opposed, but Di Cristina didn't immediately abandon the plan. He kept on talking about it for a while, and not always with the most appropriate people. In this respect I remember a meeting I attended, at the Palermo municipal tax collector's offices, during which Di Cristina spoke about the proposal to Ignazio Salvo himself. Salvo didn't bat an eye: not for nothing did he have the reputation of being an imperturbable and inscrutable man. In fact, given that he was a member of a double system of power (the mafia one and the legal one), Ignazio was troubled and worried by such a subversive plan, and he immediately informed Stefano Bontade.

Bontade vigorously protested the foolish and vulgar behavior of Di Cristina, who hadn't thought in the slightest about the fact that he was talking about kidnapping with a man—Ignazio Salvo—whose family had just fallen victim to one.

18

The Salvo cousins were the richest men in Sicily and both were men of honor. They were in a position to control ministers. But today Ignazio Salvo will deny having become a man of honor, and Nino Salvo died after being convicted at the maxi-trial. The Salvos were introduced to me by Gaetano Badalamenti, who was proud of and jealous about their friendship. Badalamenti told Pippo that if he were to introduce the Salvos around as men of honor there would be a parade of people asking favors of them. To tell the truth, a parade is what it was anyway, because their offices and companies were filled with men of honor and the friends and relatives of mafiosi. One time I asked for work on behalf of the Ramacca representative's son, who was hired for five or six months in a tax office or bank in Caltagirone.

The Salvos owned land, immense agricultural enterprises. I visited some of them. In the Gela area they had a mammoth vineyard. They were the first to exploit an EEC law that provided financial incentives for reorganizing viticulture. I think that information about the law was given to them by Salvo Lima, but it was possible that they already knew about it or had people who studied such things for them. It's a fact that the others only started once they learned about it later. For every old plant uprooted, one received, say, fifty thousand lire. And then one planted new vines under cover or against trellises and would receive another fifty thousand. So, what did the Salvos do? They bought a whole estate belonging to monks outside Gela—thousands of hectares that they developed without spending a lira of their own, by using money from banks. Then they took advantage of the EEC law and returned the money they had borrowed. They really knew how to use their money. Just imagine: they diverted a river through the huge vineyard and created six or seven little artificial lakes, then installed gigantic pumps to irrigate the whole vineyard. The lakes were no joke. Nino would drive me around them in a Jeep and boast about the operation, which was the flower in his lapel button. Nor had it cost them anything. In Sicily they say: "Money makes money."

We were closely acquainted, Pippo and I, with the Salvo cousins. We were on familiar and confidential terms with Nino in particular, an open type who liked to joke around, while Ignazio was pensive, taciturn, and reserved. Outside the Cosa Nostra they were powerful and unreachable. But inside we were all equals, and in fact we were in a sense more elevated because Ignazio was merely the vice-representative of a small town, Salemi; I was the vice-representative of a large city, while Pippo was a provincial representative and secretary of the Region. When we met, in fact, they would jokingly greet Pippo as "Mr. President." I had even been to Nino's house in Palermo. It was on a cross street off *via* Liberta, and in the same building in which the Minister of Defense, Mr. Ruffini, resided. He also was an intimate friend of the Salvos. And because Ruffini's guard was always stationed in front of the building's main door, Nino would jokingly rebuke him for forcing him to step over all those policemen every time he came home.

So that the police wouldn't see us when we came to see him, Nino would make us go in through the building's side door, next to the garage, in the section where the Salvos had an apartment in which they hid their secret account books. I once had dinner there, along with a number of other men of honor. It was a luxurious apartment, but refined, very refined. The dinner was served by two black waiters who didn't speak a word of Italian, and we all were impressed by the high standards. Another time my brother and I slept at the Salvos' villa near their inn, the Hotel Zagarella, the same villa in which Tommaso Buscetta hid out for a period of time. That villa was also very luxurious, and it was unusual too:

the beds were set in lower than the floors instead of being raised. But maybe I'm mistakenly thinking of the bathtubs.

The Salvo cousins were also important because of their political connections. We went to them around 1976 or 1977 because an assistant investigator in the Criminalpol was giving us a lot of trouble. Cipolla was the only official in the Catania police department who conducted serious investigations against us. He didn't bear us any personal animosity, he was just doing his duty: he was convinced we were mafiosi. When Pippo was operated on while in jail, Cipolla even had him watched in the hospital. Another time he sent agents to my house to look for me, and then he refused to tell my lawyer whether they were looking for me because of an arrest warrant or merely for a summons to police headquarters. I had to hide out for a few months until the situation was cleared up.

It had become difficult for me and Pippo to live quiet lives while Cipolla remained in the area. We attempted to have him transferred using our Catanian connections, but we didn't manage to. In the end we decided to go to Palermo to ask the Salvos if they could have him transferred. Those were quite different times. Given today's mentality, in such a case one wouldn't act the way we did. An investigator like Cipolla is eliminated and that's that—no wasting of time and money on recommendations and transfers.

We met the Salvos in their offices and explained the problem to them. Their conclusion was succinct: "We need Salvino"—that is, Salvo Lima, the parliamentary deputy. An appointment was fixed at the Rome offices of the Maniglia firm, a large company owned by the Maniglia builders in Palermo that later went bankrupt. Salvo Lima arrived with his already-white hair and his renown as a politician close to the mafia. He listened to us carefully (Nino Salvo was also there) and told us he would take it up with the minister. That was the only time I saw him. The Salvos subsequently passed on to Pippo that the minister of the Interior at the time had replied to Lima that he should just wait a bit since Cipolla would soon be leaving on his own; he had asked for a transfer in order to follow his wife, who was a teacher.

—

There were still other ways to exert influence over the police and the magistrature. One channel that worked very well with judges was Freemasonry. We would seek out contacts with them because we knew that many judges were Masons, and through them we could gather information about our accused men and influence trials. Someone who did this at the Trial of the Hundred Fourteen was Giacomo Vitale, a Mason who was a brother-in-law of Stefano Bontade but not a man of honor. Vitale often went to the Palace of Justice in Palermo with an aged gentleman whom he called "Uncle," a distinguished person who wore a hat and a blue overcoat and was quite intimidating. Vitale would treat him with great deference because he was a high-ranking Mason who enjoyed a great deal of esteem among the judges. They would go to the Palace of Justice building together, and Uncle had access everywhere. He would talk to all the magistrates, even those in the highest positions, and find out how things were going for the mafiosi under trial. I know this for sure because I went with them a few times to try to find out some news about Pippo, and I was present when Uncle came out of a room and told Vitale that things had taken the right direction with respect to Stefano Bontade.

I also met the chief of the Catania Freemasons, a retired major in the Army Engineers who had worked as an engineer in my brother Pippo's company. Whenever an important trial was starting I'd go to him and ask if he knew the judges and if he could plead on behalf of our people. I went to Palermo with him once to speak with the Court of Appeals judge presiding over the trial of Filippo Marchese, a man of honor who later became famous—he dissolved the bodies of the people he had killed in acid—but was a nobody at the time. He had been recommended to me by his family's vice-representative, a good friend of mine. The judge was a Mason himself. Marchese was condemned, but was very lucky. A suspended sentence, I think.

One day I said to the engineer, "Why not bring me into Freemasonry?"

"What are you saying, Antonino?"

"Induct me. I ask you. I really want to be a Mason."

He resisted. My request seemed a bit opportunist to him. At last he replied with a counterquestion: "Think it over. You'd be capable of killing someone?"

"Let me in and we'll talk about it afterward."

He didn't want to tell me outright that my request was impossible because I was a mafioso. And because I was having fun putting him on the spot, he finally said to me: "Listen. We don't want people like you. You're too cunning to be in Freemasonry." It was logical that they wouldn't accept mafiosi. They weren't naïve. They knew very well that a mafioso couldn't betray the Cosa Nostra and would have infiltrated himself into their sect with the sole aim of obtaining benefits for himself and the mafia.

And yet the mafia and Masonry get along with each other. They share a certain logic. In 1977 Stefano Bontade informed Pippo that the Masons wanted to create a union with the mafia. A person in Palermo had asked the Cosa Nostra to enroll its most prominent members into an appropriate reserved lodge whose existence was to remain unknown to ordinary members of Freemasonry itself. Two or three top men from each province were to be chosen and inducted into the lodge. The regional committee discussed the proposal and decided to accept. Stefano Bontade and Michele Greco were to represent Palermo; my brother, Catania; Totò Minore, Trapani; and so on. But it would remain clear which pledge was to come first. Faith to the Cosa Nostra oath was beyond discussion. If it came down to it, Freemasonry would be betrayed on behalf of the mafia and never vice-versa.

Soon after these events the Catania family was dropped, and when my brother asked Stefano Bontade what had happened with this Freemasonry deal he got an evasive reply. Pippo told me he was sure that the whole thing had been thrown out the window and that instead only Bontade and Michele Greco had joined the Freemasons.

How useful it is to have the support of Freemasonry and the mafia is illustrated by the case of Sindona. Who did Sindona turn to when he came to Sicily? He turned to us and to the Masons, although to the ordinary ones. I learned from Francesco Cinardo that Sindona went to Caltanissetta too, where he met a very important lawyer who was also a Mason.

—

There is no one over and above the Cosa Nostra. A third level that hands down orders does not exist. I am certain of this. The Cosa Nostra is autonomous. It is the mafiosi, if anyone, who give orders to politicians, even if indirectly, by pretending to be doing something else. The style is like Michele Greco's, who while in jail blessed the judges at the maxi-trial as well as their families. It was a terrible threat to the judges and their children, and yet it could seem like a benediction.

And it's mafiosi who give out money. How do you think that Pippo could get contracts for his firm as early as 1962? He bought the projects, giving 5 to 10 percent to the regional assessors who distributed them, and 5 percent to the lawyer Carlo Laterza, who acted as middleman. Around the end of the 1950s the Costanzo brothers ran the parliamentary deputy Milazzo's electoral campaign. And they did it through one of their employees, Giovanni Conti, whose sole task was to maintain contact with politicians and to buy projects from them. Graci, on the other hand, relied on a Socialist. I don't know if they were partners.

It's difficult for a politician to become a man of honor. There's a strong sense of diffidence toward them in the Cosa Nostra because they're untrustworthy, they don't keep promises, and they always conduct intrigues. They're people without a word of honor, without principles. This distrust has grown in recent times. In the fifties and sixties it was easier for politicians to be admitted into the mafia. Today it's very difficult, and it's even avoided for fear of repentants. The case is different with a man of honor who at a given point becomes a politician. There are no prohibitions, and in fact it is considered favorable by the Cosa Nostra.

Certainly politicians try to influence the Cosa Nostra, to use it to their party's interests, to strike at rival politicians. It could be that Ciancimino effectively influenced the Corleonesi, but more in the sense of informing them about the position toward the mafia adopted by his party or other parties than because he controlled anyone or imposed his own decisions on them. It's possible that

Ciancimino said, "There's this deputy who's boring everyone because he wants to make a law against associations [mafia associations—P.A.]. He wants to do this and that . . ." Or he could have eliminated someone who was causing him trouble by presenting things in a certain way, by inventing faults or attributing to the person qualities he didn't have.

When there were party meetings at which the political line on the mafia was discussed, someone would always run to the Cosa Nostra bosses immediately afterward to tell them about it. The politicians close to the mafia never did anything but "pump up" the Cosa Nostra bosses against their own colleagues. "You know what this minister said about you? Oooh, terrible things! At least I was there to calm him down, change the subject." "You know what this other one said about your family? Oooh, he hates you. He wants you arrested at all costs." "Watch out because they want to do this." And the mafioso would immediately get angry. "What an idiot! I'll show him, the son of a bitch!"

Or else they play the victim, like that very charming Graziano Verzotto, who told my brother about having been called to Rome by the heads of the Christian Democrats when he was the party's regional secretary in Sicily. "They told me that if I continue being involved with mafiosi they'll throw me out of the party and no longer stand me for elections," Verzotto told Pippo. "They've ordered me to stop seeing Di Cristina, Peppe Russo, and the others. You know what I said to them? I answered, 'If you chase me out of the CD I'll say that Rumore is a pederast, that the Pope's a pederast too, etc.' "

No politician has ever been on the regional commission. The rapport between the mafia and politics has always been close and still is, but a distinction has always been made between who is and who isn't a part of the Cosa Nostra, between those who can say no and those who have to perform a given action. When I was in Sicily a great many politicians were involved with the mafia— deputies, assessors, regional councillors who were helped out by mafiosi, who would ask for binding, weighty favors from men of honor. Normally the mafiosi carried out those favors, but they could also say no with impunity. But when mafiosi asked favors of politicians, there was no choice. They couldn't say no or look for excuses.

Mafiosi have always felt superior to politicians, even those who are friends. Don Paolino Bontade, Stefano's father, once slapped a deputy in public. Agatino Ferlito himself slapped the parliamentary deputy Drago during a Social Democrat assembly in Catania. Drago was always annoying the mafiosi. He slighted the electoral support of Agatino Ferlito and of his group in the SD, when it was well known that Agatino was a mainstay of the party in Catania, someone who controlled thousands of votes. Agatino's only offense had been to bestow his votes upon his nephew Orazio, who was a candidate for the city council, and not on Drago's man.

I know of one case in the sixties when a Palermo mafia boss stopped the regional parliament in Sicily from passing a law. At the time some deputies in the regional assembly were men of honor. These mafioso-deputies rebelled against their families at one point because they didn't want a certain law to pass; they felt that by blocking it they could provoke the fall of the government. But there were other deputies who weren't part of the mafia, were in favor of the measure, and were intending to vote it through. So Salvatore Greco sent one of his men to each of their houses so that they couldn't leave to go vote. And the law didn't pass.

From the 1970s on the regional commission started to indicate which parties to vote for in political elections. It was a guide and not an order because we already knew whom we should and shouldn't vote for. The Cosa Nostra has always opposed the Communist party and the left. It's against anything leftist, even Craxi's Socialists, but not the Social Democrats. They can be voted for and we did so many times. We didn't like the fascists even though some Social Movement deputies were lawyers who represented mafia people. While I was in Catania the instructions were to vote only for centralist parties, the "democratic" parties. There's no need for much explanation because it's logical: the Cosa Nostra grows as long as there's decay. The more decay, the better it is for the Cosa Nostra. If a totalitarian party comes to power, the Cosa Nostra is finished. And which are the totalitarian parties? The

Communists, the Socialists, the Fascists. The Christian Democrats were a democratic party, truly democratic. They'd share power. The mafia could get along with that; it would make it possible to do more. This is second nature to the Cosa Nostra. We've always known that we couldn't get along with the left and that we have nothing in common with the Communists.

Politicians have always sought us out because we can provide votes. To get an idea of how much the mafia counts for in elections, it's enough to think of the family of Santa Maria del Gesù, a family of two hundred active members: a force of terrific importance, especially if it's kept in mind that, between friends and family, each man of honor can muster up forty to fifty other people. There are between fifteen hundred and two thousand men of honor in Palermo province. Multiply that by fifty and you get a nice package of seventy-five thousand to a hundred thousand votes to go to friendly parties and candidates.

Around 1976, Stefano Bontade—the Santa Maria del Gesù family boss—spoke to me about Giuseppe Insalaco, the former Christian Democrat mayor of Palermo who was killed in January 1988. Stefano told me that Insalaco was winning his trust and that he was preparing his electoral campaign. His support for Insalaco was convincing and decisive, and I remember Stefano jokingly saying to me, "I've been reduced to running an electoral campaign for the son of a police inspector!"

Only recently, after 1970–1975, has the Cosa Nostra begun to understand the importance of having men of honor in politics, of using its votes to make them its own representatives—people who don't need to be asked anything because they already know what they should do, people who directly further the interests of the mafia, of the family to which they belong, and who can be candidates in municipal and regional elections, even elections to the national parliament. I had this idea before anyone. Toward the end of the sixties or the beginning of the seventies I intended to declare myself a candidate for the regional council on the Republican Party ticket. I was sure of being elected because the PRI was a small party that we could easily control. I spoke about it to my brother, but then did nothing because in reality I had little time for politics.

My head was filled with Cosa Nostra matters. I couldn't think about anything else.

This episode had nothing to do with the story of the relationship between the deputy Gunnella and Giuseppe Di Cristina. I'm referring to Di Cristina's assumption into the Sicilian Mining Council at the hands of Aristide Gunnella, who was an adviser to the council and a member of the Republican Party. I wanted to be a candidate in the PRI because only a few votes were needed to do it. Mafiosi have never had a particular sympathy for one party over any other. As long as they're centrist, they're all fine.

The example of the Di Cristina family is classic. They had been the mafia bosses in Riesi for three generations. Giuseppe Di Cristina's father was called Francesco: a good, generous man of honor, loved by everyone, who lived the traditional life of the Cosa Nostra. He died a natural death, his funeral was impressive, and the whole town of Riesi mourned him. Guiseppe was named after his mafioso grandfather, and at the beginning he and his brother Antonio supported the Christian Democrats and were CD men. Riesi was a Communist municipality, or rather was very Communist until the Di Cristinas decided to enter active politics. They defeated the Communists and Antonio became Riesi's youngest Christian Democrat mayor. Then he married the Communist ex-mayor's daughter. When the scandal of these mafiosi inside the Sicily CDs broke, Giuseppe Di Cristina was thrown out of his party. He dropped the CD deputy Calogero Volpe and joined Gunnella out of spite, and because Gunnella was introduced to him by the Salvos and the builder Maniglia. It's useless for Gunnella to deny this by saying that Di Cristina was only an employee of the Sicilian Mining Council. They were friends, and Di Cristina gave him and his party some three or four hundred votes in Riesi during the 1968 elections.

I don't know if Gunnella is a man of honor. He was never introduced to me as such. The national politicians, the parliamentary deputies, whom I knew to be men of honor were Concetto Gallo, Calogero Volpe, and another from Agrigento province. Then there was Giuseppe Guttadauro of Palermo, who was a monarchist or liberal deputy but was never particularly active in the Cosa Nostra. He and his brothers were citrus traders who had entered the mafia at a time when a number of people were doing so out of a sense of superiority and to better take care of their own property interests.

My family has supported various candidates in political elections. For a long time we stood behind the deputy Lupis, the Social Democrat I've mentioned a few times. After his death another Social Democrat deputy came to visit me at my house. He wanted to reap the electoral legacy, but it was then assumed by Lupis's personal secretary, Bonomo—of the family's "passport office"— who was a friend of both Nitto and the Cursotis.

The Costanzos would support and give money to every party, but they had a set deputy, the Social Democrat Russo, for whom even we sometimes voted.

19

Around 1973–1974 an unexpected danger appeared on the family's horizon. A series of people, mainly merchants from the city center, started coming to Nitto, Pippo, me, and others to ask for protection. They were very worried because they had begun to receive extortionist phone calls, from persons unknown, demanding a cut. The callers weren't amateurs: some merchants had already suffered attacks and damage to their businesses, and others had been shot in the legs. Everyone asked us to do something, to step in against these people.

The larger number came to Nitto Santapaola, since he was the most prominent among us, and for a time his tactic against the extortionists was the following. He would make sure he was at the business when the calls were supposed to come in, and he would answer them himself. He'd say who he was and ask the extortionists to identify themselves, to make themselves known, to show up so that he could meet their demands. Many dropped out of sight as soon as they heard his name, but others (the more stupid or the more arrogant) would appear and say: "Dear Nitto, we apologize. We didn't know it was something you're interested in, that so-and-so is under your protection, we didn't want . . . In any case, since we know you're involved, we won't do it anymore." And then Nitto would insist: "No, for goodness' sake. Don't talk that way. You asked for money? Then you should take it, because you earned it. You've been smart and brave. My compliments." He'd put money in the pockets of the scoundrels and send them on their way. Then he'd have them killed by his brother or do it himself.

From the start of our conflict with these underworld groups a rift opened between Pippo and me on one side and the Santapaolas on the other. We argued that the strength of the Catania family wasn't comparable to that of the Palermo families. We weren't in a position to defeat the underworld bands that were instilling terror through murders and violence. We needed to come to an agreement with them. Pippo and I had realized that they were in fact too numerous—a crowd of hundreds of kids that had sprung up in little *genghe* [gangs—P.A.] of ten or fifteen youths in every neighborhood and had come together slowly, one by one, and grown into powerful and warlike bands that, all together, were certainly stronger than we were.

There's no question that we were more able, more united, and better organized. But we were still, all said and done, thirty-five men of honor against a force of more than one thousand to fifteen hundred excitable youths capable of swamping us under the weight of their numbers. The Santapaolas thought, on the other hand, that after we had exterminated a good number of them and opposed them step for step in terms of extortion and other things, these delinquents would either flee Catania or come under our control. Besides, Nitto and his brother didn't believe they were so numerous. They thought we were facing a couple of scattered bands that would get frightened and take to their heels as soon as we demonstrated our firepower.

The Santapaolas had grown up in the neighborhood of San Cristoforo and thus were convinced that they knew almost all our opponents. Things, however, stood quite differently. The bands of common criminals came from many outlying neighborhoods other than San Cristoforo. Only the Laudanis and Carcagnusis came from there. The Cursotis, the Pilleras, the Malpassotis, and the Ceusis were based in other areas, even in the hinterlands of Catania province, and some had even developed branches in the North. The Cursotis, for example, had already planted groups in Milan and Turin. Besides, the bands were continually changing because they were always taking on new people. New groups would join the existing stock, and many of them were made up of faces that were completely unknown to us. And thus they had another advantage: they knew who we were because there were few of us and we were known to everyone—clear targets with first and last names. But we didn't know who many of them were.

If there was an attack on us mafiosi, the newspapers would write about it, and the whole underworld would come to know and talk about it. But we didn't know who could have carried one out, we didn't have specific people to identify or come up with ideas about, because we didn't have a complete map of our opponents. We had to fight against an enemy we didn't know. In Torino in the period from 1984 to 1986, I was accused by a certain Parise, one of the common Catanian delinquents. He claimed to know me and said I was a mafioso. But I'd never seen him before and didn't have the least idea who he was. The guy was a professional thief who had seventeen murders to his credit. Though I had lived in Catania since I was born, though I had become a man of honor at twenty-seven, I had never heard a word about him and had never met him.

The bands would work like this. In each neighborhood there were one or two squads of kids who would steal cars, or tires, or car radios. Then the squads grew a bit bigger and started to commit extortions, thefts, murders. These kids gradually specialized, since some of them were smart and determined to carve out a territory for themselves. Later on some of them even became men of honor. And they were very good at stealing. They really knew how to go about it. And when someone knows how to steal, he's ready, he can do anything. It's harder to pull off a theft than a murder. There are at least three or four minutes between entry and exit. One has to know how to move, how to act, how to control oneself perfectly for an extended period of time. A murder takes forty or fifty seconds, a minute at the most: the time it takes to aim, shoot, and leave.

Many among Catania's common delinquents were even able to pull off actions against banks with a guard at the door. One of them would come up to the guard and say to him, "Give me a light?" Meanwhile, the other would put his arm around the guard's neck from the back and relieve him of his pistol.

There was another way the family could have responded to the underworld threat. Some were proposing that we expand, that we too should become a small army of three or four hundred by letting the more dangerous bands into the Cosa Nostra. How, in fact, had they become so large? By taking in whoever showed up—without ceremony, without an initiation, without tests, without researching the blood families they came from. What did it matter to the Carcagnusi or Cursoti bosses if a young thief or robber was the son or close relative of a policeman, if his mother was a prostitute, or if his father or brother had been killed for mafia reasons? They would keep him only if he was smart, aggressive, and able to shoot. And we should do the same.

But it was an idea held by very few and to which almost everyone was opposed. To accept the proposal would mean killing the Cosa Nostra, betraying its spirit, transforming it into a rabble of street hoods without rules and without honor, who join up only when they need to and then return to their own business. Not to even mention the danger of letting in dishonest swindlers, two-bit traitors, or even people who don't understand the fact that we're totally opposed, on principle, to the state, to the justice system, to the police. We don't even denounce someone when he steals something from us. A man of honor cannot set foot in a police station if he hasn't been charged or arrested. There was a long discussion in the Cosa Nostra about reporting stolen cars. In the end it was decided to make an exception and allow men of honor to report them. But not for insurance purposes; it was to prevent the police from blaming people after their cars had been used to commit murders and thefts, and to discourage the Corleonesi's growing habit of masterminding criminal operations to make them look like they'd been committed by someone else.

This was the kind of dilemma that meant nothing to the Catanian underworld, to ordinary thieves and extortionists. I can't even imagine a delinquent from San Cristoforo thinking about such things, posing himself such complex questions. The Cosa Nostra's investigations into the backgrounds of young men who wanted to become men of honor was extremely thorough; we would learn everything about them, even the history of their parents. It even reached a point where Michele and Salvatore Greco were re-proached for the fact that during a trial in the twenties or thirties their father had demanded justice for the murder of his brother! Michele Greco was the subject of discussion on this point around 1975. A man of honor doesn't ask for justice from anyone, much less from the state. He must be able to serve justice on his own, alone.

We couldn't widen the nets and allow people we didn't know, sons of nobody, into the family. The Catanian Cosa Nostra was always something restricted and secretive because it had always upheld a policy of very thorough selection, even more thorough than in the Palermo families, which grew quite large after the seventies. So much so that all the way up until the second half of the seventies the police didn't know that the mafia was in Catania at all.

—

But in the meantime the underworld gangs were growing day by day. The Cursotis had become so numerous that they were ex-porting their handiwork all over Italy and doing things just about everywhere: people would catch a plane in the morning, go to Milan or Bologna, commit a theft, and return home that night. The underworld also had far fewer problems making money than we did. The people in the bands would take whatever they could find. They tilled every field. They organized not only extortions, but even prostitution and loan-sharking. They stole and robbed from whomever they could.

So it was decided to increase our firepower and to make a slight amendment to our policy of not adding to the number of associates in the Catanian Cosa Nostra. Five new members were admitted, chosen from among the best faces in the common underworld. One of these was Salvatore Lanzafame, whom I've already mentioned. The new members accepted the promotion proposed to them after having struggled for a time between the desire to become men of honor and the fear that it was all a trap devised by Nitto Santapaola to kill them. It was my brother's intervention that convinced them there were no tricks, just a recognition of their worth as fighters.

209

The group of five, however, remained very leery of Nitto Santa-paola, all the more so because the strongest and most resourceful of them, Alfio Ferlito, had barely joined the family before he got into a conflict with him. It thus became obvious to all of us that eventually one would kill the other. Besides, Ferlito had no sooner developed a picture of the dispositions inside the regional Cosa Nostra than he joined the Inzerillo-Bontade group, while Nitto was already closely linked with the Greco-Corleonesi one. Their Palermo exponents then began to push—for opposite reasons—Ferlito and Santapaola to eliminate each other.

Overall, the group of five was not a success. It always remained a bit apart, distanced from the rest of the family, and instead of encouraging internal solidarity its presence increased antagonisms. After a short time the five young men realized that we had in a certain sense bluffed them. From outside the family they had thought that we mafiosi were very important men in Catania. Once inside, they realized that we were what we were: no more powerful than the others. They were disappointed.

But what incredible killers! They were all highly experienced in theft and murder. They weren't cowards, and they were precise, prepared. We sent a pair of those young men to kill someone who was in a car filled with women, and he was seated between two of them. The young men went up to the car and shot calmly, without hitting anyone else. They killed, these five, but they were good and high-spirited. They didn't kill out of malice. They killed because they knew that they would die, that they were destined to die.

The young men were born under a bad sign; in fact, all ended up being killed except for one, Turi Pillera, who now commands a formation of four hundred men and has always been miraculously lucky. When he was seventeen the Carcagnusi had laid an ambush for him but didn't manage to eliminate him. They filled him with machine-gun holes, but Pillera didn't die, unlike his father, who was with him at the time. On another occasion, after his entry into the Cosa Nostra, I saw him drive up to me in the countryside, at my brother's house, with his Fiat 126 riddled with bullet holes and a handkerchief around his neck. "They shot at me," he said to me. "They hit me in the neck. The bullet's still inside." I looked at his neck, realized that the projectile hadn't gone in very far, and extracted it with the tip of a knife. I went out and bought some medicine and treated him with antibiotic shots. And he survived for the second time.

But let's look a bit more closely at the makeup of the principal bands. Obviously, I can talk only about the ones I know. We'll start with the Laudanis, who I'm familiar with because their family boss, Sebastiano Laudani, nicknamed *"Mussu i ficurinia"* (Prickly-pear face), lived in my old neighborhood and herded goats. It was a humble occupation, goatherding, but it wasn't the lowest. The lowest was shepherding. There was a distinction between shepherds and goatherds in Catania. The goatherd was considered superior to the shepherd because the latter kept his animals in the country and turned their milk into cheese, while the goatherd kept his goats in the city and sold fresh milk every morning walking around the streets with his animals and stopping for whoever called out to him. Sebastiano Laudani was one of these urban goatherds, and as a child I remember him walking through the streets with his small sons, who would trot behind him along with the goats. The five children all grew up to be criminals. The Laudani family had a great deal of respect for Pippo, and at one point, sometime in the seventies, we even thought of making one of them a man of honor. But then they moved to the city's northern outskirts, broke with us when Nitto decided that we had to come down in force on everyone, and set up a pair of butcher shops and a small neighborhood racket. Later they created a group of their own by allying themselves with a few clans in the area, and they developed into both extortionists and meat traders. Today they control the city's trade in butchered meat and a racket that extends even outside of Catania into several provincial towns.

The Cursotis were called that because they come from *via* Antico Corso, a street outside the center of Catania, and were led by a certain Manfredi, a friend of Nitto Santapaola and a close friend of Aurelio Bonomo, the secretary to the deputy Lupis. The Cursotis were a somewhat unusual group in that they expanded or contracted according to the moment. The members of this band would undertake whatever activity on their own account, independent of all the others, and become a true, proper clan under the command of one recognized boss only under particular circumstances. In these cases—for example, when they had to pull off a large heist—they would even ally themselves with the Carcagnusis, the Laudanis, or others. The heist pulled off, each would return to his own business. We knew the Cursotis well, and we were always careful not to make them men of honor. They were too undisciplined, too loud, a bit unstable. And, in fact, they'd kill one another off every now and then. I read in the newspaper that fifteen of them died last year because of an internal conflict.

The Carcagnusis came from San Cristoforo and were as poor as the Laudanis. The father was a drunk, a good-for-nothing. He was a thief out in the countryside. He tried to give himself the airs of a mafioso and said he knew my uncles, but he was just a pack rat who stole cheese, oil, grain, and a few chickens to feed his children. No one respected him. He wasn't anything, even within his own family. When he saw his father in the distance, one of the sons would call out his name and then shoot him in the buttocks with pellets from an air rifle. The one who really counted in the family was the mother. In the families of many criminals from the outer quarters it was the women, the mothers, who always counted most, especially because they were often the only parents.

The Carcagnusis' mother was also a thief; it was she who organized them, she who pointed them down the road to delinquency. She would send her sons—three kids of fifteen to sixteen years of age—and their friends out to steal. They brought her back the stolen goods, which she would then sell. Or cook, if it was chickens or edible goods. When they grew bigger they started small-scale extortion and stealing more valuable things. One of them set up a small shop to repair Vespas, but it served above all as a place to receive stolen motorcycles and to sell spare parts cannibalized from them. Then they moved on to Fiat 1500s. They became specialists in stealing, dismantling, and then reselling 1500s piece by piece. In Catania in the seventies there existed a very large market in stolen spare parts.

At the beginning of the seventies the Carcagnusis were already a significant presence with a well-defined character. They were the first to shoot people in the legs. They'd put ski masks on and shoot store owners who refused to pay the cut. They grew larger in numbers, and aroung 1970 or 1971 they invited me and Nitto out to the country, to "have a big dinner" with them, and on that occasion they let us see that they had more than forty young men at their disposal.

The invitation was for a banquet organized expressly to show us mafiosi what they had become. The Carcagnusis were still scared of us. They saw us as a model to imitate and as a target to strike, perhaps, in the future. With this invitation they had already taken a big step, and Franco, the clan's eldest brother who came to ask us to the "big dinner," was afraid of being refused, of being snubbed. "Come to our place, in the country around Cardinale, past the highway exit. We'll have fun. Our group has prepared everything. You mustn't refuse. We'd be very happy. You'll offend us if you don't come. . . ."

Nitto turned to me, winked, and said under his breath, "You want to go be the guest of honor? You want to go to the feast of thieves?"

It was thus partly out of curiosity and partly out of compassion that we went. The "big dinner" was held on a somewhat isolated property, and it was a very casual, very simple affair. Up the driveway in front of the farmhouse came, at great speed, one after the other, kids of eighteen to twenty riding Vespas. There was a radio playing at full blast, demijohns filled with wine, and an open fire over which chickens were roasting. Everyone was laughing and joking, many were sitting down on the ground and eating from the dishes with their hands, without utensils, and someone was shooting a few rifle or pistol shots into a tree out front, on the other side of the entryway.

Nitto and I looked at each other and exchanged smiles, as though to confirm to each other that we were thinking the same thing. It was truly a feast of thieves. Everything around us, everything we were using—none of it belonged to the Carcagnusis. The Vespas were stolen, the chickens were stolen, the wine was stolen, the radio had just been stolen, the pistols and rifles were stolen. Even the land on which we found ourselves didn't belong to the Carcagnusis: the watchman on the property was their friend and had allowed them to have their party in the owner's absence. All of it looked like a scene from one of those old movies with gypsies eating a lot and dancing in front of the fire, only in the movies there would be women dancing, and here there were none. After dinner everyone went off to shoot. They set up a tin can as a target and began a contest to see who could shoot the best. They were very bad shots and didn't know how to hold a firearm. We declined to take part in the contest and left immediately afterward.

I saw Franco, the head of the gang, again a few months later. He was now a fugitive. He had urgently asked to see Nitto and me. We found him crying his eyes out. He told us that his father had just died and that he and his family didn't have the money to pay for the funeral. I immediately thought that he wasn't crying for the loss of his father, who hadn't ever meant anything to any of them, but because of the shame of not being able to pay for a proper funeral. And I also thought that he was trying to fool us, in the sense that he did have money for the funeral and was trying to take us for a few lire. In any case, we gave him a hundred thousand lire each to help him in his flight.

———

Nitto's logic was this: "How many of them have we killed up to now? Good. Now we have to kill their sons too, otherwise it'll be their sons who'll kill us." If their sons hadn't done anything to us, we had to find a pretext, some excuse for killing them, as if it were a question of chickens and not human beings with names, families, and houses they went home to at night. And this is how scores of people lost their lives.

Inside a mafia family everyone must be capable of murder, and soldiers carry out the order to kill eagerly because an assassination adds to their reputation, advances their career. While cruelty in the execution of a murder is not particularly appreciated in the Cosa Nostra, a man who is not affected by blood, who manages to remain calm and cool while taking a life, comes to be held in high esteem.

The fact remains, however, that some prove to have a taste for killing and others don't. There are sick people who find pleasure in killing, like Francesco La Rocca, who would turn into an animal every time he took a life. After a murder he would go berserk. He'd kick the corpse and scream like a beast. That was how he'd vent his feelings. La Rocca was truly half-animal. He had lived in the woods for many years because he had been a forest warden. He preferred to strangle people to keep things quiet, and because it was more feral, with the victim struggling and biting and making terrible faces.

I've heard it said that people who commit a murder build up a great amount of rage, of tension, and that afterward they have to discharge it. At such moments they don't think; nothing exists for them. I think that something springs loose inside them, something that gives free rein to the brutality, the bestiality inside us that we hold back in our normal transactions. It's something that not even they can explain, but it happens. And in time murder begins to be pleasing; it becomes a vice, an illness.

Nino Santapaola, Nitto's brother, is the cruelest man I've known. He needed to kill. When someone had to be eliminated he would be the first to step forward, and he had to go immediately. Some said that Nino was crazy, but I don't think he was. Nino Santapaola would become crazy only when he didn't kill. He was impelled by something stronger than him. When I read in novels that an assassin feels a need, that he has to return to the scene of a crime, I believe it. Because I think of Nino Santapaola, who had to kill at all costs, no matter who the victim was, even if afterward he had to find a thousand reasons to justify the perverted, criminal acts he performed, which finally disgusted his brother Salvatore, and even Nitto. Every now and then Nitto would send him off to eliminate someone, but he wasn't pleased by Nino's excesses and a few times reproached him sharply. Nino Santapaola has a scar under his lower lip precisely because Nitto threw an ashtray at him in the course of an argument about the problems he was causing.

Every Saturday night that madman would leave his house to go hunting. He amused himself looking for people to slaughter, and he would drag along with him the first person he found. He was often accompanied by Alfio Amato, another person suffering from the same illness, and a few of his nephews would also go with him, young men of eighteen or twenty whom Nino was teaching to sow death. The parents would feign protests, but deep down they were proud of it, as were the young men.

Every Saturday it was the same story. During the week Nino would get it in his head to rub out a certain person, and he would find out where he went at night. When Saturday came, Nino would get someone to go with him and they'd steal a car that they'd park near the place frequented by the victim. They'd hide and wait until the target showed up and came into their sights. Then they'd shoot and escape in the car, which they'd immediately abandon somewhere. If one looks at the chronology of murders that took place in Catania around 1976 and 1977, one finds that many of them happened on a Saturday. In my house on Sunday morning we'd open the paper and say, "The madman was out working yesterday." We knew some of the assassinated people. My wife knew them, and she'd be angry and frightened every time she read about their deaths. It was then that she started thinking the situation was impossible, and started pushing me toward the decision I later made.

Our family's conflict with the common delinquents was like a godsend to Nino Santapaola. In Catania in those days it could take very little, almost nothing, to die, like that butcher's boy who was in the company of two underworld types one night in 1975. Nino Santapaola and Alfio Amato were going past a café when they saw them. They ran home for their guns, and since the two underworld types were no longer there upon their return, they shot and killed the poor boy.

They say that the mafia has a code of justice. But what sort of code is it that inflicts the death penalty for almost anything, even for minor vices, eccentricities, like that of Nicola Maugeri's brother-in-law, a Peeping Tom knifed to pieces by Nino and his men in Catania's Boschetto section, where pairs of lovers went? Peppe Orazio, on the other hand, was a mechanic who had had a fight with Nino Santapaola. He was executed in his shop by a squad composed of the usual killers who drove up in a Fiat 600. The life of Turi Fabiano, a small-time smuggler, was snuffed out by Nino Santapaola and others in front of another café near the residence of Catania's governor. The police guard in front of the governor's villa hid behind a car to keep from being hit by stray shots. In the same period a fellow nicknamed *"Cola dei Cani"** was killed; his fault was to have been close to the Carcagnusis. He was invited to lunch by Nino Santapaola and Alfio Boccaccini at Salvatore Santapaola's restaurant, La Capricciosa. After they fed him they drove him to the Leutinis', strangled him with steel wire, and threw him down a well. On the *via* Laucatia they killed a greengrocer, who tried to dodge his fate by throwing boxes of vegetables at his assassins. He was throwing boxes while they, with Nino Santapaola in front, shot at him.

An underworld type had been foolish enough to speak ill of Salvatore Tuccio, one of Nino's "hunting partners." The man said he was going to cut off Tuccio's head and hang it up in front of the Bellini villa. Instead it was Nino Santapaola who killed and decapitated him, then placed his head at the base of the Garibaldi monument on *via* Etnea.

Nitto too would commit his murders, many of them. But the difference between him his brother Nino was that Nitto didn't kill out of sickness or amusement, but to eliminate someone with whom he had a conflict, who was annoying him for whatever reason. He was obsessive about it.

I remember a double murder that Nitto committed on February 5, 1975. That day, while driving past a café on the seaside road, he spotted two extortionists of his acquaintance who had tried to take a cut from a company he was protecting. He stopped the car and told the two people with him to wait for him outside and then to follow him, because he was going to get a ride from the extortionists and kill them during the trip. And he did, shooting them in the head from the backseat. That same evening there was a reception at my house. It was the feast of Catania's patron saint,

*"Dog-drowner" in dialect (translator's note).

Agata, and we had invited the families of our brothers and even Nitto's, who arrived all out of breath and went off into another room with my brother. Pippo came out and begged me to go to the piazza Verga with Nitto. I knew nothing of what had just happened and refused because I couldn't abandon my guests. Nitto went off on foot, annoyed, even though there was a driving rain. Pippo later told me about the murders but didn't explain Nitto's reasons for having to go to the piazza so quickly.

Neither Pippo nor I knew about the greater part of the murders committed by the Santapaola brothers. What little I'm telling you is what I found out later. The Santapaolas kept the family in the dark as to their decisions. There was never any discussion with the family leadership. Assassinations of Catania's small-time criminals were decided upon and carried out by whoever felt strongest, and our mistake was to have tolerated this without energetic protests, without trying to lay down the line. But Pippo and I could not, perhaps, have done otherwise because we didn't have a group of highly faithful people prepared to do whatever they were told. We respected the laws of the family, while the Santapaolas were building up a following of people who answered to them alone. Nitto in particular had many young men who followed him. He had established very close relations with Giuseppe Pulvirenti, a member of our family who had at his disposal an additional forty-odd very active people. Although they weren't men of honor, they were entirely available to Nitto. Pippo and I thought we were still strong, because yours truly was the family vice-representative and he was provincial representative, but in reality we were generals without troops, and were under the control of other clans inside the family. Pippo Calderone was the most prominent member of the Catania family, but at a certain point his strength came to depend more on the powerful support he had in Palermo than on his local "patrimony." Once he was abandoned by the Palermitans, killing him was child's play.

When Pippo was elected boss of the regional commission he asked to be allowed to have under his direct command a troop of fifty men of honor that he would have drawn in twos or threes from each family. But everyone replied in unison: "Nooo, it can't be done! Are you joking? You want to have a real army under your command! It's too dangerous." And instead, I think, given how things turned out, that was precisely what the Corleonesi and Michele Greco did after the elimination of Pippo and the decay of the Cosa Nostra.

20

I should continue relating the developments in the Catania family and the Cosa Nostra, but I no longer feel like keeping quiet about the serious crimes that I'm personally responsible for and that I haven't talked about in the first months of my confession. I've said nothing about them, not out of fear of punishment but because I was and am deeply ashamed of them. For my own self-respect I need to tell everything I know, not so much to show others as to show myself that I have recognized my errors.

I'm a believer, and I feel that I can't partake in the sacrament if I haven't paid my debt to earthly justice before atoning to divine justice. I am responsible for seven murders. Whatever the legal consequences of my acts, I feel morally guilty for these crimes, even if I did much to keep them from being more heinously carried out. I'm not asking for anyone's pardon because I don't deserve anyone's pardon. I only hope that after hearing what I say, everyone finally understands who these so-called men of honor really are and what horrors they are capable of.

The first assassination I took part in was that of "*Saro u bau*"*— Saro Grasso, a man of honor in the Catania family who had plotted, along with four others, to overthrow the family leadership and to install himself in power by eliminating my brother, me, and Nitto. He had pulled together a small group; they were going to attack

*"Saro the barker" (translator's note).

221

us with hand grenades. But one of the conspirators, Nino Condorelli, the chauffeur of one of the Costanzo brothers, became frightened by the project and at a certain point went to seek the advice of his father, an old man of honor. His father said: "The plan won't work. Run quickly to tell the Calderones everything, or you're dead!"

Condorelli came to look for me at my service station, but didn't find me because I was out hunting. He waited for me there even though he was a fugitive, and when I returned I found him in tears. I asked him why he was crying. He answered that he was sorry because he was about to betray his friends, and he was also frightened of our reprisal. I told him not to worry about that but to make sure he kept me informed about his companions' movements. The plotters soon abandoned their plan and tried to reestablish themselves in our eyes, but they remained very worried about a possible retaliation on our part. *Saro u bau* fled to Milan with the excuse that he needed "to make a bit of money" and then returned saying that he hadn't been able to find work, while the others stayed on their guard and hoped that in time their disloyalty would be forgotten. Actually, Nitto was continuing to ponder a harsh, exemplary punishment for them.

The chance arose when Giuseppe Madonia, who had just come back from Milan, told us that Saro Grasso had barely escaped being lynched after he had molested a little girl in a movie theater. This information left us perplexed. Madonia had a reputation for exaggerating facts, and he was capable of turning hearsay into an event he'd witnessed with his own eyes, so much so that in Catania he was called "Piddu the Chatterbox." In this case, however, the news was confirmed by someone else, and so Nitto seized the opportunity: the punishment that the Cosa Nostra rules set down for this kind of transgression had to be meted out. I was opposed and told Nitto to let the matter drop. He accused me of defending a shameless person like *Saro u bau,* and I had to give in.

The trick used to eliminate Saro was the usual one. The operation had to involve people Grasso trusted so that he wouldn't suspect anything and the killing would be easier. Nitto approached two of his ex-companions in the plot and revealed our intentions to them.

Salvatore Guarnere and my cousin Salvatore Marchese quickly betrayed their friend and joined us. It was they who would draw the victim out of his house and participate in the whole shameful affair. The pretext we found was that volunteers were needed to pull off a job damaging a property in the countryside; the action was supposedly commissioned by an agricultural concern. In exchange for a few million lire we were to kill some cows, destroy some fields, and burn down some buildings. In reality we were to gather at the country house of a friendly man of honor, Ciccio Cinardo, the Mazzarino representative, and eliminate Grasso there.

The presence of his friends reassured Grasso, who drove to the site of the "job" with them, while Nitto, Cinardo, and I arrived later. We parked the cars at the beginning of a short path that sloped up toward a shack, and there we joined our other accomplices, among them a shepherd from San Cono and Francesco La Rocca, the killer I spoke about earlier. Grasso went up the path with his friends, La Rocca, Nitto, and the others. I stayed below with Cinardo. After a few minutes, the desperate scream let out by Saro Grasso the instant before being strangled and the loud blows of La Rocca venting himself on the body were the signals that the horrible day was over.

The second bloodletting I took an active part in was the murder of two members of the Cursoti group: one of them was nicknamed "Marietto"; the other, "the Scientist." We were convinced that the two had received orders to kill Salvatore Lanzafame, who was already with us at the time, and we figured we'd hit them first. While they were trying to kill Lanzafame, we'd be arranging their own elimination.

One day the two of them showed up at Lanzafame's house, where they found his mother, who told them that they'd surely find him in the next day. So we laid out the whole plan, and the next day Marietto and the Scientist were greeted by Lanzafame and Turi Palermo. Reassured by the fact that their hosts were unarmed and very cordial, the two Cursotis fell into the trap and agreed that they'd all go to have a coffee at the motel at the start of the Palermo highway. To put them even more at ease, Lanzafame and Palermo proposed taking Marietto's car. He climbed in behind the wheel.

The two Cursotis could have thought anything but that this was their last drive. Nothing is more normal than a group of mafiosi or gangsters going off in a car and driving around the city, talking about people and things, stopping every now and then at a café, a shop, or a house. We've always liked driving around.

Turi Palermo climbed in beside Marietto while Lanzafame and the Scientist settled in on the backseat. They began talking about handguns and guns. Then Lanzafame said to Marietto: "I know that you've got a nice pistol. Why don't you give it to me as a present?"

"I'll give you a gift later. I'll give you the pistol afterward," Marietto answered, calm and sybil-like. The idea had already struck him of killing Lanzafame and Palermo the moment they were outside of the car. After all, hadn't they gone to Lanzafame's house with precisely that in mind?

But Turi Palermo absentmindedly pulled out his pistol, showed it to Marietto, and said, "Look at this. You should give him a pistol like this one."

"No! Like this! Like this!" Lanzafame suddenly yelled, shooting from the backseat into the driver's head. Then he immediately turned to the Scientist and said to him, "Don't move or I'll kill you. I don't have anything against you. If you don't move, nothing's going to happen to you." In the meantime, Turi Palermo had gained control of the car and pulled it over to the side of the road. He got out, moved the dead man over into the front passenger seat, and then headed the car back toward us, who were waiting in another car no more than five hundred meters away. When they stopped, the Scientist got out, ran toward me, and clutched me, saying, "Nino, Nino, I want to be with you guys! Take me with you, I'll do whatever you want!" He was torn apart with fright. He seemed like a hunted, wounded animal.

"Yes, yes. Calm down. You'll be okay. Don't worry. Don't think about anything," I replied, inviting him to climb into our car, where Lanzafame and three other people were already seated. And so we headed toward Gela, toward the Mazzarino country house; Turi Palermo followed us in the Fiat 126 with the dead man next to him. It was really something. He was driving on a national highway in broad daylight with a corpse lying back against the seat. To avoid being suspected by truck drivers when they overtook him, Turi Palermo pretended that he was transporting a sick man; he covered the head up with his hand.

During the trip, the people in the car I was driving convinced the Scientist to hand them his pistol. Then we stopped to wait for nightfall at Francesco Cinardo's property. At last we reached Riesi territory. We hadn't told Di Cristina of our presence because, given the friendship between him and my brother, it wasn't necessary. We turned off onto an unpaved road that we drove along at walking pace and with our lights out. The road followed the slope of a valley. I remember seeing lights through the darkness below: a Rendo construction site. There was deep silence, and one could hear noises coming from some nearby livestock pens. The sad procession came to a stop in the courtyard of a large farm. Marietto's body was thrown into a well a little ways off, while the Scientist was strangled by Lanzafame and the others. Up until the end the Scientist kept screaming, insanely, "It's me who's choking you! It's me who's suffocating you!" And so Lanzafame started pummeling him and shouting at him and kicking him until he saw that he was dead. The body of the Scientist was dropped into the same well his friend had been thrown down, and their clothes and papers were burned.

—

What did I feel on these occasions? Nothing. My soul wasn't there. My conscience didn't exist. It was as if the fact of having taken the lives of human beings hadn't happened. The only time I was somewhat affected was when I saw my assassin friends wildly punching and kicking the victim while they were slaughtering him. Remorse came later, very slowly; only then did I begin to feel uneasy.

But the episode of the four little kids was something else entirely, something that turned me inside out immediately, from the very first. It's the worst thing I've done in my life. It's the most shameful thing the mafia has done from the year 1600 to now, since the day it was born. I spent two days and a night talking about it, saying no, continually repeating, "No, no. Let's send them home. Let's send them home." But there was nothing to do about it. The mafiosi, the defenders of the weak, wanted to eliminate them. And I went along with them.

Everything began around five-thirty one morning in 1976. My friend Ciccio Cinardo telephoned to tell me that I had to come pick up a loan, a sum of money I had lent him. "Is this guy crazy?" I immediately thought. "At this time of morning he calls about re-paying money?"

"What are you talking about, Ciccio? What loan?"

"No, friend, no and no," Cinardo insisted. "I don't want your loan, I don't like it. Come take it back." And he hung up.

I got dressed thinking that Ciccio Cinardo must have gone out of his mind. But the event had disturbed me and I decided to talk about it with Pippo, who lived on the same landing. Pippo was still asleep, but he got up and we had coffee together.

"Ciccio isn't crazy. If he spoke like that he had a reason. Maybe he wanted to say something else. Or maybe something bad came up. This is what we'll do. You go down to the office. I'll meet you in a bit, as soon as I'm dressed," Pippo said. I preferred to wait for my brother and so we went down together. In front of the office door we found Nitto Santapaola waiting for us. He had come to tell us what had happened, probably because he too had had a phone call from Cinardo. The night before, his brother Nino and other men from the family had abducted four purse snatchers and had locked them up in a stable in San Cristoforo. Then, that same night, they had brought them to Cinardo's property in Mazzarino because they wanted to kill them. The delinquents were there under the eyes of Pietro Paterno, the San Cono shepherd who had helped us strangle our victims and get rid of their bodies. But the problem was that Ciccio Cinardo was categorically refusing to keep them on his property and in his territory, and it was for that reason that he'd called us.

Pippo reproached Santapaola: "Cinardo was forced to act like that. It stands to reason. You always go *bam-bam-bam,* and then you ask for permission. You couldn't care less about the rules, and Cinardo is tired of your arrogance. What can I say? Go to Cinardo, go to Mazzarino, and talk it over. I can't move because I'm under close surveillance."

Nitto asked me to come along with him, and no sooner did I see Ciccio than I realized that something very serious must have happened. Cinardo was livid, furious: "You get them out of here right now. I don't want to see anyone. I don't want to know anything about this godforsaken business."

Then, noticing that I was looking at him a bit blankly, he turned to me. "Why make that kind of face, Nino? Are you pretending you don't know we're talking about four little kids?" Nitto interrupted and tried to contradict him, but faced with my firm refusal to agree to the elimination of the abductees, and with my subsequent refusal even to go see them, he told us to wait because he wanted to return to Catania and talk once more with my brother. He returned toward evening and told us that the question had been discussed up and down, and that the kids could be killed. They were guilty of having robbed and beaten his mother, who had fallen down and broken her arm.

I know these situations, and I know how easy it is to make a mistake identifying those responsible, how many errors can be made. San Cristoforo was full of little kids who stole, snatched purses, broke windows, hung around the post office and waited for poor pensioners to come out so they could grab the few lire they had just collected. Poor old people were thrown to the ground and reported fractures and cuts during robberies. But these little criminals were like bees. There were swarms of them on the streets. Had it been precisely these kids? And did they realize that they were robbing the Santapaolas' mother? Did they know what they were doing? And even if they did know, was that sufficient reason to kill them? Does one kill a child of thirteen for that?

Ciccio Cinardo held his ground firmly: "If you want to throw me out of the Cosa Nostra, do it. Try it, do what you want. But I'm not budging an inch."

Nitto looked at me and asked, "You don't want to do it either, right? You won't agree to lend a hand to punish these little shits?"

"No. I've already told you. I think we should let them go."

"Fine, I don't give a fuck," Nitto answered. "I'll go against everyone, but I'll do it myself. So this is what I'll do. There's a cattle trough near where they're locked up. Tonight I'll take them there and cut their throats. Afterward I'll throw a few necklaces and some gold jewelry around to make it look like petty thieves someone caught and punished."

"So you're absolutely set on killing them. But if you bring them to the cattle trough you'll be running a huge risk. Even if they're little, there are still four of them, and one could get away from you. And you could also run into someone while bringing them there or cutting their throats." I spoke to him in a conciliatory tone of voice, because I wanted more time to think of a way to save the kids' lives.

"I don't care about the risks. They have to die. I'll kill them whatever the cost."

"At least wait until we hear Di Cristina's opinion. We're on his territory and we have to ask permission."

While we were talking, Salvatore Santapaola, the owner of the rotisserie on the piazza San Cristoforo, left the group and went out alone to his car. In his trunk he had pans filled with baked pasta, roasted meat, and other foods, which he carried into the stable on Cinardo's farm where the little kids were locked up. When the stable door opened and the little kids saw Salvatore Santapaola with the pans in his arms, their faces lit up. They had been seized by hostile strangers, brought to a place they didn't recognize but was surely isolated and remote, and left there for two days without food. They had cried a lot and were filled with anxiety and terror.

"Uncle Turi! Uncle Turi from the Capricciosa!" the poor little kids shouted out, heartened, as if they'd seen their father. At last a familiar face that was even bringing them food! So that meant they weren't lost, that they'd be safe!

But Turi Santapaola came back to us and said brusquely: "Nothing more can be done. They recognized me. At this point we absolutely have to kill them."

See how evil these people are? Turi Santapaola hadn't gone to the kids because he was bothered by the fact that they were hungry, but with the aim of forcing us to eliminate them.

I was furious and asked Santapaola, "Why did you have to go into the stable and let yourself be recognized?"

"I had to bring them something to eat. They hadn't had anything for two days."

"But if you mean to kill them, what sense is there in giving them something to eat?"

No reply. I tried again with another suggestion. "Listen. We'll give them each a hundred thousand lire. We'll tell them we abducted them to make them unload cigarettes for us, but then the boat didn't show up. And so we're letting them go home. Since they know who we are, they'll never give us any trouble. They're just children of twelve or thirteen."

"No. We have to kill them." Nitto and his men were implacable.

The way I see it, a lack of respect toward their mother wasn't the real reason for the Santapaolas' fury against the abducted kids. It was an accumulated resentment, a desire to vent their anger and avenge themselves; it had to do with the Santapaola family's tenuous reputation in the San Cristoforo neighborhood. Not every member of the family was in fact feared and respected like Nitto. Many of them were wretched people who were made fun of for their poverty. Turi Santapaola in particular was an object of scorn on the part of the young people in the neighborhood because he was vulgar, dirty, clumsy. Turi was a man in his fifties, a mafioso, who would make raspberries and things like that in front of everyone, and then he expected to be looked up to. But instead the young people of San Cristoforo would treat him for what he was, would bait him constantly, returning his raspberries and throwing firecrackers and stink bombs into his rotisserie.

Nitto was aware of his brother's and his other relatives' defects, but this served only to sharpen his hypersensitivity toward whoever offended his family's name. Only one maternal uncle of theirs had been a man of honor who played with a complete deck. But he died young, and the Santapaola brothers grew up in the shadow of his renown, since their father was a nonentity everyone referred to as "the bore." And they had also been very poor, so much so that Nitto had even been sent to a seminary for some time so that he could keep studying.

For these reasons the abduction of the little kids was something that had been planned for a long time, and the robbery from their mother was merely the pretext that the brothers—and above all Turi—used to make the coiled spring of revenge against San Cristoforo go off inside Nitto.

My opposition to eliminating the hostages resulted in a request for authorization from Giuseppe Di Cristina, in whose jurisdiction we were. It was Pippo who had recommended that I ask the Santapaolas to make the execution of the little kids dependent on Di Cristina's assent. I went to Riesi with Cinardo and there found Di Cristina in the company of Luigi Annaloro, the Riesi district boss, who had already been informed by Cinardo and had even gone to the stable to assess the situation. Annaloro too declared that he was firmly against killing the kids, and told Di Cristina that one of them was only twelve, the age of Di Cristina's own young son.

But, having heard out all the parties, Di Cristina gave his definite consent to the execution. There was nothing left to do. After the declaration by Di Cristina, who was the provincial representative, any other attempt at dissuasion would have been useless. I didn't want to do it, believe me. I'm not saying that to justify myself, since I was more guilty than the others. But I absolutely didn't want to do it.

Night fell, and a few of them telephoned Catania for other men of honor to come lend a hand in the massacre. I'll never forget the caravan of four cars that pulled up in the dead of night to take the little kids away. Two of them rode in my car, and one of them was so small that he was almost invisible behind the seat. Their lives came to an end in the same place the bodies of Marietto, "the Scientist," and *Saro u bau* had been dumped. They were strangled, and my cousin Marchese told me that he had been in so much anguish carrying out the order that he hadn't had the heart to squeeze the rope fully around the neck of one of them, who was thus still alive when he was thrown into the well.

During the execution I stayed in the car, waiting with the windows rolled up so that I wouldn't hear anything. One of my killer colleagues came up to my door all excited and called in to me, "You're not coming? You're not coming to watch?"

———

Can someone tell me if there are judges capable of judging us? Wouldn't someone be doing something very just, very laudable, if they were to shoot and kill me as soon as I left this room? How could I have stayed inside that cursed organization? And yet I stayed for a number of years more with this wound, this weight inside me that's still there and will always be. That's why I'm ashamed every time I go into a church. Because I can't raise my eyes.

———

The killing of the four little children was briefly discussed during an ensuing meeting of the regional commission. Bontade berated all of us Catanians, but especially Nitto and his brothers, for the disproportion between the accusation against the victims and the punishment inflicted on them; he didn't forget to mention that they had been very young, practically children. Nitto raised a few weak words in his own defense, saying that they weren't that young, they were nearly adults. No other members of the commission had any reproaches to make. It was, in sum, a normal administrative action that didn't cause a big to-do, and the discussion moved on to other topics. The press and the police, for their part, didn't make much of a fuss about the disappearance of the four children. They thought it was the usual story: wild young people who had run away from home. Their families were also very humble, and the whole business was quickly forgotten.

21

The Santapaolas' tactic of exterminating common delinquents ended up provoking a revolt against us by the bands of the Catania underworld, which formed a coalition to fight us more effectively. The little neighborhood squads had in the meanwhile become small forces of three to four hundred men each. Thus a full-blown war broke out. Toward the end of 1976 it became clear that they had the upper hand and that it would be better for us to go away for a while to ease the tension. We all left Catania: Pippo, me, the Santapaolas, everyone.

As far as I was concerned there was another reason to leave. The police had started to become interested in me and, using various pretexts, kept me under constant surveillance. In reality it was the inspector Cipolla who was after me. He was convinced that I was a mafioso and that the mafia was in Catania, while the other leaders in the police and the carabinieri, even the magistrates, thought otherwise. Cipolla wanted to take away my gun license, and in any case didn't allow me to renew it, even though I had a good reason to have it due to the large sums of money I carried around from managing the heating-oil distributorship.

And so I went to Palermo, where my friend Salvatore Rinella had put a seaside villa at my disposal, and where a short time later I was joined by my wife and children. We spent the Christmas and New Year of 1976 at Stefano Bontade's house. It was very nice. A number of families gathered together, all of them belonging to men of honor and close friends: more than fifty people, with children playing and jumping around all over the place. Pippo came with his wife and children, Stefano's brother and sister with their families, as well as Mimmo Teresi and "Tweezers" and his wife ("Tweezers" was Totuccio Federico, who later disappeared). There were also other friends and relatives of Stefano's who lived in Santa Maria del Gesù. We were a carefree group filled with life and joy.

Stefano's house was a villa that had a huge underground room with a kitchen, a stove, and a long mahogany table where we ate, played cards, and had fun all night long. One of the most popular games was called The Plate. Everyone put up an ante to create a bank of 200,000 to 300,000 lire, then each person staked a sum of money: if one drew a card less than a six, one lost, and if greater, one recouped one's bet from the pile. If one drew an ace, one paid double, and if a king, one drew double. Even the women and children played. There was great excitement whenever someone put down a big stake, and a burst of talk and laughter when the cards were dealt. At various points there was a bank of 10 to 20 million lire because of everyone drawing negative cards, but there were a few who played for high stakes. Stefano Bontade would put up huge sums—he wasn't scared of taking risks—and if he lost 10 million in one hand he would get it back sooner or later, by continuing to take risks. There were no great winners because in the end everything came out even, and I would stake only 20,000 or 30,000 at a time since I wasn't interested in winning or losing. I liked the atmosphere of the game, and the delight that arose in the circle of players.

At midnight we sat down around the table and ate the food the guests had prepared. The men cooked, as is the custom at mafia banquets. Some of them were excellent chefs, and the best of them all was Giambattista Pullara, who was able to produce truly exquisite foods: lamb, kid, mutton, desserts, etc. We ate and laughed into the morning. No one thought about danger and death.

In the spring of 1977 we went to Naples for another celebration. Ciro Mazzarella had asked Pippo to be his son's godfather. The war was still raging in Catania and it was better to stay far away, to let ourselves be forgotten. The Neapolitans were perfect for us. We Sicilians arrived with our families in two brand-new luxury cars. One of them, a Mercedes, had been a gift to my brother from Ciro Mazzarella himself, who had just pulled off an enormous swindle—four billion lire—from the agents of the cigarette companies (the large companies, the ones with their names on the packs). The agents were furious. They had already sent a group of delinquents to kill Mazzarella. But he had been cleverer and had hit them in time; his men eliminated them. The swindle had, however, caused much grumbling among the other men of honor because the companies no longer wanted to sell to the Italians. Everyone was hurt and was trying to claim compensation from Mazzarella. Since my brother was the commission boss, he more than anyone else was expected to straighten out the situation. Hence the attack of generosity, and the Mercedes, from Ciro Mazzarella.

The celebration was a very big deal. There were more than four hundred guests. Giuseppe Di Cristina and my friend Francesco Cinardo also showed up from Sicily, and almost the whole Naples family was there. Only the Nuvolettas and Michele Zaza were missing, but Salvatore Zaza, Michele's brother, was there. The feast lasted twenty hours. The church ceremony was in the afternoon, and then we went to a large restaurant in Posillipo, where we stayed until nearly mid-morning on the following day. We ate until we couldn't eat anything more, and we listened to music. There wasn't any dancing. We just ate and listened to the succession of singers and orchestras. The best singers in Naples were there: Anna Luce, Peppino Di Capri, Mario Merola, and others. Each of them would come into the room, greet the guests, and receive a great round of applause, then perform for an hour or two and leave. Then there would be a break, we would have a gelato or sweets, wait for a few hours, and then start all over again.

We Sicilians would also entertain ourselves in the same way. We wouldn't go overboard like the Neapolitans, but we organized huge events as well. I remember the party for the baptism of Stefano Bontade's son, and for that of his brother Giovanni's daughter. On those occasions Mario Merola and Peppino Di Capri came too. We gathered at a seaside restaurant near Palermo. The Neapolitan singers would come expressly for parties thrown by the Cosa Nostra bosses—the Inzerillos, the Bontades, and so on. The baptism of the little Bontade was attended by Franco Franchi as well, who was a close friend of Mario Merola. Franchi and Merola acted out a scene from a play: Franchi played the role of the mother and wrapped a shawl around his head, and Merola knelt down at his feet, making us all laugh to the point of tears.

After the Neapolitans' giant party we didn't go back to Sicily. Mazzarella was so insistent we stay for a few more days that he ended up convincing us. He brought us to the Barra district in Naples, where he introduced us to a prominent camorrist, a builder, who didn't belong to the family. The man invited us to dinner at a tavern that in reality wasn't a tavern but quite an elegant place, and he too asked us to stay in Naples.

"I asked my friends here to stay, but they won't hear of it," Ciro Mazzarella said.

We tried to slip out of it: "How can we stay? It's too complicated. We're with our families, our children. . . . We'd have to find a house. . . ."

"The house isn't a problem. I have a villa in Ischia that's at your disposal. You can stay here for as long as you like. You have no excuses left!"

Pippo and I looked at each other and decided to stay. The next day we and our families moved into the villa, where we lived for almost three months. It was a huge building with three stories. The ground floor was entirely ours, and the others belonged to the camorrist builder's family, who came for the summer. Pippo traveled to and from Catania, where the conflict with the underworld was blazing away, and I stayed at Lacco Ameno in Ischia, going for walks, doing crossword puzzles, and poking around in shops, where no one asked me to pay out of respect for our host, who was called "O Schiavone," Umberto Schiavone. What a life! What entertainment! But every afternoon the Sicilian Gazette on the radio would bring terrible news . . .

During the stay in Ischia two things occurred that made me very uneasy. One of them was a premonition of events that would, very soon, upend the Cosa Nostra and my life.

The first episode could seem a bit irrelevant, and in fact it was, or rather would have been under normal conditions. I was with Pippo on the villa's veranda one day when Ciro Mazzarella told us that Michele Zaza and Mario Merola were staking large sums of money playing cards at Lacco Ameno's Hotel Regina. My brother continued the conversation, but I was intrigued by the news and went off to watch the game. At its conclusion Zaza came to the villa with me to say hello to Pippo, who greeted him with a strong reprimand, chastising him for the vice of gambling, deploring the fact that he was putting such high sums at risk, and warning him against following the example of "that druggie," his friend Alfredo Bono, a large-scale trafficker who lived in Milan.

Zaza didn't reply. He took his licks, mumbled a few words of apology, and left. I didn't feel good about it, and immediately told Pippo that it hadn't been wise, his position as commission boss notwithstanding, to make such serious accusations about Bono, to whom Zaza would certainly relay them. My brother repeated that that sort of gambling didn't suit men of honor, but the episode still left me with a vague sense of uneasiness, as if something threatening had been set in motion against us.

The second episode was much more significant. When Gerlando Alberti was released from internal exile and came to Naples, a banquet to celebrate his arrival was held at the restaurant Il Cafone. Since I was in Lacco Ameno, I went to Naples to take part in the dinner, where a few other Sicilian men of honor were also present. I took a seat next to Ciro Mazzarella, and after the toast, Pippo Ferrera, one of the Cavadduzzi, who was in Naples for smuggling purposes, proceeded to cut and distribute pieces of cake. When he reached me he ostentatiously neglected to serve me and moved on to my neighbor. Ciro Mazzarella stood up immediately and re-proved Ferrera sharply for the slight. Ferrera denied any ill will on his part and raised the feeble excuse that he thought I had already been given cake.

The event seemed serious to me because at that time I was vice-representative of the Catania family and Ferrera had allowed himself to express scorn toward me, and in the presence of people who didn't belong to the family. I thought about the matter again and again, and at last, when I was back in Catania, I expressed all my worries to Pippo, who shared my assessment that danger was hanging over us. In the meantime, taking advantage of a good deal, I had acquired an armored automobile in Naples.

22

On August 18, 1977, my son turned two and we were once again in Lacco Ameno. We had barely returned to Sicily when, a few days later, the carabinieri colonel Giuseppe Russo was assassinated in Corleone territory. For my brother it was a cold shower. A prominent member of the forces of law and order had been killed without him—the secretary in charge of the regional commission—knowing anything about it. It was unthinkable that a colonel of the carabinieri could have been killed by a run-of-the-mill shepherd: the execution bore the unequivocal stamp of the Cosa Nostra and had taken place in the jurisdiction of the Corleonesi. Over the preceding days and weeks there hadn't been any warning, any word, talk, or allusion that could have foreshadowed such an important event. Pippo knew that his authority had suffered a mortal blow, and with it all the work patching up the Cosa Nostra that he had undertaken three years before. What was the interprovincial commission for, what were the statutes for, if afterward nothing was changed, and the most important decisions were still taken inside individual families or internal cliques without anyone being notified?

As was to be expected, there was an immediate deluge of protests from every part of the island. There was a general heightening of defenses. Everyone was saying that the Palermitans had once again lied. After *viale* Lazio they had pretended to accept a more "democratic" leadership in the Cosa Nostra, but only in order to gain

239

time to reorganize and gird themselves to return to the old habit of doing things alone, to tend only to their own interests without heeding the damage they could cause others. What did it matter to the Corleonesi or the Grecos if, the day after the murder of a state authority, the police started arresting and jailing men of honor all over Sicily—people who didn't know about it, who left their houses in the morning and were caught at a roadblock, or were seized without having had the time to save themselves, to watch out, to establish alibis for the day of the murder?

Many mafia bosses came to Pippo, furious about the sudden wrong that had been done to them and troubled about the consequences of the unexpected move. "We have to be informed before certain things happen," many of them objected. "It's our right. Seeing that we created the commission, we should discuss everything together. We can decide whatever, but we must know if we're facing arrests, trials, orders for imprisonment. If someone acts on his own and doesn't warn anyone, then he has to pay. We must establish the principle that anyone who slips on this point has to pay."

Giuseppe Di Cristina came too, in the company of Francesco Cinardo. The first thing he asked Pippo was: "Who did this? Who decided it?" My brother answered that he didn't have a clue, but that he thought an explanation should immediately be asked of the Palermo people; a meeting of the regional commission should be called. Di Cristina told him that he was in favor of it. Cinardo and I were thus set to inform Michele Greco of the meeting's time and place, and to get him to furnish any useful information about the elimination of Colonel Russo.

We went to the Favarella property, and Michele Greco offered us coffee in the parlor, where there was a writing table whose upper surface was inlaid with twenty-centime coins. It was the same table I later described to the judges to refute Greco's claim that he had never laid eyes on me.

"We've been sent by Pippo and Giuseppe Di Cristina. We want to find out about this Colonel Russo matter."

"Bah! It was probably an act of bravado. Something done by people we don't know."

It was obvious that he was hiding something. We informed him that the meeting would be held in Falconara, at Antonio Ferro's farm, and we went away. Di Cristina and my brother agreed on a course of action. The official request for an explanation of the incident would be made by Di Cristina, and Pippo would step in only if necessary.

But on the day set for the meeting, Di Cristina was late, and Pippo had to speak in his place. Michele Greco replied: "I asked for information from Totuccio Riina because the murder took place on Corleone territory, and he answered that when a cop is killed there's no need to ask permission." It was a useless reply, evasive, almost provocative. But no one objected. Only Di Cristina—who showed up three hours later because, he said, his town was surrounded by carabinieri roadblocks—thought of insisting to Michele Greco, in private after the meeting was over, that he reveal the reason for the colonel's killing. Greco answered that the carabinieri officer had tortured Franco Scrima, a Palermo man of honor, while he was in a holding cell. He'd twisted his testicles and had started asking about the kidnappers of Luigi Corleo, Nino Salvo's father-in-law. At that point Di Cristina accused him of letting himself be manipulated like a puppet by Totò Riina. Michele Greco didn't respond. He remained silent and then left.

A few days later two men in Riesi lost their lives during an attack whose real target was Giuseppe Di Cristina. It happened like this. Every morning Di Cristina would commute to work at the Sochimisi—the group in the Sicilian Mining Commission, where Gunnella had given him a job—with a couple of colleagues who would pick him up in front of his house. But on the day of the attack he had an appointment with me, Pippo, and Cinardo. We were in his villa when the two employees drove by, and Di Cristina told them that he wasn't going to work, or that he'd get there on his own later. I remember one of the two employees, the one who was driving. He was wearing a little beret and looked just like Di Cristina. A half hour later someone arrived and said, "The two men you were meant to go with are dead. Someone got them into some kind of accident and killed them."

Di Cristina reacted immediately, setting up a meeting with the

Palermitans and sending word to Michele Greco that his attendance was imperative. The meeting took place in Riesi, on the Salvo cousins' large estate, because for reasons of personal security Di Cristina didn't want to leave his own territory. Various prominent mafiosi arrived, among them Stefano Bontade, but Greco didn't show up. The attack was still "hot," and it wasn't wise for him to venture out as far as Caltanissetta. Bontade said, "Michele Greco couldn't come and asked me to stand in for him."

The session opened with a statement by Di Cristina: "I've called this meeting, and I sent for Michele Greco because I wanted to say that I'm speaking from among the dead. A dead man is talking. I would have been dead. And now I want to know why on earth I was attacked. Why was I attacked? Why did they want to kill me? Can someone tell me why I've been condemned to death?"

"Michele Greco came to me," answered Stefano Bontade, "to ask me why you called this meeting. He told me he doesn't know anything about the attack, that perhaps it was the Cursotis who did it. It could be that they have it in for you."

If there was any need for proof of Michele Greco's responsibility for the attack (and there wasn't), this stupid justification was it. The Cursotis were from Catania and had nothing to do with Caltanissetta or Riesi. They were at war with us, not Di Cristina, who didn't even know them. Nor were the Cursotis men of honor, and this meant they couldn't have been even indirectly involved in our disputes. Michele Greco's assertion thus meant something else. Everyone understood that it was a provocation, a barely disguised challenge.

The internal relations in the Catania family were in the meantime deteriorating in an ever-more disturbing way. Nitto was becoming stronger by the day, allying himself more and more closely with the Corleonesi and the Grecos. The war against the common underworld was continuing, even if after our return from Naples things had begun to get better for us, given that the opposing front was no longer as solid as it had been before. Some groups, like the Malpassotis and the Cursotis, had dissociated themselves from the antimafia alliance and had become less hostile. But then the inclusion of the group of five into the family constituted another big problem, because Alfio Ferlito didn't accept the authority of Nitto Santapaola, was very touchy, and argued with others about anything and everything.

It was Ferlito himself who furnished one of the pretexts that led to the family's disintegration. Nino Santapaola, Ferlito, Romeo, and Alfio Boccaccini were in Sant'Agata Li Battiati for one of the usual death missions. They were armed with carbines, pistols, and machine guns. During the wait for the target Ferlito fell asleep. When the doomed victim arrived he woke up with a start and instinctively fired off a machine-gun burst, which hit the target but also struck Boccaccini. Before dying the victim managed to return fire and hit Alfio Ferlito. The two wounded men were brought back to Catania by the other two killers, who called for Pippo's help and advice. My brother couldn't leave his house at night because of police surveillance, so he replied that there was nothing he could do. Given that the two were both in serious condition, he told them to take the wounded men to the hospital. In fact, it was the only thing that could be done. We had few reliable doctors at our disposal, and the two could only be taken care of in a hospital since they were nearly dead.

Boccaccini died a week later because a bullet fragment had cut his spinal cord, while Ferlito survived and managed to escape from the hospital with Nitto Santapaola's help. I remember the episode very well because on that very day I was in Palermo—substituting for Pippo, who because of the surveillance couldn't move—at the marriage of Salvatore "the Senator" Greco's daughter to a man of honor named Giovanni Scaduto. It was a magnificent ceremony, with all the Cosa Nostra luminaries (except, of course, the ones in jail and the fugitives) standing side by side with all of "good" Palermo, the elegant society the mafia has always admired and protected.

This fact aroused the resentment of Ferlito and the group of five against my brother, who was accused of not caring about the fate of two soldiers wounded in the line of duty. Nitto fanned the fires of protest and agreed that the limit had now been reached: the Catania family was ungovernable and needed a general overhaul before the regional commission. The request was not very orthodox and Pippo was puzzled. What did the Region have to do with Catania's internal disputes? Did Alfio Ferlito realize that Nitto was supporting him out of opportunism merely to annoy us, to break off with us?

But Giuseppe Di Cristina convinced him not to oppose the request, especially since he himself had another claim that was as anomalous if not even more so. He wanted the whole Catania family, excluding no one, at the meeting. He had conducted an extensive investigation into the attack on him, interrogating a number of witnesses, including a few peasants, who had told him that one of the two assassins had been hurt in the shoulder in the collision with the victims' car. The wound was serious, so much so that the other killer alone had done the shooting. Since Di Cristina suspected that someone from the Catania family had helped Michele Greco out in the executive phase of the operation, he intended to find out if one of the men of honor might show up at the meeting with signs of a wound or fracture in the shoulder or arm. Pippo consented, and fixed the meeting in Bagheria, at the villa of Prince Vanni Calvello, a man of honor in the Alia family and a business partner of Michele Greco's son. Alexandre Vanni Calvello is the same person who hosted the queen of England at his Palermo palazzo during her last trip to Italy in 1984, a few weeks before he was arrested.

I had once spent a couple of nights at the Bagheria villa, where the group meeting of the Catania family and the regional commission took place. The prince took care of security for the session, greeting everyone at the front door and searching them according to the usual protocol at mafia meetings. Di Cristina watched restlessly as each person arrived, and when he saw Nicola Maugeri with one arm in a cast he asked him sharply, "How did that happen?" "Ah!" Maugeri said, "I fell down some stairs." Pippo went up to Di Cristina and made an imperceptible gesture to him that he should stay calm. There would be time and the right occasion to look into it. The ideal would have been to bring in the witnesses to the attack and show the suspect to them, but they were ordinary people who couldn't be admitted into a meeting of men of honor.

The meeting opened with a series of accusations against us Cal-derones. Alfio Ferlito accused my brother of not having had him taken care of clandestinely after the Sant'Agata Li Battiati attack, and of having exposed him, by forcing him into the hospital, to serious criminal charges. Nitto reproached me for not having gone with him to piazza Verga the year before, on the night of the feast of Sant'Agata, after he had killed the two extortionists, and he claimed that I hedged and made myself scarce every time guns had to be used. I retorted that it was better to hedge if acts of war consisted of strangling little kids.

"Fine. Seeing that it's impossible to reason here, I don't want to be in the family anymore," Nitto pressed. "I want to be let go. The family isn't working anymore, and I don't feel bound by any of its decisions."

Michele Greco stepped in at this point and said: "Listen to me, everyone. Do we want to settle these disputes once and for all? Let's dig a huge hole and bury all our disagreements inside. Let's try to forget everything, and let's leave here after we all trust one another again and have shaken hands." Nitto and Alfio Ferlito shook their heads, disapproving of the proposal. Michele Greco then saw the opening and declared, "Do you know what you're saying, then? Saying there's no possibility you'll come to an agreement, the only thing to do is dissolve the family. We'll set up a three-man regency until you're prepared to take care of your own affairs. After you've made peace, we'll reconstitute the family."

I knew that it was a comedy, a scene previously staged by Greco and Nitto Santapaola to reach this very point, this base violation of the Cosa Nostra's rules. A family can be dissolved only by its immediately superior authorities, that is, by the district boss or regional representative. The process is calm and orderly. Michele Greco meant nothing, in these terms, to the Catania family. In that he was the representative of another province he had no power over us. The boss of Catania province was my brother, who was also secretary of the regional commission. Because we didn't have a district boss, only he could make the decision to dissolve our family. Michele Greco's role in the meeting was that of peacemaker, mediator; he had no rights or power over us and our family.

Nitto changed his tone and consented to Greco's illegal decision, even claiming (hypocritically) that he didn't want to be given any higher rank. Pippo and Stefano Bontade also took Nitto's position, which made me shake with fury. They hadn't realized, the two big bosses, where it was all leading: to the automatic withdrawal of every office my brother held, beginning with that of regional representative.

And so it happened. Pippo was deposed, as was the provincial vice-representative, Calogero Conti.

Afterward I protested to Stefano Bontade, asking him why on earth Michele Greco had been allowed to be so arrogant, and stating once more that only Pippo, as the provincial representative, had the ability to dissolve the family. He answered that it wasn't a question of arrogance, since it was precisely Pippo's behavior that had been under discussion, and thus it wouldn't be right if he, as a claimant in the suit, sat in judgment of himself.

In any case, a council made up of my brother, Nitto, and the old Adelino Florio was constituted. Nitto kept up the pantomime of feigning reluctance to accept any appointment, and it was established that until there was a new round of regional offices, relations with the regional commission would be maintained by Giovannino Mongiovì, the boss of the neighboring province of Enna.

—

I was arrested on January 21, 1978. I was coming back to Catania from the house in Monterosso Etneo, where for a few days I had hosted a fugitive, a young man from Palermo who had arrived in Catania with my cousin Marchese. I was bringing him back to Catania to arrange, through the family, some kind of work for him. A few kilometers away from the village where we'd hidden Luciano Liggio years before, we passed an Alfa Romeo Giulia with a big antenna on the back that was going the other way. The young man sitting next to me saw it and said, "Aren't those guys cops?"

"It's a yellow Giulia. If they're cops, they're from the Finance Guard," I replied, looking back through the rearview mirror and noticing that the Alfa Romeo had turned around and was now following us at a certain distance.

Before entering the next village I swerved sharply onto a country road that should have brought us to its other side. But I unexpectedly found myself heading toward none other than the yellow Giulia, which was sideways to us and blocking the road. I braked quickly and saw the doors of the car in front of us open; two men armed with machine guns and pistols got out and immediately started shooting at us. My car's windshield turned white from the bullets striking the glass, and bullets were hitting the sides of the car and the passenger windows too. But nothing shattered and we were unhurt because the car was very well armored.

"Hands up!" the two men shouted.

I didn't believe it was the police. I thought it was someone's setup to kill us. Then I saw that they were flashing their badges and I breathed a sigh of relief. My companion and I climbed out of the car and immediately obeyed their command to lie back flat on the ground with our arms outstretched. They kicked us in the side, searched us, and asked us our names. When I told them mine they replied, "Ah, Calderone! Great. End of the road. You're finished." Then they found a pistol on the fugitive's back and started shouting. "He's armed, he's armed!" They contacted their command by radio, then continued to beat us. I guessed that they were carabinieri from the fact that they had spoken with Captain Licata, the official I've mentioned before and who was later, when he was a colonel, arrested by the Torino magistrates. After a while other police and carabinieri cars arrived, and they brought us to the Catania command post. There they asked me, obviously, about the person who was in the car with me.

"I don't know him," I answered crisply.

"What do you mean, you don't know him?"

"Five minutes before I was stopped he asked me for a ride and I let him in."

Then they asked me to explain the bedding and suitcases that had been in the car. "I sell machinery oil and drive around to construction sites all over Sicily. At night I roll out the bedding and go to sleep wherever I am." I improvised that sort of defense while waiting for my lawyer to arrive. When they asked me why I needed an armored car, I replied that I was frightened and had bought it after reading a headline in the newspaper: LARGE-SCALE TRADER FEARS ABDUCTION AND ACQUIRES ARMORED CAR.

They took me to jail, where I was visited by the officer in charge of the arrest squad. He apologized for the fact that the men who stopped me hadn't recognized me and had behaved very badly. He also explained that they'd opened fire on sight because they had received a bulletin about a car identical to mine carrying weapons and a fugitive. In fact, in Naples Turi Palermo and I had acquired similar cars, with the last number on our license plates one digit apart. And Turi Palermo was a fugitive at that point.

Our enemies in the underworld had struck again, using the old trick of ratting to the police. But when news spread that along with Antonino Calderone a dangerous member of the Palermo mafia had been arrested, they grew scared. Many figured that people from Palermo were around and had come to support us in our war against them. A few bosses from the Carcagnusi, Cursoti, and other groups then opened talks with Nitto and other members of the family, and there was a temporary peace. And to think that the young man from Palermo was a fugitive only because he didn't want to do his military service—he wasn't even a man of honor!

I was jailed for forty days on charges of abetting a fugitive, then I was acquitted in court. I would like to specify that the president of the judiciary panel was Judge Inserra, a severe and upright man, and that there wasn't the least pressure on him from the family, even if this was because he was impossible to approach.

━

While I was in jail Salvatore Greco Cicchiteddu, just back from Venezuela, arrived in Catania. A meeting was arranged to discuss another problem that had cropped up in the meantime: the conflict between Francesco Madonia and Giuseppe Di Cristina for supremacy in the Cosa Nostra of Caltanissetta province. Under normal circumstances a question of this sort would have been handled locally, without involving representatives from outside the province. But the rift between the Greco-Corleonesi and the rest of the Cosa Nostra had by now reached such a point that every problem of a certain weight became the occasion for an antagonistic confrontation between the two sides. Francesco Madonia was in fact backed by the Corleonesis. Other than Giuseppe Di Cristina, at the Catania meeting Gaetano Badalamenti, my brother, and Salvatore Inzerillo were on the opposing front, as well as the two influential Palermo mafia bosses who were not with us, in so many words, but were well disposed toward our positions—Tommaso Buscetta and Salvatore Greco. The latter had great authority over Pippo as well as Giuseppe Di Cristina.

The meeting was held in the Costanzo offices and under conditions of maximum secrecy. Pippo didn't tell me about it because in those days he would not inform me precisely of his movements for fear of being reproached by me. I didn't think much of his friendship with Di Cristina, who tried to exploit my brother's generosity to resolve problems he should have dealt with on his own. It was my cousin Salvatore Marchese, the lookout outside the room in which the discussion was held, who informed me of everything.

Cicchiteddu heard out the complaints against the Palermitans and Francesco Madonia, who was considered the accomplice of his cousin Michele Greco in the attack on Di Cristina a few months before, but he vetoed the proposal to kill Madonia. When the meeting broke up, Cicchiteddu told Di Cristina that it would be better if he gave up his posts in the Cosa Nostra and followed him to Venezuela for a while. Immediately after his return to Latin America, Salvatore Greco died a natural death, and it seems significant to me that Madonia was killed only after Cicchiteddu passed on to a better world.

The elimination of that man, who was his strongest internal opponent, became an obsession for Di Cristina. He would talk about it constantly to my brother, trying to involve him in the plans he would time and again devise to strike his adversary. One of these plans revolved around Francesco's son Giuseppe Madonia. Di Cristina tried to make up a "tragedy" according to which Giuseppe had disobeyed an order of Stefano Bontade's that had to do with punishing a breach of trust by Gaetano Grado, a man of honor living in Milan. He convinced Pippo to go with him to Bontade to tell him about the grave infraction. Stefano Bontade grew extremely angry because he had never asked Madonia to do anything of the kind, and he wasn't pleased with Di Cristina's interference in his private business. But Di Cristina persevered with the imbroglio and went to Giuseppe Madonia's father to tell him that Bontade was furious because of the disrespect his son had displayed toward him, and he heinously dragged my brother into it by adding that it was Pippo who had denounced his son to Bontade.

It was very clear to me that my brother was being exposed to danger by Di Cristina. I tried in as many ways as I could to keep him from getting involved in the insane projects that were constantly being proposed to him, and finally I threatened to leave Catania if he consented to the elimination of Francesco Madonia on our territory. But nothing could be done. One day in the spring of that unfortunate year, 1978, I was in the house of Pippo's sister-in-law when I saw Turi Pillera arrive, all worked up, his clothes stained with blood. Pillera went aside with my brother, who immediately afterward confided to me that Francesco Madonia had been killed by Pillera and a Riesi man of honor who lived in Rome and worked as a jeweler. Madonia had been eliminated through the most classic of mafiosi stratagems: he had been called by Di Cristina to a meeting at Antonio Ferro's farm in Falconara and was killed on the spot.

The Corleonesi's answer wasn't long in coming. A few weeks later my brother was in Palermo, along with Franco Romeo, a man of honor from Catania, and was staying in an apartment on the *via* Leonardo da Vinci that had been placed at the Catania family's disposal by the Palermitan builder Piazza, who was closely tied to Salvatore Inzerillo. I don't know the reason for Pippo's trip to Palermo: after the murder of Francesco Madonia our relations had become even more strained. Pippo would leave the house alone, and at night our families no longer ate dinner together.

I had lived in the apartment on the *via* Leonardo da Vinci during my long stay in Palermo the year before. Now Alfio Ferlito, a fugitive after his escape from the hospital, was hiding there, and

Giuseppe Di Cristina also stayed there whenever he went to the capital. Franco Romeo was in Palermo because Di Cristina, who was aware of his skills with a blowtorch, was planning a robbery at the Banco di Sicilia with the complicity of a man of honor from Sambuca who was the chief cashier there. And thus, on the morning of May 30, 1978, Di Cristina left with Franco Romeo while Pippo and Alfio Ferlito stayed at home. At a certain point Pippo and Ferlito heard explosions, and through the windows of the second floor they saw two men shooting at Di Cristina, who—kneeling either because he was wounded or to keep from being wounded—returned the fire with a revolver, hitting one of the assailants in the leg. Frightened by his response, the assailants were about to run away when they realized that Di Cristina's gun was empty. Then they retraced their steps and finished him off with a series of close-range shots. In the meantime, Franco Romeo, who was unharmed, managed to get back into the house in a state of shock, and started vomiting all over the place. From that point on I have had suspicions about him, but Pippo said he was too scared to have been involved in the murder.

That day I was the guest of my friend Cinardo in Mazzarino, where I had gone with the brother-in-law of one of the men in the family. He was acting as my driver because my own license had been revoked. A telephone call came from a mafioso in Riesi informing us of Di Cristina's death. We turned on the radio and the news was confirmed. I started to become restless because I knew that Pippo was in Palermo with Di Cristina, and I was afraid that something had happened to him, especially since the radio had mentioned other people being hit in the attack. I telephoned Catania and asked my cousin Marchese to take me to Palermo. Evidently my cousin had immediately informed Nitto Santapaola, who called me up to tell me it wasn't wise for me to go. I answered that Pippo was my brother, and that I wouldn't listen to reason.

I telephoned Gaetano Fiore, the owner of the Baby Luna, a place frequented by the Palermo mafia general staff, but didn't reach him there. I then called Giovanni Bontade, who reassured me about Pippo and told me that he and the others were at the Bontades' Magliocco estate. I arrived in the evening and found a great deal of animation. There were many Inzerillos, a number of Bontade men, Alfio Ferlito, Rosario Di Maggio, and many others. That night Ferlito and I slept at a country house that belonged to Nino Sorci, while Pippo spent the night at the Magliocco estate. The next day Michele Greco arrived and met with Stefano Bontade, Salvatore Inzerillo, and Rosario Di Maggio. Ferlito and Pippo weren't invited to the secret conference; this was natural for the former, but not for my brother, and Ferlito didn't let the fact pass unremarked. In the afternoon the meeting of the Palermo provincial commission was held, as usual, at the Favarella property. Stefano Bontade was furious about Di Cristina's killing, and Salvatore Inzerillo was even more so, since the murder had been committed on his territory and without his knowledge: he wanted to find out at all costs, the poor man, who the assassins had been. Gaetano Badalamenti didn't show up for the meeting and his absence was criticized severely. It was said that he was hiding out in the countryside, surrounded by his most trusted men, because he was afraid that he too would be killed. I subsequently learned that Di Cristina had been eliminated because it was found out that he had become a carabinieri informant.

After the elimination of Di Cristina there was a moment when everything seemed to straighten itself out. A regency for the province of Caltanissetta was composed of Giuseppe Madonia, Francesco Cinardo, and one Peppe Nasca. The families appeared to be very earnest about working peacefully on drug trafficking. But for us Calderones the situation in Catania was promising nothing good. Every day Nitto Santapaola was becoming stronger, richer, more arrogant. He continued to commit murder after murder of our underworld opponents with the goal of assuming, once the war was concluded and our family was back in order, a position of preeminence.

My brother was attempting above all to resolve the family's internal problems. He had taken its dissolution as a personal defeat and humiliation. He held meeting after meeting to preach peace and harmony. "Let's avoid these constant struggles. If it simply isn't possible to get back together, let's form two separate families. Catania is big, very big, and we are very few. There's room for everyone. Let's divide the city in two. The half north of *via* Etnea, for instance, could go to the Santapaolas. The south side to us. It's silly to fight like this," he would repeat.

But Nitto would never accept that solution. The family, he said, had to remain a unit. Because in that way he could dominate, he could be the only one in command. Had the family been divided into two parts, there would have been no winners or losers. My brother would have been reelected provincial representative and we would have returned to the previous situation, to the old mafia order, and all the work that had gone into demolishing Pippo, Di Cristina, Badalamenti, and the others would have been wasted.

The big mistake Stefano Bontade and Pippo made was to have too much confidence in their own strength. Pippo never thought Nitto would dare to go beyond a certain point. Stefano went around saying that the Corleonesi would never do anything against him or the Inzerillos and the others. He felt safe, and was always boasting about his two hundred men. But while he was reveling in his own power, his adversaries were slowly, slowly sowing weeds inside his and the other families. The weeds grew slowly, and day by day the house's walls were crumbling. The soldiers, the *decina* bosses, and the vice-representatives saw the growth of the Corleonesi, made their calculations, and started to head in that direction. Pullara, for instance, one of Stefano Bontade's men, ended up going over to them. And many other lieutenants who had been faithful and loyal to their bosses followed suit. The order of the Cosa Nostra, the ties to family bosses, counted for nothing before the supreme law of the mafia: the law of the strongest.

Until the end Pippo hoped he could make Nitto see reason, all the more so because a definite break would have spelled the end of a very deep bond. There was a difference of fifteen years between them. My brother had watched Nitto grow up. He had made him. He couldn't bring himself to believe that Nitto would conspire to murder him. Dispute with him, sure. They would call each other every name in the book, but beneath it all was a longtime and deep friendship. Pippo never spoke to me, not even hypothetically, about killing Nitto. Had he wanted to he could have had him killed at any time by his friends in Palermo. But it was something that never even crossed his mind.

Nitto had baptized my daughter. My brother had baptized two of his sons. Three months after the arrest of Pippo in 1971, he had a son and I a daughter. In 1972 Nitto had another daughter. Well, Nitto had asked that we wait until Pippo's release in the summer of 1973 to baptize all three children. My daughter was already walking at the time. But Nitto wanted Uncle Pippo to be his girls' godfather. In 1969–1970 the Catania family had two tried and tested *decina* bosses. Against everyone's advice Pippo removed them from their positions to nominate one single *decina* boss: his pupil Nitto Santapaola. There wasn't a Sunday when our families didn't get together for dinner. Our wives were friends and our children played together. We often visited one another on the spur of the moment.

—

The post-Di Cristina calm didn't last long. Not quite two months afterward, in July 1978, my brother was in the countryside, at his mother-in-law's house. One day he spotted two men of honor from the Madonia family driving around the place, and they vanished as soon as they'd realized he'd seen them. Later Pippo and his wife took out the armored Mini Minor that Turi Palermo had let Pippo use while he himself was in jail. They were going shopping at a supermarket. Pippo got the car out of the garage, and when he flipped the driver's seat forward to put the empty shopping bags inside he found a strange-looking packet on the floor. Next to it was a tin can. He called me and we concluded it was dynamite. This time we both agreed that the present could have come from no one but Nitto. Our ties had deteriorated. We didn't see one another anymore, and his alliance with the Grecos and Corleonesi was by this time common knowledge.

Pippo immediately telephoned him to see what his reaction would be. Nitto answered coolly, as if he already knew everything or even wanted to let it be known that he was aware of it. Pippo cursed. It was terrible for him. What little friendship was left evaporated instantly. Not only that, but behavior of that sort was, in the oblique and twisted world of the Cosa Nostra, tantamount to an admission of responsibility and a threat. Nitto added that it would be best to meet quickly because he had a solution in mind. The device had to be defused, because if the car blew sky-high the police would analyze the wreck and easily trace it to Turi Palermo.

Before running to Nitto for help, my brother had the idea of telling Carmelo De Luca, the Costanzos' secretary, who in his presence called a friend of his, a carabinieri colonel, and asked him to step in and defuse the bomb. The colonel answered that he could only step in officially—after Pippo reported it—since the work of a specialist would be needed. But it was beyond discussion that Pippo, a high-ranking figure in the Cosa Nostra, could violate one of its most ironclad rules and report the incident like any man on the street. So Pietro Rampulla, a man of honor from the Mistretta family who was also a leftist terrorist and thus familiar with explosives, was called in. Rampulla realized that he was dealing with a remote-activated device and disconnected it so quickly that Pippo and I grew very suspicious. The ease with which he had laid hands on the packet meant that he himself was probably the person who had built it. Pippo then remembered that sometime before he had left the key to the garage with Franco Romeo, thus giving him the chance to have it duplicated.

A few days after the attempt Pippo and I were in Trabia, outside Palermo, to talk with Stefano Bontade, Gaetano Badalamenti, and Rosario Riccobono. We laid out the facts, but I couldn't get anything out of them, these great Palermitan mafiosi who didn't understand the Corleonesi strategy of clearing out the provinces— Catania, Caltanissetta, Agrigento—before concentrating on a frontal assault on their adversaries in the island's capital. They were now hitting us. How much time did they think it would be before they hit them? The Palermitans listened in silence. After an embarrassed pause Rosario Riccobono concluded, "We can't step in openly on your behalf right now. We have to be cautious, we can't show our hand. We can't take the mask off our faces. If we do they'll let loose."

At this point Pippo became very irritated toward me. He

launched into me because I had painted a compromised picture of the Catanian situation in which we were the weakest and had already lost. It had made him look bad in front of his peers, and he told me to shut up from then on. I felt humiliated and left the meeting. While I was leaving I saw Gaetano Badalamenti sitting, a bit aloof, on the house's veranda. He hadn't spoken the whole time, and while I was closing the door I saw him looking ironically at Pippo and heard him sing a little song that was very popular at the time: "Shoot, Gonzales, shoot 'cause otherwise they'll shoot you!"

The noose was tightening. I had understood that we were doomed to die, and I said to my brother, "When are we going to get out of here? How much longer do you want to stay in this hell where no one can be trusted? Why do we have to get ourselves killed?" The enemy group was no longer hiding its intentions. Franco Mangion expressed them to me outright a few days after the attack: it would be better if Pippo pulled out of the fray and resigned from the scene honorably. At the time Pippo was hiding from the authorities. He had been served a warrant, but it had been rescinded in appeal on a technical point, and Pippo was afraid that he would be served with a warrant for close surveillance. Instead of trying to avoid it, Mangion said, all Pippo had to do was accept it; he would then have a valid excuse to retire. Mangion also told me that he had a police official we could rely on to get the scheme going. He was a deputy police chief whom I knew well.

But Pippo didn't want to listen to reason. It was as though he were hypnotized by the prospect of his own death. Toward the end of July, I and my family went on vacation to Gioiosa Marina, near Taranto, and every two days I would talk to my brother. In August, Pippo moved for security reasons to the Costanzos' hotel, La Perla Jonica, and he brought Turi Lanzafame with him as a bodyguard. He would never move from the place, where he had a little room in which he received the men of honor who came to see him. One day Pippo telephoned me, elated, and said, "At last, after all these misfortunes, something good has happened. You know what we've done? We've reconstituted the family!" He led me to understand that he had been elected representative, Nitto

was vice-representative, Condolleri was *consigliere,* and Lanzafame and Salvatore Tuccio were *decina* bosses, while Salvatore
Ferrera was the new provincial representative.

"Maybe we've made it. We've reorganized the family. We've
stopped fighting among ourselves and shedding one another's
blood," Pippo said hopefully. And he didn't realize that he'd been
had, that they'd staged the recomposition of the family only to
reassure him, with the aim of killing him more easily. In fact,
Pippo would no longer leave the place unless he was armed, had
an escort, and was in an armored car.

In the waning days of August my wife returned to Catania to go
back to her job at the university. I intended to join her a few days
later, hitching a ride with two of my cousins who were on vacation
with us, but one morning she telephoned me: "Nino, I have to tell
you something. I don't know how to tell you. Your brother's been
wounded, he's hurt, he was hit in an arm or a leg. But it isn't
critical."

"How do I get back to Catania?" I immediately thought. I was
alone with two of my children, and I didn't have a car or a driver's
license. My cousins had for the moment gone back to Sicily for the
hunting. I told my wife that I'd be in touch later, and hurried to
a grocery store where there was a telephone on which I could talk
without fear of being recorded. Along the way I ran into my cousins,
who were coming back to tell me what had happened. Pippo had
been shot the night before, while he was on his way to an appointment in Aci Castello. Lanzafame had been with him and was
wounded in the head, although not seriously, while Pippo had been
hit in the stomach. They didn't know what condition my brother
was in. Pippo was recovering in a private clinic whose owner was
a professor related to the Costanzos.

I called the professor, who told me that after initial treatment
there Pippo had been transferred somewhere else, but that he had
come into the clinic on his own two legs, because he hadn't been
in serious condition. He'd asked Lanzafame to drive him to the
clinic and then go off into hiding.

I decided not to move from Puglia, and followed the progress of
Pippo's recovery by telephone. The doctors told me that he was

getting better. Our lawyer told me that the authorities had tried to ask Pippo some questions, but that Pippo had used his throat operation as an excuse not to talk. An arrest warrant for contempt was perhaps on the way. I then decided to ask Ferlito or one of the other trustworthy men to go down with me to Catania to retrieve Pippo from the hospital. But three days after his admission into the hospital my brother died.

Turi Lanzafame then described the whole event to me: "Uncle Nino, we were all together at La Perla Jonica because we'd reorganized the family. Nitto was there too. All that remained to be done was to straighten out the question of the Madonia men Pippo had seen driving around his house before the attempt. We were to go to Salvatore Ferrera, the new province boss, to meet with the Madonias and officially clarify the question. The appointment was to be set up by Nitto and we were to wait for his call. Nitto telephoned and told us to be at Ferrera's house in Aci Castello at six or seven that evening. We went off calm and secure. We weren't even armed. When we took the turn off the main road, at the railroad crossing, we were ambushed."

23

I stayed away from Sicily for a few weeks, and since I had no money left I telephoned Pasquale Costanzo. We met a few days later in Rome, in his firm's offices, and he gave me two million lire. After having had ample assurances about my safety from Francesco Cinardo, I returned to Catania with Salvatore Marchese. I arrived home to find enormous agitation both inside and outside the family even though twenty days had passed since Pippo's assassination. The group of five (which had in the meantime been reduced to three because of the murders) wanted to leave the family, since it maintained that under these conditions of constantly broken rules it was impossible to get anywhere. Without concrete proof of the Santapaolas' involvement, no accusation could be made before any Cosa Nostra body. All one could do was clench one's teeth and take one's blows. Or else make plans to run away.

The first thing I did was, in the company of my cousin Marchese, to go see Nitto. He came across as very unhappy about the loss of my brother and declared that even he hadn't managed to explain who killed him or why. Cinardo informed me that Stefano Bontade had arrived in the area and wanted to see me. Bontade was afraid of coming into the city, so the appointment was set up outside it, at a dog kennel owned by one Pippo Aiello. Bontade told me that he was crushed by what had happened, that he knew nothing, and that he was trying to find out who was to blame. He asked me what I intended to do. Did I want immediate revenge? Was I planning reprisals against whoever I thought was responsible for the attack? I replied that I wanted to be left alone. I had nothing against anyone and no one to turn to. I was tired, and I had seven children to feed (my three and Pippo's four). I didn't intend to think of anything else in the future. Stefano embraced me and gave me ten million lire in Italian and American currency. He told me that the money belonged to Pippo but didn't explain any further. I knew what it was. The money came from my brother's involvement in smuggling and drug-trafficking activities.

It was precisely three months later, during the delivery of a second payment, that I had the chance to learn what had been, above and beyond the real reasons I was clearly aware of, the formal justification, in terms of the Cosa Nostra's so-called "rules," for my brother's murder. In January 1979 Nitto informed me that Salvatore Inzerillo needed to give me a sum of money that belonged to Pippo, and since he was on his way to see Michele Greco in Palermo, he asked me to go with him. Inzerillo gave me two checks for ten million lire apiece and thirty million in cash. On the drive home we stopped in Canicatti, at the house of Antonio Ferro, the Agrigento provincial representative, having picked up Francesco Cinardo on the way. We stayed at Ferro's for about an hour, where I was soon left on my own; the others went into another room to confer animatedly. I noticed that while before Pippo's death Antonio Ferro referred to me with the familiar "*tu*," he had now switched to the formal "*Vossia*," and thus forced me to do the same to him. On the other hand, while before Nitto had addressed Ferro as "*Vossia*" and Ferro had addressed him as "*tu*," they were now both calling each other "*tu*." On the way home to Catania, Nitto asked me what I knew about the failed attempt on Di Cristina's life and his death, as well as Francesco Madonia's. He told me that he didn't think they had been the work of "peasants," that is, of locals outside the Cosa Nostra, and he said that he was sure a few Catanian men of honor sent by my brother had been involved in the killing of Francesco Madonia.

His assertion was on target, even if I was very careful not to confirm it. Nitto was telling me all this to say that it had been right to kill Pippo. By collaborating in the killing of someone in another person's territory without permission, my brother had committed a serious violation of the "rules." Madonia had in fact been eliminated in Falconara without the knowledge of Antonio Ferro, the Agrigento province boss.

"Smart Nitto!" I thought. Like a good schoolboy he was applying the lesson he had learned from the Corleonesi: kill your adversaries one by one as soon as a favorable opportunity arises. And do everything in a "formally" correct way. In such a way, in other words, that not even the victim's closest friends can respond because they are on the side of wrong. Di Cristina had been killed because, alas, he had become a carabinieri spy (what did it matter that at the time of the attempt on his life nothing of the sort could have been said about him, and that his contacting the carabinieri had been the effect and not the cause of his death sentence?). Pippo had condemned himself the moment he began plotting with Di Cristina to kill Francesco Madonia without telling anyone and in someone else's territory (what did it matter that every Greco-Corleonesi murder was done that way, in other people's territory?). And now this degenerate, this evil and ferocious being, was trying to convince me that they'd eliminated my brother for the common good, and oh so reluctantly!

During our meeting Stefano Bontade also announced that the Cosa Nostra regional commission had decided to call a meeting to commemorate my brother, and that the whole Catania family had been invited to show up. The meeting convened a week later in San Nicola l'Arena, a town in Palermo province where Tommaso Spandaro, the smuggler, had a villa. The participants were to gather at a castle in which Prince Vanni Calvello ran a nightclub in partnership with Franco Di Carlo, the Altofonte family boss who lived in England and was later implicated in the Calvi murder. We were to park our cars in the lot adjacent to the castle and wait for other men of honor to take us to the meeting place. It was Di Carlo himself who showed up to greet us, and he came into our car with a man from the Corso dei Mille family nicknamed "Dog Killer," whom I suspected had an active role in Pippo's murder.

A few months later, in fact, my cousin Marchese and I went to see him in Palermo, and when we didn't find him we asked his father (also a man of honor) where he was. His father went pale and said he didn't know. Dog Killer was part of the powerful squad of men that Michele Greco had drawn from among the individual families and that acted under his direct orders. Dog Killer would often come to Catania, and on one occasion—during a dinner at which he tried to be brilliant by recounting anecdotes about his illustrious friend in Catania—he betrayed himself. In my presence he started talking about Aci Castello, thus proving that he was well acquainted with the place where Pippo was killed. Nitto Santapaola skewered him with a glance, and the conversation trailed off into silence and general embarrassment.

To return to the commission meeting, it opened with a short speech by Salvatore Riina, who, claiming that he was expressing everyone's sentiments, recalled the figure of my brother, his reputation as a generous and capable man of honor, and his work toward building a more ordered and harmonious Cosa Nostra. Pippo was great because he had united the Cosa Nostra, but all the troubles had come from Di Cristina. Pippo had believed him, it's true, but in good faith. He couldn't be blamed for that. Now it was time to sweep all conflicts and venom aside and start wishing one another well. I watched Riina grow excited from his speech, and then I realized that I was now a stranger to that world, since I was looking at it with detached eyes and an impassive heart, as though from behind a window of icy pain.

It was difficult to tell whether Riina was play-acting—whether his elevated and noble words were coming from sincere grief for the death of a worthy man or from the base satisfaction of a victor who has just eliminated a dangerous enemy and is proud of the victim's qualities because they increase his own barely established reputation for bravery. I didn't torture myself for long with such thoughts. It was useless to try to dissect, understand, make sense of it. It's always like that in the Cosa Nostra: no fact ever has only one meaning.

My reflections were interrupted by a burst of irrepressible grief from someone sitting next to me. I turned and saw Giovanni Mongiovì, a man of honor who had been very close to my brother, and whom I remember coming to our house before every Christmas with his gifts and his sincere best wishes. I comforted Mongiovì, and realized that the tone and subject matter of the meeting were rapidly changing. They moved on to other topics, and after the meeting I was invited to dinner at Michele Greco's house. The session had concluded without anyone explaining to me why my brother had been killed. It was a clear hint to not make much of a fuss and to accept the new reality of things.

—

Over the following months, in the course of 1979, I didn't do anything but think of what step to take next. It was clear that Pippo had been assassinated by the Santapaolas and their allies in Palermo. But I had no proof against them, neither real nor contrived, like the kind the Corleonesi would pull out to justify their infamies. I had no young people ready to do anything and everything to support me, and our friends in the rest of Sicily had either been killed or didn't have the courage to act. After the loss of Pippo even my relations to the Costanzos had changed; or rather, had been broken off. They were now dealing with Nitto. I had major difficulties in even getting them to see me. As if a spell had been cast over it, our "anteroom" had emptied of ordinary people asking for favors. No one would come anymore to ask anything of a mafioso so disgraced as me. I was a has-been, a relic, useless, forced to coexist with the assassins of the person who had been dearest to me—with my future executioners.

I could have killed Nitto Santapaola by shooting him on sight the first time I ran into him, sure. But they would have murdered me immediately. And no one would have avenged me. My wife and children would have cursed me and been ashamed of me. Then I thought of leaving the Cosa Nostra, of abandoning everything. Nitto came to tell me that there was going to be a meeting about once more redistributing positions within the family, and I said to him, "Listen, would you do me a favor? You're telling me I should be there when the family's being rearranged. But I don't want to be in the family anymore. Leave me in peace. Set me free. All I want to do now is enjoy my children. I don't want to hear anything more about the Cosa Nostra."

"What are you saying, Nino? You know that's not possible! What I can tell you for sure is that if you need something, you don't have to go through your *decina* boss, you can come straight to me. But to leave the family is out of the question," Nitto replied.

He wouldn't let me leave, and it made sense. Apart from the fact that the mafia doesn't allow resignations, there was the fact that I knew too much. I absolutely had to be kept in the family, even if everyone was aware that I knew roughly who had murdered Pippo. Either they killed me or they kept me in the family. There were no other alternatives. My position with respect to the Santapaolas and the others, however, had become difficult. Given that we had to maintain this sort of forced cohabitation, it was impossible to hide much information about the family and its activities from me. They were trying to keep me off to one side because they no longer trusted me, and they were involving me as little as possible in their operations and secret intrigues, but they couldn't avoid many compromising facts from coming to my knowledge.

Over the course of 1979 I received another couple of installments on the sum owed to my brother for his participation in the family's smuggling and drug businesses. The last payment was given to me by Francesco Cinardo on behalf of Stefano Bontade at the end of the year. It was a figure of around 30,000 dollars. Cinardo told me that the amount should have been greater, but the confiscation of a suitcase containing 500,000 dollars at the Punta Raisi airport had cut into the operation's profit margin. In any case, according to my dear friend, the payment of those sums constituted a display of respect toward my brother and of loyalty to me. But when I asked why I wasn't involved in new business in Pippo's stead, they replied that the partnership with the Neapolitans had ended, that there were also difficulties with drugs, and they raised a series of excuses to guarantee my exclusion from that area too. Overall I received some 110 million lire in checks and cash as the Calderones' payoff in one of the Cosa Nostra's most lucrative businesses.

Picturing what Pippo's behavior would have been under the circumstances, I gave part of the money to the needier men of honor in the Catania family. As far as the money Di Cristina could have expected from the same source goes, however, I have to say that things went differently. His family didn't get anything, because Di Cristina had behaved shamefully by talking to the carabinieri. The money they were expecting was divided in two and assigned to Caltanissetta's two district bosses for distribution among the various families. And it was on this occasion that my friend Cinardo committed a serious error. The other district boss was Giuseppe Madonia, who called on Cinardo to allot the money to the families under his jurisdiction, and who then sent Francesco La Rocca, a Corleonesi man, to ask Cinardo for an account of the distributed sums. In comparison to Madonia's half, it emerged that Cinardo had not distributed the whole sum but had retained a portion for himself. The Corleonesi were, as usual, implacable: Cinardo was accused before the commission, degraded from his rank as district boss, and even thrown out of the family notwithstanding Stefano Bontade's intervention on his behalf.

The period between Pippo's killing in September 1978 and my escape to France in February 1983 was the worst in my life. It was almost four and a half whole years in which I stagnated, hiding out, living in the shadows. I was bitter, poor, reduced to the shell of a man. Since I was excluded from most of the more profitable illegal activities, I threw myself back into legitimate business. I set up a construction company with a person from Messina and my cousin Marchese, reserving a third of the proceeds for my brother's family, and set about getting a few contracts from our friends in the business and in local government. Then a really good idea struck me. I intended to start a partnership, along with my cousin Marchese and another man of honor, for the distribution of beer, mineral water, aperitifs, and soft drinks. It would have been enough to go around to bar owners in the city and make a very simple pitch: "What do you sell? Beer? Orangeade? Good. Then, you'll take our brands. At the same price as the others, of course. This is by no means extortion." We would have pulled off a coup. We would have made piles of money without causing difficulties or harming anyone. But I never managed to set up the company. One of the partners pulled back, started having doubts, finding excuses to postpone committing, etc., until I finally grew tired of it and lost interest in the project. Now, when I read in the newspaper that the idea was brought to fruit in Catania by Carlo Campanella for coffee and by others for other goods, I feel angry.

In 1980 it became clear that the Santapaolas' next step after eliminating my brother had to be the destruction of Alfio Ferlito and his group. The conflict between Nitto and Ferlito arose out of a struggle for supremacy in the Cosa Nostra and out of commercial competition in illegal business. The conflict of interests had started a number of years earlier, in the days of cigarette smuggling, when Ferlito managed to corner a good slice of the market and thus became a troublesome competitor to the gang led by Nitto and Mangion. Ferlito's entry into wholesale distribution in the Cantania area had increased the supply of cigarettes and made prices sink, with proportionate damage to the preestablished suppliers. It was especially for this reason that Nitto had opposed Ferlito's admission into the family, and he hadn't been wrong. As soon as he became a man of honor, in fact, Ferlito started smuggling and drug-trafficking partnerships with some members of the Santapaola clan, among them Pippo Ferrera, who, though being Nitto's cousin, couldn't stand him at all. A conflict immediately arose about the division of a colossal shipment of hashish.

The strife between the two groups lasted nearly three years and caused some forty deaths. There were phases when one or the other was on top. A couple of attempts at peace were made. Everything ended with Alfio Ferlito's killing, on June 16, 1982, in a horrible bloodbath on the ring road around Palermo.

From the outset of the new war I remained on the sidelines. I withdrew, stayed in my house, and wouldn't leave it anymore except for family meetings, in which I participated as a ghost, always saying yes. I had to attend these meetings because, given the former links between Ferlito and my brother, if I didn't the Santapaolas would have interpreted my absence as a sign of distance from or betrayal of them. But I was in danger even if I went, because it was while going to appointments that one was killed.

Over the course of 1981 the family's internal war became interlinked with the one that broke out in Palermo that same year. The killing of Stefano Bontade at the end of April forced everyone to accept that the rift would close only after one of the parties was beaten by force of arms. After that murder, Ferlito and his men precipitately tried to attack and kill Nitto at the Renault dealership, but they missed their target and became the subjects of a massive reprisal. Twenty days after Bontade's death, the Corleonesi struck another decisive blow by eliminating their second great opposing leader, Salvatore Inzerillo. The justification in this case was that he and Bontade had swindled twenty billion lire from the consortium the Palermo families had created to finance large-scale drug trafficking.

The ripples this event created in Catania were immediate. The Santapaolas' power increased, and thus also my anxiety about my fate. My life was changed. I often slept in different places, and got by on Valium. I could no longer fall asleep without it. When I was at home I took the telephone off the hook. I didn't want to answer any call asking me to carry out an order such as hiding a fugitive or taking part in an armed action. I excluded myself from the family's activities, and my situation thus became more dangerous. By keeping apart, one lost touch with the news and was put in a weaker position with respect to the police. If one wasn't aware of an imminent murder, one didn't have the chance to "get proof," to create a workable alibi. When Pippo was killed, everyone was ready with their proof. Nitto was in America, Mangion in Greece, Lillo Conti taking the waters in Fiuggi. For a while it was suspected that I or one of Pippo's closest friends had assassinated him.

Meanwhile, my legal situation was becoming precarious. In the course of the same year, 1981, Judge Falcone called my wife in to ask her why some checks from Inzerillo had been deposited in her accounts, and to recommend that I come see him as soon as possible. I knew that Falcone arrested anyone who couldn't come up with a plausible explanation for payments made or received. Thus the police were also on my tail.

Immediately after Ferlito's murder, the Catania carabinieri indicted a vast number of men of honor for criminal association. I was the target of an arrest warrant and became a fugitive. In September 1982, after the assassination of General Dalla Chiesa, the Rognoni–La Torre law was passed for the confiscation of illegally obtained property and of firms that had secured contracts through our group. I was also out of work. The bank canceled my line of credit and that of the company I was a partner in, and in addition asked me to pay back a loan of eighty million lire immediately. I was completely, hopelessly ruined.

Around the beginning of February 1983 my arrest warrant was revoked. The judges had realized that the trial was slipping out of their control because of appeals, objections, and pressure, and they acquitted almost every one of the defendants. Even fugitives like me were acquitted. On the morning of the day after the cancellation of my arrest warrant, a Sunday, I put my wife and children in the car and brought them to a cathedral. It had been years since I was last in a church, and I was moved by being amid all those people who had something to believe in. Then, like so many times before, we went to Nitto's house. I was the one who proposed it, and my wife was hesitant because she didn't think it very wise, given the collapse of our relations with the Santapaolas after Pippo's death. But I wanted to show everyone that nothing had changed, and I wanted to give myself courage and to comfort my family on the eve of something that was ending, or about to begin.

Nitto's wife greeted our visit with something like consternation. She received us cordially but was a bit more glum than usual, which she attributed to the fact that her husband was a fugitive, even if she did manage to see him without undue problems. She apologized for not being able to invite us to dinner, and I told her not to worry about it. We ate at a restaurant in Zafferena Etnea, then went to my cousin Salvatore Marchese's house. I had my suspicions about him too, and the purpose of our visit was to set him at ease about my intentions and to gain some time. In the paranoid environment of the Cosa Nostra, a targeted victim like me couldn't display nervousness in the presence of his own persecutors. A show of fear would have served only to convince them to accelerate the pace of the execution. I was sure that my time had come, and the next day it was confirmed to me by Francesco Mangion.

I went to his house without warning and started talking with him about the killing of Franco Grillo, one of Nitto's men, who had been captured by the survivors of Ferlito's group and brutally "interrogated" before being eliminated. Under torture Grillo had, Mangion said, very probably revealed that Nitto and his men were responsible for my brother's murder. It was thus obvious that if Nitto's friend Mangion was aware of Grillo's talking, then Nitto and the others in his clan were too. I wasn't surprised by Mangion's revelations, and even felt something like a sense of relief: the long-awaited pretext to kill me had arrived. Since at this point it was legitimate to expect vendetta from me, it was also legitimate on their part to forestall it by getting rid of me as soon as possible. And not only me. I had also considered that Nitto, my personal friend, whose wife was a friend of my wife's, knew me well enough to realize that a thorough job would also have to entail the elimination of my wife, to whom, it was logical to think, I confided everything.

I said that I had fallen ill, and for a week I stayed at home to prepare an escape. I was a hunted animal who had looked at the sky and seen clouds gathering and threatening, and was hoping to find shelter before the storm. I didn't think anymore; I wasn't alive anymore; I was scared of everyone but didn't know where to go: my life had been spent entirely in Catania and in Sicily, in the hallucinatory world of the Cosa Nostra and its intrigues. Outside, everything was darkness. One night I was talking with my wife and it emerged that she knew of a place in Switzerland—a hospice, a sort of inn run by priests. "Listen, who knows if you'll find work. Find out when you're there. But just leave! We'll join you afterward. But it's time to go. Get away from here!"

It wasn't easy to leave like that, on the spur of the moment. We had no money. We no longer had liquid assets. We had a house and other property, but they couldn't be sold in a couple of days. My wife had her salary, which would just cover feeding the children. So she sold the children's baptismal gold, our silver, and everything of value in the house to scrape together a small sum for my escape. I left Catania with 1.7 million lire in my pocket. At the Swiss border I had a little more than 1.5 million left, the most one could take out of the country. I slipped the rest into an envelope with a letter to my wife and mailed it to Catania. I looked for work in Switzerland, but in order to work there you need to be a resident, and to get residence one needed a job. It was all pretty strange.

My wife then suggested that I move to France, to Menton, where she knew the sister of a colleague who was studying for her doctorate. "Go to her. Who knows, maybe she can help you." I went to Menton, where I stayed in an inn for nearly a month. My wife joined me as soon as she was able to scrape together another small sum. I fell sick and was treated in the Menton hospital. Then we decided to move once more, this time to Nice. We had already been to the city and had good memories of it; during childbirth our son had suffered from low oxygenation and needed a specific treatment that they performed very well there. We rented a furnished apartment, where I stayed with my eldest daughter while my wife returned to Catania to settle the rest of our affairs. She sold the house through a notice in the newspaper, waited out the children's school year, and arranged for her pension, since she had completed twenty years of service. She and the children joined us in June. The family was again reunited, and the sale of the house had been providential. Bit by bit we brought the proceeds to France, and we were set for the immediate future.

In the meantime, I tried to sell the building equipment and earthmoving machinery that belonged to me as owner of the construction company. I did everything by telephone, through my nephew Salvatore. I had to pay off the 80-million-lire debt to the bank, and the machinery was worth more than 250 million. I offered it to the Caterpillar franchise in Catania, which showed an interest in buying it for 200 million. But a couple of characters in Nitto's circle stepped in and forced me to hand it over to someone they had chosen for the paltry sum of 115 million lire, value added tax included: little more than the amount of the bank loan.

Now our problem was what to do in France. We didn't know the language, and obviously we avoided any contact with the Italians living in Nice. Apart from the possibility of being recognized, it was too much of a bother to have to make up stories about where we came from, who we were, why we were living abroad, etc. During the time I lived alone I had brought my laundry to *laveries,* the launderettes that are very common in France. Why not set up our own? And so we did. We bought washing machines, rented a place, and opened at the beginning of January 1984. We started working and were happy, happy, happy. Every month my wife would pick up her pension in Ventimiglia in Italy. She'd exchange currencies and come back to Nice. We managed to live on a couple of million lire a month and were even able to save money.

We then moved into a larger house that we rented, and we bought some furniture. We were very, very comfortable. We worked hard and were content, even if the work was menial. The children acclimatized without problems and were happy too, with their friends and games. I found life again in Nice, I was reborn, I grew morally. I discovered my children there. I learned what it means to teach them, follow them, watch them grow up. When we settled in France the girls were twelve and ten, the boy eight. They had to start school one class behind, but they did very well. They learned French immediately, to the point of being able to help us out. In my whole life as a rich man in Catania—as a powerful and respected mafioso—I had never been as serene and happy as I was during those three years in Nice.

In my prior life I had cared for my children, but the fear of being killed at any moment made me think of them in limited terms. The only question I would ask myself was, "Who can I leave them to? What will their life be like without me?" My mind wasn't free to consider anything else. And I was in no state to understand what a huge treasure they represented. I've already told you that many men of honor have children principally to make themselves feared by other mafiosi, to increase the strength of their own clan. But is any of this logical? Isn't it perhaps abnormal? Those men of honor live like dogs and don't know it. Even when they're very rich.

One night in 1985 I was sitting on the back steps of the launderette and chatting with my elder daughter, who was then fourteen. She was inquisitive and started asking questions. She wanted to know, she wanted to be told why our life was so unsettled. My wife and our other children were also there. "Dad, why did we come here? Why did we leave Sicily? I like Sicily," she said to me out of the blue.

"Listen, my sweet, and I'll tell you something. By now you've realized who I was, who I could have been there in Catania. You're grown up, almost a young lady. If we had stayed there and someone like me, a mafioso, had come to ask for your hand, I couldn't have said no. You would have been married to someone like me. And you've seen what kind of life we led in Sicily. I was never at home, always sleeping somewhere else, coming and going unexpectedly in the middle of the night. Does it seem like it was a good thing to you? You see, if one day you marry a boy who doesn't have a lira, but if you both work hard and you love each other, well, that's an enormous step up from our situation back there. You can be free, independent. You can study in peace, find a job you like. And then if you want to get married you can: it's you who decides. You're not obligated to marry anyone. You don't have to become the wife of a mafioso and lead a hard life. I don't mean hard because you don't have money. I mean the hardships and suffering that come from fear. You know very well what I'm talking about." I had barely finished saying this before my daughter threw her arms around my neck and burst into tears.

To tell the truth, a few shadows from my recent past continued to haunt me, although without giving me serious troubles. One morning in 1984, around the end of summer, I was leaving the launderette when I saw, on the sidewalk opposite me, Michele Greco's cousin Pino walking along, followed by another man carrying two expensive plastic suitcases. I seemed to remember him as a soldier from Stefano Bontade's family. Luckily, neither one of them looked like he was going to come up to me, and I even thought that they might not have recognized me. After all, I had lost a lot of weight and was wearing, contrary to habit, a pair of ordinary blue jeans. A few weeks after that ugly encounter, a person showed up at the launderette door and my blood froze: a small, thin man whose name I couldn't remember but whom I had seen at Michele Greco's house. I remained expressionless, forcing myself to contain my fright. He handed me clothes to be washed and didn't seem to recognize me. I gave him his receipt, and on the day he was due to pick up his clean laundry I made sure I wasn't behind the counter. My wife took care of him, remaining calm and reserved for the whole interminable moment. The mafioso never came to our launderette again, but both my wife and I saw him pass by almost every day like an unsettling ghost.

I ran into Pino Greco a few other times, but always under circumstances when I couldn't be identified. Only once was I recognized by a Catanian, a small-time hood who hung around the fish market. He came up to greet me. I pretended not to know him, not to know his language, and I responded in French to his declarations of respect. He insisted, and then, after a while, when he realized I wasn't going to get involved, he said, "Fine, I understand," and left.

Bit by bit, working and saving, we managed to get a mortgage and buy a home—a small apartment, but it was ours. The mortgage would have been paid off in 1995. In December 1984 an arrest warrant for criminal association was handed down against me by the procurator of Torino. In February 1985 the repentant Salvatore Contorno revealed that I was a mafioso, and Judge Falcone indicted me and signed another warrant for my arrest. Thus I found myself in Nice with two arrest warrants on my head, but still happy. I was living a normal life by this time. My lawyer in Catania told me not to worry because at any moment everything would be settled, would turn out in my favor.

Even on the Cosa Nostra side, things didn't seem to be going badly. Neither my friends nor my enemies knew where I was because I had truly cut off my links to everyone. I hadn't received any sort of word that they were looking for me. The only serious problem that could have arisen out of my absence was the possibility that I would decide to collaborate with the police. But a certain amount of time had passed by now and nothing had happened. In fact, I had no intention of repenting. For that reason it was probable that they had forgotten about me, that they no longer considered me a threat, an imminent danger.

The new house was ready. We were to move in on May 20, 1986, but on May 9 I was arrested by the French police. It was a Friday, and I stayed in the Nice jail until the following Monday morning. On the day of my arrest I was questioned by a judge, who asked me if I wanted to stay in France or return to Italy. I replied that under no circumstances did I want to return to Sicily, and he set the trial in motion. If I hadn't made that declaration, the Catanian policemen who had joined their French colleagues to make the arrest would have taken me away. Or at least that was what I was afraid would happen.

They had tracked me down by intercepting a conversation between my wife and her brother in Sicily, in which she had referred to the hospitalization of our daughter in Nice. They searched all the hospitals in the city and found the dates of her stay and our address. They certainly would have found it earlier had they looked through the list of residence permits. I had requested and obtained one, in fact, at the end of 1984. I was legally registered as a resident alien, and under my own name.

One of the policemen who arrested me said to me, "By now we know you well. We've been filming you for a month or more." He was referring to the fact that he had been stationed with a video camera in a house opposite ours. I answered that I was happy about that, because it meant they knew I left for work at seven-thirty every morning and didn't have any contact with anyone. I worked and that was all. And I was perfectly aboveboard in terms of both Italian and French law. I didn't know about the arrest warrants, I was running an honest business, I had a current bank account and the documents necessary to obtain a residence permit. My family was normal and quite like any other.

From Nice I was brought to Aix-en-Provence, near Marseille, and was put in a cell with some Calabrians. They had me read a book on the mafia that was made up of documents from the Palermo maxi-trial and in which Pippo and I were mentioned—specifically, the recording of a phone call made in Toronto, Canada, from Paul Violi's dairy bar in 1974. In the intercepted phone call it was mentioned that Pippo was the Cosa Nostra provincial representative and that yours truly was representative of "the town," that is, of Catania. I immediately thought that more than ten years had passed since the phone call and that someone must have hidden the document in a file to pull out later at a convenient moment. In any case, the description of my role in the Cosa Nostra agreed with

Contorno's accusation. The judges had fairly strong evidence against me. No doubt about it: I was in trouble again.

All that notwithstanding, I didn't decide to collaborate until December 1986. I spent nearly eight months in jail, hoping for the impossible, confident that one fine day my lawyer would tell me, "There's nothing against you. The matter has been settled. You're free." In the meantime, my wife continued to run the launderette, but things were no longer what they once had been. The spell had been broken, and when I looked at her during our talks in jail I noticed a few small signs of exhaustion, a kind of sadness when she spoke about our future and our children's. But it was the situation inside the prison that worried me most. The other inmates didn't set me at ease. I was in a special wing where those awaiting trial were housed in individual cells and placed under closest watch. Every door had a double lock. I was never, for any reason, allowed to walk alone. There was always a guard next to me. During my talks with my wife the guard would stand in the doorway and not budge until the moment came to bring me back to my cell. One inmate in the prison was a Corsican, the killer who had murdered Judge Michel in Marseille in 1981.

At a certain point I realized that messages from Sicily had started coming in. My jailmates were planning a bizarre breakout and asked me to escape with them. They said they had grenades and other weapons. I refused, because I thought they'd kill me first and then escape. It was a plan contrived to kill me without arousing suspicions. And, in fact, the day after the date planned for the breakout, I found them all there, wandering calmly around the courtyard. "Still here?" I asked them sarcastically, then revealed to the warden that there were grenades in the jail. All the inmates in that wing were brought out to the courtyard and made to strip naked. It was winter and very cold. Their cells were inspected and all their bedding was tossed out into the corridor.

On the morning of December 31 I was assailed by paranoia and started to raise hell. I shouted and shrieked as hard as I could, demanding to speak with the warden. They brought me to another wing, but the guards didn't show any intention of listening to me.

The prison's social worker came, and during our talk I picked up the telephone that was on the table, hurled it at the wall, and started smashing everything within reach. "I don't need a social worker. I want to talk to the warden now! I have something important to say to him. I have a lot to tell him before they kill me!" I screamed like a madman. They put me in a straitjacket and locked me in a room. In the afternoon the warden came in, and I told him I urgently needed to speak with Judge Falcone. I had decided to collaborate and to tell him everything I knew about the mafia in Sicily.

"It's New Year's Eve. Where could we find Judge Falcone now?"

"I don't care. Look for him. I have to talk to him now."

Later, toward 8:00 P.M., two French policemen came in, one of whom spoke Italian. I told him, "I'm not joking. Listen to me carefully. Before anything else you have to take my wife and children and hide them. They must be in your hands, under your responsibility, because they want to kill us all. Then you should know that Nice is full of fugitive mafiosi. Greco, and many others with him. Follow him and you'll arrest lots of them. Those are just the first things I'm going to tell you. Just to show you I'm sincere and not lying to you."

I was waiting for immediate reactions, different treatment. But instead, from that point on they didn't pay any attention to me. They transferred me to another jail and kept me in a cell for eight terrible days during which I barely ate and never slept. The prison director had personally chosen to put me in with an inmate who was meant to create no problems for me. And instead that lunatic put me through the tortures of hell. Every night the guards would open the cell door and come in. And I didn't sleep. I would sit up for the whole night with the television in my hands, ready to throw it at whoever came in. I was convinced that they were coming in to kill me. I was absolutely positive that someone had paid the guards off to kill me, to keep me from talking. So my custodians were doing it on purpose: slowly moving, up and down, the two steel dowels that slid into the lock, as if they were going to open it. I would sit there, eyes wide open, staring at the two tabs moving slowly, slowly, slowly . . . And my cellmate was acting strangely, as though he were in on it with the guards. They were trying to drive me crazy.

In the end I was forced to tell the warden that I wasn't appealing anymore, that I was no longer going to oppose extradition. "I'm going to Italy. If I have to die, better it be there. I don't want to look at anyone here!" Then, one night, they stripped me and beat me with sticks, kicks, fists, all over my body. The warders went wild; they seemed like animals. They even kicked me in the head. They wanted to punish me because I had barred myself up in a cell to avoid being transferred to another place that was even worse, at the mercy of other prisoners who could stab me, strangle me, cut me to pieces at will. I had barricaded myself in by leaning my bed up against the entrance to the cell. The guards all threw themselves on me, hurting me badly. They systematically beat me in the head and face. A few hours later I was told that my wife and children had arrived for our talk. I was still reeling. I didn't know what to do. I didn't want them to see me in this condition, covered with bruises, swollen, bloody. But if I didn't go to meet them, who knows what they could have thought.

At last I decided to wash, straighten myself up a bit, and go. As soon as my son saw his father looking like that, he burst into tears. I was humiliated and furious. I said to my wife, "Go see the judge now!" She went and raised hell. A functionary from the Italian consulate arrived, and the same day I changed prisons. They sent me to Marseille, among crazy people in an insane asylum. There I was better off. They were all completely crazy. They didn't understand anything and there was no danger. Two months later I was called in to see the doctor who ran the asylum. He declared, "I'm discharging you. You're better."

"Fine. Where are you sending me now?"

"Where you were before, naturally. To Aix-en-Provence."

I didn't sleep the first night. On the night after that the people in the cell next to mine fell completely silent. I was terrified. I had been told that the previous occupant of the cell I was in had been found stabbed sometime before, and that this was a jail where warders stabbed prisoners. I felt like it was over. At 6:00 A.M. they brought me food. I knew that the guard changed at 6:45. I pretended to swallow something, and when the guard went off to be relieved I took a razor blade and cut myself in the stomach. I gave myself two deep gashes. My intestines were visible. I called the guard and told him to have me brought to the hospital, but he didn't move from my side. He notified a colleague, and more than an hour passed before anyone appeared. The warden arrived in the company of other prison officials. They made me strip because they thought I was hiding a message to send out of the prison. I dressed again and didn't reach the hospital until 11:00. I had little blood left and was very weak. I could barely think straight anymore. I was on my way into the next world. I was driven to the hospital by firemen, or rather by superfiremen, a special detachment, who signed me over to the gendarmes and said, "Stay on your toes, he's a repentant." No one should have known I was a repentant, and yet even the firemen knew about it!

I was laid out on a bed with bars, bound hand and foot, and sewed up like a stuffed goat on a spit. The surgeon had barely finished putting the stitches in before they wanted to bring me back to jail. The doctor wouldn't allow it: "He can't go back to prison. He has to be kept under observation here."

"But he's a special inmate, a repentant. He can't stay in the hospital. We have orders to bring him back," my custodian replied.

"I won't allow it."

"We have to bring him back to prison. He can't be watched properly here," the gendarme insisted.

"Do you have a hospital inside the jail?" the surgeon asked, losing patience.

"No, there's no hospital there!" I interrupted with a shout.

"Yes. There's a wing equipped for it. If you want, Doctor, you can talk to the penitentiary director," the gendarme said.

The doctor telephoned the warden, who assured him of the existence of a hospital inside the prison. I went back to jail at two in the morning and recuperated in a sort of infirmary, where I was given a transfusion, and where I was forced to endure the head guard's bullying for the whole night. That too was punishment for my repentance.

The only thing I got out of cutting my stomach open was a

transfer to another prison, where I spent another few weeks before I was finally, in April, called before Judge Michel Debacq of the Marseille Tribunal, who asked me, "You want to speak with Judge Falcone, right?"

"Yes. Absolutely."

"Where's your lawyer? Have you hired a lawyer?"

"I don't have a lawyer anymore. I don't want one."

"So, you declare, on your own responsibility, that you don't want a defense lawyer?"

"Yes. That's right."

"Good. You can go. We will call for you."

I wouldn't have been able to resist, after December 31, 1986, the physical attacks and the nervous tension of prison life in France had I not had a security, a certainty, just one. That was essential for me. After my repentance a very thorough protection plan was set up. My wife had sold the house and launderette and moved to another city with the kids. The French police kept them under vigilant watch, and even the Italian police—the Central Anticriminal Center led by Mr. Gianni De Gennaro—was collaborating in the protection program. Mr. De Gennaro had even put an inspector, Giovanni Natella, at my family's disposal. He lived with my children, who were extremely happy with him. He almost became a second father to them.

Even before I spoke with Judge Falcone, Mr. Antonio Manganelli, De Gennaro's deputy, came to France to talk to my wife, to reassure her about the fate of our little family, give her courage. My wife greatly admired him. She was always talking to me about him. One day she said to me, "You know, Nino, Mr. Manganelli told me that I'll be here on the day they interrogate you."

That day finally came. On April 16, 1987, Judge Falcone arrived with two other Palermo judges, Natoli and Sciacchitano, and we all met in a room along with Judge Debacq, an interpreter, and a stenographer. Mr. Manganelli was there too.

"Where's my wife?" I asked.

"Your wife is coming, don't worry."

"I'm not worried. I trust you. But I'll only start talking when my wife is here."

I wanted her there because I had prepared a brief speech I wanted to make in front of all these sober characters, these men of the law. I didn't know where my wife was. Perhaps she was just outside the door but Judge Debacq didn't want to let her come in, or perhaps she really was on her way. In any case, I wouldn't have opened my mouth had she not come. Finally, when it was already night, they brought her in.

"Before I begin collaborating with you, I want to say one thing," I said calmly, and turned to Mr. Manganelli. "Are you married?"

"No," Manganelli replied.

"Then listen to me carefully. As of tonight you have a wife and three children. Do you feel capable of saving the lives of these three little ones and that woman for me?"

"I give you my word. For you I don't know, but for them I give you my word."

"Agreed. I thank you from the bottom of my heart. We can begin now."

—

Debacq and Falcone questioned me together. From that time on I saw them regularly every month. They would question me for a week at a time. After the first session with Debacq my treatment in prison improved. I was held in Lyons, in a prison where no one recognized me and where I was safe from dangers coming from Sicily. It was the same jail where they had locked up that person who had exterminated all the Jews in France during the war, the Butcher or Killer of Lyons, he was called. But for the weeks I was to meet with Debacq and Falcone I was to be transferred to Marseille, to the insane asylum in which I'd been before. I would be put in a room with no bars on the window, in the midst of all these madmen settled down on mattresses on the floor with their bedding scattered all around them. They'd piss on themselves, do their business wherever since they couldn't understand anything. Every morning they'd be hosed down along with the floor. They would be showered down with jets of water. But I wasn't crazy, and every month I'd spend a week in a nightmare. The fact that I was a repentant, that I was revealing things that hadn't been known before, hadn't produced any significant benefits for me. When I spoke about it with Falcone, he answered, "What can I say, we're guests here. We don't have any say abroad." When I spoke about it with Debacq, he said, "I can't do anything. The prison system is independent."

In any case, from the month of June onward they no longer brought me to the asylum, and I was transferred to yet another cell in the Lyons prison. I myself let the warden know where I wanted to be. But one day I had just returned to my cell from a talk when a cataclysm hit—a mutiny of the entire inmate population. They burned everything, the whole prison. They destroyed everything that had been inside. Only the walls and things made of steel remained. The cell doors were stacked up in the corridors, ready to be burned. Hot water poured down on me from the ceiling of my cell, which was below a stationery supply room that had caught fire. All the inmates, nearly two thousand of them, escaped. I was the only one who couldn't, since the key to my door wasn't among the general mass taken by the mutinees, but was in the possession of only a couple of guards, who had fled without me. I was trapped like a rat. For three hours I sat there with a basin full of water and a towel that every now and then I draped over my face to fight off the heat of the fire. The smoke had just about suffocated me when the gendarmes broke into the prison along with the firemen. The deputy warden and a few prison officials came to free me. I was livid: "It's great that you freed me. But why didn't you take me with you? Why did you leave me behind to die like an animal in a cage?"

Their only reply was to put me for two days into another cell, empty and bare, without a cot or mattress. All I had was a towel. I refused to eat. The warden arrived and asked what he could do for me. "Send me back to the cell I had before," I replied. I went back there and saw a disgusting sight: all my clothes had been soaked and charred, and there was blood all over the place—on the walls, on the floor, everywhere. The bathroom door was smashed. It turned out that in the intervening time my cell had housed someone else, who had either tried to commit suicide or been badly wounded. I changed rooms again, but the new one was empty like the preceding one, and I had to sleep on newspapers. After another three or four days they brought me a mattress, which I threw myself down on at night.

After a bit of time, an encore: another fire, another mutiny, another threat to the life of yours truly. They had tried to incinerate me twice. Then I understood. I thought that no one knew I was hiding in Lyons, but one fine day I was sent a letter by a lawyer in Cannes. He claimed to be speaking on behalf of my nephew, who wanted me to hire him for my defense, and he asked me for an urgent meeting. He also told me that someone would approach me to try to get me to say things I wouldn't want to say. I didn't reply, and they sent me an express telegram. They were clearly on my track. Letters and telegrams were merely the first salvo, the first direct threats. Since they hadn't managed to have me killed inside the prison, it was better to move on to direct action. And, in fact, at the very same time four Catanians were stopped on the French side of the Italian border, among them two of my cousins, Giuseppe and Salvatore Marchese. They were probably returning from a preliminary reconnaissance. I warned my wife through the prison's social worker not to come see me, and I showed the telegrams to the judges. I asked to leave Lyons and to be sent to the prison in Marseille for the duration. Given that my assassin ex-companions were onto my movements, I might as well stay there.

While I was in Marseille, Mr. Manganelli said to me: "Listen, we've made arrangements for your wife and children. We can send them overseas. We're set up; they can take all their things and leave immediately. I can't make you any promises, but I can also tell you that there's a chance you can join them in the future."

I couldn't believe my ears. But I had no reason to doubt what a person as sober and upstanding as he was telling me. "Have them go as quickly as possible. And may God bless you," I replied emotionally.

▬

I too am overseas now, with my family, safe. In a normal, well-tended town. Far from the turbulent island of the mafia, of the Cosa Nostra. Far from your world, mafiosi, and from your twisted way of thinking and living. And now I want to shout, as loudly as possible, to all of you: if you have ten million lire in your pocket, or twenty or thirty or a hundred million—some mafiosi have that kind of money today—then get yourself a passport. Take your family and run away from there, disappear. Go somewhere else— another continent, another world, as far away as possible from Sicily. Because there you'll always end up the same way. You'll end up dead. You'll die and your sons will die too. And your wife will cry, and the wives of your sons will cry, and so on with the sons of your sons. The generations to come will cry even more bitter tears because it's all one big chain. Death calls forth death like blood calls forth blood. It's endless.

Nitto Santapaola had an insane dread of this fact, but the only thing he knew how to do was to say, "We must also kill the sons of those we've killed." He would say that because he was afraid that the sons of the dead would grow up and kill him or his sons. Your greatest fear, mafiosi, springs from this: you know that a human being is not alone, but lives surrounded by affection. He's cradled by many bonds, and when that man is gone because his life has been taken away by someone else, not every part of him is lost. The people who loved him remain, those links remain. An assassination is like a hole in a web, but a web of human emotions. Haven't you seen how people cry for the dead, even those dead from car crashes, accidents? Have you ever been with the family of a man who has just died? Have you seen them crying? Or have you swallowed the oath to the Cosa Nostra so completely that you don't see the tears and suffering of the people you exterminate?

A murdered man has parents, brothers, friends, and above all sons who feel the loss, and who will, many years later, when one fools oneself into thinking that they've forgotten, leap to their feet and shout, "You killed my father! Now I'm going to kill you!" Many powerful mafiosi die that way. They've killed too much; they have too many enemies. No one dies a natural death anymore today, in their beds, like the men of honor in the old days. Nitto Santapaola, Totò Riina, Bernardo Provenzano, and the others like them have condemned themselves. There's no hope for them. They'll die because they'll all be killed.

Some men of honor believe they can protect themselves from this curse through power. They try to remain above everyone, because if others think they've come down, even just a little bit, they'll be killed. And so they continue to kill. They kill to stay in command, and at that point there's no way out. They cannot exist without commanding because they live to command, and when they no longer command they die. They think that no one would be crazy enough to strike at them. As long as they have power they believe themselves invincible. And they claim that no one has the right to strike at them and their sons.

But—excuse me—why? If you've killed my father, why shouldn't I kill your sons? If you, Nitto, have offed someone's father, doesn't that person have the right to off your son? Even in secret, without letting you know, for the sheer sake of making you suffer. You've made others suffer? Fine. Then you have to wait for someone to kill one of your sons, for the sake of making you suffer.

It's for this reason that life in the Cosa Nostra is so short and unhappy. There's no security; one lives on the brink of an abyss. Today Totò Riina is on high, on top of the mountain. Tomorrow he could find himself on the ground, in the dust, shot and with his head eaten by dogs, like what happened to my friend Francesco Cinardo. And yet Riina is as strong as Jesus Christ, because he wields supreme power. He holds a man's life in his hands. With a nod he can take or spare someone's life. He's above everyone. But at the same time he's been reduced to misery because he can't travel, he can't move, he can't sleep, he can't sit down in an orange grove and enjoy the freshness and perfume of the orange blossoms: he can't rest. He's drowning in the terror of being killed. And when he dies and everything is added up, what could one say about someone like him? His life was led in hiding, being on the run, being alone. What, after having been a fugitive for twenty-five years, never having left Sicily, can Totò Riina claim to have seen of the world, even if he was very rich and owned villas and palazzos: fields, caves, the company of animals among which he was born? What does he know of the beauties of nature and the beauties created by man?

Men of the Cosa Nostra, many of you are fugitives and know